THE GREATEST OF THE BORGIAS

ST FRANCIS XAVIER
A KING OF SHADOWS
UNCERTAIN GLORY
DON JOHN OF AUSTRIA

MARGARET YEO

* * *

THE GREATEST
OF THE BORGIAS

LONDON

SHEED AND WARD

1936

PRINTED IN GREAT BRITAIN
AT THE ALCUIN PRESS
WELWYN HERTFORDSHIRE
AND FIRST PUBLISHED
IN FEBRUARY 1936 BY
SHEED AND WARD
FROM 31 PATERNOSTER ROW
LONDON EC4

FOREWORD

AMONGST those who have greatly helped me by personal kindness, information and introductions, my sincerest thanks are specially due to Father Melchior Balaguer, S. J., Father Miguel Barqueto, S.J., Father James Brodrick, S. J., and Father Vincent Baker, Cong. Orat., and to Betty Williams for help with the index; also to Monsignor Edwin Henson, Rector of the English College, Valladolid, who has supplied photographs of the two portraits of St Francis Borgia in the English College (one of which is reproduced as the frontispiece), that in the church of San Miguel, Valladolid (formerly a Jesuit church), and those of the statue of the saint by Martinez Montañes in the University church at Seville.

CONTENTS

vii

PART III
IN AUTHORITY
(1565-1572)

SAINT FRANCIS BORGIA

PRINCIPAL DATES IN THE LIFE OF
ST FRANCIS BORGIA

1510 (Oct. 28) Born at Gandia.

1520 Death of his Mother and Flight from Gandia.

1520-1527 Zaragoza, Baza and page to Princess Catherine at Tordesillas.

1528-1539 At Court of Emperor Charles V. (1528 [May] meets Ignatius of Loyola at Alcalá de Henares.)

1529 (July) Marries Eleonor de Castro.

1536 (Summer) Campaign with Charles V in Provence.

1539 (May 1) Death of Empress Isabel at Toledo.

1539 (June 26) Appointed Viceroy of Catalonia. Viceroy till 1543 (April).

1543 (January) Becomes Duke of Gandia on death of his Father.

1543 (April)-1550 (August) At Gandia.

1546 (March 27) Death of the Duchess.

1548 (February 2) Professed in Society of Jesus.

1550 (August 31) Leaves Gandia for Rome. Rome 1550 (Oct.)-1551 (Feb.).

1551 (May) Arrival at Oñate.
(May 23) Ordained priest.
(Aug. 1) First Mass at Loyola.

1551 (Nov. 15) First public Mass at Vergara.

1553-1561 Commissary General for Spain, Portugal and the Indies. (Journeys through Spain and Portugal.)

1561 (July 12) Leaves Spain for Rome.

1561-1565 Vicar General and Assistant for Spain and Portugal.

1565 (July 24) Elected General of the Society of Jesus.

1571 (June)-1572 (September) Last journey from Rome to Spain, Portugal and France.

1572 (September 28) Returns to Rome.

1571 (October 1) Death.

[1624 Beatified.

1671 (April 12) Canonised by Pope Clement XI.]

PART I
IN THE WORLD
1510-1550

CHAPTER I

THE HEIR

THE spring of 1510 faded to summer. The Valencian sun blazed from a sky of cloudless sapphire. The air had that marvellous clearness which gives a sharpness of vision, physical and mental, unknown in the misty north. The narrow streets of Gandia, shadowed by the tall, grim houses, were like dark ravines. The high church, the huge square façade of the palace over the walled terrace above the banks of the Serpis, the brown, ridged roofs, the old city walls showed hard and brilliant as enamel. The fertile *huerta*, with its quaint white cottages and their steep thatched roofs, was like a fantastic jewelled chess-board, gold of ripe corn shot with blood-red poppies, green of tall sugar-canes, dun grey and golden green of olive and orange orchards.

It was too hot now to stay on the wide, red-tiled terrace of the palace, whose view swept over the flat, fruitful plain to the sea two miles to the east, away to the mountains, range behind range, almost transparent in the dazzling light, unreal as a background of painted gauze. The long afternoons when streets and fields were deserted, when even animals refused to stir, the Duchess, Doña Maria Enriquez, and her young daughter-in-law Doña Juana de Aragon, went down to the little sunk garden which Maria's husband, Juan de Borgia, second Duke or Gandia, had designed to pretend he was home again in Italy. It was deep and cool, shaded by thick orange-trees and tall feathery palms, set with little round stones underfoot, ringed with a tangle of roses and geraniums, red and white. The last roses scented the still air and the only sound was the splash of water into the moss-greened stone basin of the fountain.

Doña Maria folded her hands over the rosary which she had said for the grandchild, hoped for since her son's marriage a year and a half ago and now to be born in the autumn. No one could know, as she knew, how many prayers the longed-for heir would need, the boy in whose veins would mingle two streams of such fierce, passionate, lawless blood. The girl beside her, a little pale and weary, long lashes casting a shadow on smooth cheeks, was the bastard daughter of Alfonso, Archbishop of Zaragoza, himself the bastard son of King Ferdinand of Aragon. And her own husband had been Juan, second Duke of Gandia, son of Pope Alexander VI and his Italian mistress Vanozza. Surely the child would be no mediocre nonentity, but something vital, arrogant, impassioned, a great sinner or a great saint. His birth would bring her one step nearer her secret desire, to hide her bruised heart under the rough serge of a Poor Clare in the convent at Gandia where her daughter was already a nun.

The four years of her married life came back to her. Far away they seemed but the memory still agonized, like the searing of hot iron on quivering flesh. After her quiet childhood at Baza, she had been betrothed at the age of nine to the eldest son of Alexander VI. Pedro-Luis de Borgia had fought with Ferdinand and Isabella in the last campaign against the Moorish kingdom of Granada. The king had made him Duke of Gandia for his services and the young man had bought the town and lands of Gandia with the fifty thousand ducats given him by his father. Then he had died in Rome (1488) and his younger brother Juan had succeeded to his title, estates and promised bride. Maria had been barely fifteen when she had come to Barcelona with her mother, Maria de Luna, and her father, Don Enrique, uncle of the king. Juan, four years older than his bride, had just landed from Rome and the wedding had been a magnificent affair, graced by the presence of Ferdinand and Isabella and the court.

Pedro-Luis had been a daring and brilliant soldier.

Juan was wicked, reckless and a fool. Hating Spain, caring nothing for his young wife, he ran wild in the streets, brothels and gambling-hells of Barcelona, chasing dogs, cats and women with equal gusto. The Pope sent stern reprimands and elderly advisers. In vain. Red-haired Cesare, with more brains in his little finger than Juan in his dark head, wrote sage counsels to his elder brother. The little Duchess sounded the depths of shame, misery and neglect. Forced to retire to Gandia and the palace which had been a Moorish stronghold and then a royal Aragonese castle, the Duke still contrived to fling money and morals to the wind and sat down at table served by thirty-five gentlemen gorgeously attired.

At last (1496) he received the welcome permission to return to Rome. Doña Maria, left at Gandia with her two babies, felt as if the shadow of hell itself had lifted to let in clean sunshine and fresh air. Juan, who showed himself as great a fool in the field of battle as in the city, was laden with titles and riches by his doting father. Then (June 15, 1497) his mangled body was dragged from the Tiber filth in a fisherman's net. Roman rumour branded Cesare as the murderer, but that astute fox had nothing to gain by his brother's death and history has laid enough crimes at his door without adding fratricide to them.

The tragedy which sent the old Pope nearly mad with grief was the order of release for Maria. Of the brilliance, splendour and beauty of the Italian Renaissance she had known nothing. It had shown her only incest, murder, adultery, lust, cruelty and blood. Tragedy and misfortune which crush weak characters only make strong ones braver. The widowed Duchess had vowed to make her life one long reparation, to foster in her children a holiness which should in some degree compensate for the sins of her husband and his family. Her personal service and alms to the poor and sick of the town were only equalled by her generosity to the Church. Alexander VI had erected the parish church of Gandia into a collegiate church with dean and canons (1499). She enlarged it to twice its original size, melted down the immense statues of the Apostles given by the Pope, and used the proceeds to furnish new sacred vessels and found larger endowments for the prebendaries. She spent lavishly on the interior decoration of the church, with its cliff-like yellow buttresses overlooking the market-place and the view of its noble Gothic door blocked by the tall houses of the narrow street. The fine triptych and reredos of the high altar were painted to her order. The beautiful bronze tabernacle was not made till thirty years later by a monk of the neighbouring monastery of Cotalba.

But all this pious generosity did not denude her of worldly wisdom. She regulated business, bought and sold land to such good purpose that her son Juan, when he came of age, succeeded not only to greatly increased estates but to a yearly income of thirty thousand ducats (in modern purchasing power a ducat is roughly equal to a pound sterling). She arranged good marriages for her son and daughter before they were in their teens. Isabel was betrothed to the son of the Duke of Segorbe. Then one day, as she was wandering with her brother in the rose garden and he was planning their future, she answered unexpectedly: "You may marry if you wish to, but I will have no bridegroom but the Maker of these flowers." He was furious at such folly but, a little later, she went into the Convent of the Poor Clares behind a priest carrying the Viaticum, and refused to leave it. The convent, founded by French refugee nuns fifty years before, was already famed for the holiness of its inmates. Sister Francis of Jesus, as Isabel became, soon acquired the reputation of a saint.

The Duchess's plans for her son's marriage were more successful. Though only fifteen he was already the father of an illegitimate son by a young woman of noble birth, and when sixteen he married at Valladolid Juana of Aragon, two years older than himself and granddaughter of King Ferdinand, his mother's cousin (January 31, 1509). When the succession was assured, his mother felt she could leave the world with a clear conscience, sure that the young Duchess, a model of common sense as well as of generosity and piety, could be trusted to keep her husband faithful and train her children in such a way as to minimise the danger of that wild heritage.

The golden October day was ending as the men returned from work in the bare vineyards, the orange orchards and stubble fields. The streets of Gandia were dark, except where a yellow pool of light from an open door fell on rough stones and piled dust. The cavernous kitchens, lit only by little earthenware lamps which had not changed since Roman times, were full of an appetising smell from stews of garlic, rice and goats' flesh. There was a buzz of talk, not only among the women, but among the men too, as they gathered at street corners or drank crude red wine outside the *fondas*. Dark as Africans, most of them, they looked like the Asiatic figures on archaic Greek vases, lean, bare legs almost black under their wide linen drawers, short velvet jackets open over homespun white shirts, gaudy belts and gay silk handkerchiefs bound round their sleek black hair. There were Moors too, in baggy trousers, turbans and white linen tunics. The slaves of the great nobles who worked on the land were all Moors, and it was said that half the population of Valencia were Mahometans in secret.

The 'old' Duchess (she was only thirty-two now) and the young were both of them beloved by the people, and the prayers of the poor reinforced those of the Poor Clares that the birth now expected should be that of a boy. But still the eagerly awaited news was delayed, and rumours began to filter through the city that all was not going as it should in the palace.

Juana lay in the huge canopied bed in the 'Duchess's Room', with its tapestries on the walls and its floor gay

b

with *azulejo* tiles. Waiting-women ran in and out, flustered and tearful. Only Doña Maria sat still, her rosary in her hands. She knew, as they all did in their hearts, that human aid, poor and inefficient at its best, was now useless. The girl's strength, drained by long hours of agony, was ebbing fast. It seemed humanly impossible that her child should be born alive or that she herself should survive. "The sins of the fathers shall be visited on the children." Doña Maria saw the words as if written in blood. Surely not thus, after her long years of reparation and prayer. God was a God of mercy, not vengeance.

The young Duchess spoke suddenly, in an almost inaudible whisper. "Fetch St Francis's cord from the convent."

It came at last, the hempen girdle that had bound the coarse grey habit of the little Poor Man of Assisi, frayed and worn with veneration and the passage of three hundred years. It was apparently too late. Juana lay as if dead, waxen-faced, without sign of heart-beat or breath. The chaplain stood by her. She seized the cord, bound it round her agonising body and invoked the saint with a fervour amazing in one so worn out (October 28, 1510).

In fulfilment of his mother's vow and in gratitude to the saint of Assisi the boy was baptised a day or two after his birth by the name of Francis. It was a scene of colour and splendour. The new-born baby was carried by one of the civic dignitaries, as was customary in Gandia, and baptised by Don Fernan Gomez, Dean of Gandia and Provost of Valencia, in the collegiate church, in the rough, cup-shaped stone font which still stands there. Gothic pillars and font were garlanded with wreaths of laurel. The banner of the city, two towers and battlemented wall surmounted by a six-pointed star, the Borgia arms, a vermilion bull on a ground of gold, the scarlet liveries of the palace servants, the bright surcoats of heralds, the purple of the canons, the dimmer, yet warm hues of frescoes and reredos, the shadows of the tall church were all aglow.

The picture of the ceremony shows the Duke, looking older than his seventeen years, his dark, bearded face framed in a small ruff, one lean hand on his gilt sword-hilt. Beside him, the dominant figure here as in palace and city, stands his mother, white-veiled, hands clasped, her long, high-collared black cloak sweeping from neck to ground.

She sees the breaking of the last chain which binds her to the world. She will wait for the birth of one more grandchild before she withdraws to the convent which is to be a spiritual power-house moulding the character of Francis and the fortunes of his house.

CHAPTER II

EARTHLY PARADISE

FRANCIS'S home for the first ten years of his life was at Gandia. The old Moorish, Aragonese castle, built for strength and defence rather than for comfort, had been transformed internally by the first Duke, Pedro-Luis, into some resemblance to an Italian Renaissance palace. The old front stood — as it still does — showing a gaunt and windowless face to the street, the only entrance, under the stone archway, through enormously thick double doors, heavily studded and hinged with iron. The first court, the *Patio de Armas* (court of arms), was flanked by the stables on the left (now the church), while opposite the entry the whole side was occupied by the noble open stairway, supported on three pointed arches, its three slim columns springing to the wide-eaved, ridged roof. The original red tiles of the steps, worn and uneven, are still in position. The Gothic window over the stairs, with three trefoil-headed lights, is the only one left from the Aragonese building.

The rooms inside were a strange mixture, typical of sixteenth-century Spain, of splendour and discomfort. Here and there bare stone walls were covered with tapestries or Italian brocades, bright with Moorish *azulejo* tiles of yellow, green and blue, or painted with fourteenth-century frescoes whose stiff, geometric patterns recalled Arab inspiration. The wooden ceilings, heavily beamed and dark with age, had no trace of richness of carving and colour such as rejoice eye and mind in the Audiencia of Valencia. The floor of the smaller hall of reception, like that of many of the rooms, was of small red tiles of plain design.

The gayest corner of the palace, and a favourite haunt of Doña Maria and the young Duchess, was the terrace above the river, with its view of the distant mountains and the plain stretching east to the sea. The five doors leading from the long series of halls on to the terrace are still bright with their porches of blue tiles, and the wall, up to the wide-eaved roof, is covered with coloured tiles and huge paintings, in Italian style, of conventional flowers and foliage springing from double-handled Greek vases.

Moorish, Gothic and Italian Renaissance were incongruously mingled in the great building, the centre of whose life was the little chapel of St Michael, patron of Gandia. A child, though unconscious of its surroundings, is deeply influenced by them, and Francis was an intelligent and precocious child, as eager to learn as a puppy to try his teeth on a hard bone. The sixteenth century had no theories about the advantage of leaving a child's brain fallow for the first six or seven years. Francis knew his prayers when he was three. By the time he was four he had mastered the whole of his catechism, which he was made to recite daily, uncomfortably on his knees. He knew enough too to be able to follow Mass, and his first school was the convent of the Poor Clares.

His grandmother was there now, as well as his aunt. He could not remember her in anything but the coarse habit of black serge, for he was not yet two when, after the birth of her second grandson Alfonso, she had joined her daughter. The doctors unanimously prophesied her death within a year of such austerity, so she had waited till her son was away on a visit to her mother at Baza. When he returned he had found her gone. She had made her profession as Sister Gabrielle in March, 1512, and later that same year was born her first granddaughter, Luisa, who, after his mother, was to occupy first place in Francis's heart and was to be his devoted shadow and imitator.

The young Duchess had no intention of allowing her eldest and favourite child to grow up in bucolic ignorance. Canon Ferran, a learned theologian, was appointed the boy's tutor, but grandmother and aunt continued to pet and teach him. He heard from them of St Francis of Assisi, his own patron, of St Michael, captain of the hosts of the Lord and patron of Gandia, of St George, patron of Valencia. The two warriors, with the conquered dragon writhing under their feet, were more calculated to appeal to a child's imagination than the Poverello. He heard too, though not from herself, how Isabel, when about to be betrothed to the Duke of Segorbe's son, had been one day alone in a garden outside the city walls, when a beautiful youth had come through the tangle of roses and had put into her hands a little mother-of-pearl cross, with the words: "Thou shalt have no bridegroom but an eternal one." The angelic visitor had vanished, but Sister Gabrielle still had the cross and, later, was to give it to Francis, always to be worn round his neck.

The child's memory was remarkable. He could repeat almost word for word anything he had once heard, and the nuns loved to put him in the refectory pulpit (the convent had as yet no chapel) and listen entranced while he reeled off secondhand sermons and meditations. It was only natural that in such an atmosphere the small boy should develop a precocious pietism. With the natural childish love of drama and mimicry he began to erect miniature altars and to imitate liturgical ceremonies, helped by his pages and, as soon as she could toddle, by Luisa.

The Duchess, with sound common sense, checked this tendency. "I asked God for a son who was to be a Duke, Francis, not a friar. You need arms and horses, not statues and sermons." The Duke, a blunt countryman with a passion for the chase, was a good landlord and a truly religious character with a special devotion to the Blessed Sacrament; he did not mean his heir to grow up 'sicklied o'er' with a hothouse piety. "Clear away those altars, boy," he said, with the brusqueness of his Aragonese blood. "Your great-grandfather, King Ferdinand, was busy with valour in the field, not with altars."

Action followed words. Francis was given an instructor

in riding and fencing and soon proved himself as apt a
pupil in the *Patio de Armas* as he had done in the convent
parlour. Mounted on a mule or pony he now accompanied
his father with hounds and hawks, and the Duke found
that the boy had inherited all his love of hunting. They
had to ride to the lower slopes of the mountains which
sheltered the *huerta* of Gandia from the cold winds of the
high plateau of Castille, for every inch of the plain was
under cultivation, sometimes yielding as much as four
crops a year.

'A little bit of Paradise fallen to earth' was what the
Moors had called the kingdom of Valencia. Their own
industry and scheme of irrigation had played no small
part in making it so. The river-beds, except in times of
heavy rain or snow melting in the mountains, were dry
long before they reached the sea, for as soon as they came
to the plains the water was drawn off into a network of
small canals and large reservoirs. In that wonderful climate
where rain was rare, snow and frost unknown, wheat
planted in November was ready for the sickle in June.
There were miles of sugar-canes, in earth-walled squares,
the tall, sword-like stems and leaves topped with insigni-
ficant little grey flowers—one of the richest sources of
revenue for the Duke. The men working in them looked
like Chinese coolies, in their short, full, blue tunics, wide
straw hats and bare brown legs. Sometimes they sat perched
on the handle of the plough as they guided horse or mule
through the blue water.

There were, of course, endless disputes about the
supply of water for irrigation. Those the Duke could not
settle as he paused on his way to the hunt, had to he taken to
Valencia to be decided by the Tribunal of the Waters, a body
of peasants which sat every Thursday (as it still does) outside
the great west door of the cathedral and, with a singularly
unlegal charity, charged nothing for its judgments.

Winter in this earthly Paradise was gay as the people.
Fields were snowy with wild daisies, the ordered ranks of

orange trees white in December with heavy-scented blossom, laden with glowing fruit in April and May. February threw a rosy veil of peach and almond blossom across the orchards. Poppies and Adonis anemones splashed the ground with blood-red. Carob-trees with their drooping evergreen leaves and long brown pods, mulberries, their leaves food for the million of silkworms which swarmed in every cottage, were succeeded on the lower mountain slopes by gnarled olives, the colour of the rocks. Here and there clumps of palm-trees rose above their fellows, their slim trunks a golden-brown, their feathery leaves swaying gently in the soft breeze from the sea.

The Duke would stop, as they rode out, to talk to the men in the fields or the half-naked brown children playing in the dust outside the *barracas*, white, thatched homes without chimneys or windows, quaint as dolls' houses. Francis, not yet ten, could scarcely be expected to take much interest in endless talks about a new manure, silkworm culture, a fresh method of pressing oil, the prospects of the grape-harvest, for the new vine leaves already showed their green-gold bright as polished metal against the blackness of the sheltering hedges of close-set cypresses. "*Valencia es tierra de Dios*," quoted the old men: "*Pues ayer trigo y hoy arroz*" (Valencia, God's country, rice to-day where yesterday grew corn). Francis fidgeted as impatiently as the leashed hounds or hooded hawks, till at last the long talks were ended and they headed for the hills. The barren slopes were broken here and there by a straggling olive tree, piled grey stones, sparse scrub and tangles of gorse, blackberry and bilberry, all dusty-grey but excellent cover for game. Then came the blissful moment when hounds were in full cry after doubling hare or wily fox, or the hawks, loosed from hoods and bells, were only still, black specks against the dazzling sky till, swift and straight as falling stones, they swooped on the quivering mass of soft brown feathers.

Sometimes, in the very instant of tensest excitement,

the Duke would pause abruptly and lift his hand for silence. He had heard, through the dry, still air the tiny tinkle of a distant bell which meant that the Viaticum was being carried through the streets of Gandia to some poor soul in its last agony. He would gallop back, Francis with him—leaving pages and huntsmen to call in hounds or hawks—to dismount and follow bareheaded the priest carrying the Blessed Sacrament.

This pious custom took deep root in the boy's heart. He kept it up all the years he spent at Gandia and, like his father, trained his sons to do likewise. There was another custom, too, at the ducal court, which was a special favourite of his. Every member of the household annually drew lots for a patron of the coming year and, on the vigil and feast of his saint, served a dinner given to two poor people. Francis carried out his service with special enthusiasm and continued to do so long after he had left Gandia and the world.

The years slipped by. Francis was in his tenth year, tall as well as intelligent for his age. He had the proud bearing and easy grace of the Borgias, a happy disposition, a quick response to sympathy and, under this pleasant surface, a capacity for passion and suffering unusual for his age. He now had six brothers and sisters, Alfonso, Luisa, Anna, Isabel, Henry and Maria, but he remained dearest of all to his mother, whom he loved with a devotion he accorded to none else.

There was peace in the 'earthly paradise' of Valencia, and in far-off Europe too there was one of those brief halcyon moments so rare in a century of endless wars and religious strifes. Henry VIII of England, Francis I of France, Charles I of Spain, all young, eager and ambitious, were soon to prove rivals for the imperial throne, but the romantic knight-errant, Maximilian I (Charles's grandfather) did not die till the new year of 1519.

Charles, whose heart was in Flanders, his birth-place, had offended the majority of his Spanish subjects by his unwillingness to visit his kingdom, his preference for Flemish counsellors and courtiers, his ungrateful treatment of the great Cardinal Ximenes, and the apparent callousness with which he regarded his mad mother, Queen Juana, shut away in the castle of Simancas.

Giovanni de Medici (who had greeted his elevation to the chair of Peter as Leo X with the remark: "Since God has given us the Papacy, let us enjoy it") was a typical child of his age, and his reign has been called the Golden Age of the Renaissance. He had dismissed news of Luther's revolt as another quarrel among German friars. The completion of the new St Peter's was far more important than ninety-five theses against indulgences nailed on the door of a church in the barbarian north.

The Duke of Gandia, like Gallio and Leo X, "cared for none of these things." His horizon was bounded by Valencia city, twenty-two miles to the north; by Denia, twenty miles to the south; by the peaks of Monduve and Barel to the west and by the Mediterranean to the east. Italy, France, Germany, England were as far outside his sphere of interest as Mexico, where Cortes, his ships burnt to prevent retreat, was fighting with his handful of battered veterans against the mighty Aztec empire, or the uncharted western ocean where Magellan and El Cano were starting on the first voyage round the world.

There was enough at home to keep a man busy, a yearly increasing family to be provided for, and though the Gandia estates, thanks to his mother's careful nursing, brought in thirty thousand ducats yearly, more than a third of this was given in alms. The Duke answered the remonstrances of succeeding majordomos with his usual bluntness. "Money had better run short in the palace than among the poor. You would say nothing if I spent it on my own amusement, so do not reproach me for giving it away in charity."

He was more than satisfied with the way Francis was shaping. The boy had outgrown the passion for pious

mummery, was a keen horseman, fencer and huntsman.
He had begun, when seven, to learn Castillean, instead of
the rough Catalan dialect of Valencia. He was getting on
well with grammar, Latin and perhaps Italian as well,
while Canon Alfonso of Avila was grounding him in
mathematics and music, in both of which he was to make
a name for himself afterwards.

But earthly paradises, like everything else in this world,
are not everlasting. The Duke, who had interests in the
city of Valencia, where his uncle had built a palace in the
Plaza San Lorenzo, was conscious that lately all was not
well in the labyrinth of crooked streets of *'Medina-bû-
Tarab'* (the city of joy). The river Turia, usually a wide
expanse of dry pasture at the end of summer, had risen
after four days of torrential rain in September, 1517, had
flooded a large part of the city, had completely swept away
a hundred of the poorer houses and had left others in
ruins. A terrible storm in the spring of 1519 had burst
over Valencia. The tall Miguelete tower of the cathedral
had been struck by lightning and the wooden roof over
the only public clock set on fire.

Men began to murmur, to remember and repeat the
prophecy of Pedro Sanchez, who, five years before, had
burst into the sanctuary during High Mass in the cathedral, and brandished a naked sword, crying: "Wake !
Wake ! for city and kingdom are threatened with dreadful
calamity !" Worse was to come, for in July, 1519, plague
broke out and raged for two months with such violence
that nobles and rich merchants fled, leaving palaces and
big houses deserted. A rumour spread that the Algerian
pirates under Barbarossa were about to land and, with the
help of the local Moors, to reconquer Spain for Islam.

Terrified, strung up to an hysterical pitch of anger and
madness, the people were as a powder magazine, and the
match was set to it by the folly of a friar who preached in
the cathedral a wild denunciation of local vice. The fate of
Valencia would be that of those other cities of the plain,

Sodom and Gomorrah, if this cancer were not eradicated from its midst. The hunt was soon in full cry. Foiled of its prey the mob broke into the cathedral. The high altar was defiled, silver statues and rich stuffs pillaged. Episcopal entreaties, an interdict proclaimed by the Vicar-General, the armed force called out by the Guilds were powerless to prevent one wretched man from being burnt in the market place.

Few, if any, of the nobles were as good landlords as the Duke of Gandia. They had abandoned Valencia in its hour of need. Incidents were remembered when slaves had been put to death, brides torn from their husbands' arms at the church doors. A certain Juan Lorenzo put himself at the head of the Guild, proclaimed a Germania (brotherhood), was named dictator and proceeded to declare a state of revolt. He and two others caught Charles at Barcelona, about to embark to be crowned emperor as Charles V (January 4, 1520). Equally unwilling to be delayed or to make things worse by infringing the cherished liberties and Fueros of Valencia, Charles named as his representative his old Flemish tutor, Cardinal Adrian of Utrecht, and sailed from a kingdom where he had found nothing but independence and discontent.

Though most of the kingdom of Valencia was now in revolt, peace still reigned at Gandia, but in February public affairs were forgotten in a more personal anxiety, for the Duchess was dangerously ill. It was the first sorrow of Francis's life. Like most children who feel deeply he was incapable of relieving his feelings by expressing them. Life without his mother seemed too dreadful a thing to endure. He went away and shut himself alone in his room to pray. Then it seemed to him that prayer, however passionate, was not enough. He knew there was no love without suffering, that the greater the love the greater the suffering. He tore off doublet and shirt and tried to scourge his own tender shoulders. It was the foreshadowing of that greater sorrow under this same roof twenty-six years later, a faint echo of his own words then: "I desire naught but in all to deny my will that Yours may be done."

This was his first meeting with death, the sight of the room where he had been born, tapestried walls and high bed hung with black and, in the yellow light of the tall flickering candles, his mother lying as if asleep. He could not believe that never again would her long lashes lift, the dark eyes open, the curved mouth smile, and the soft voice murmur the endearments which were kept only for him. The light had been extinguished. Gandia, from henceforth, would be no longer home, but an exile of sad memories.

CHAPTER III

WIDER HORIZON

NOT only was the whole kingdom of Valencia in
open revolt. The Communeros had risen throughout Spain, had even forced their way into the
castle at Tordesillas to get the poor mad Queen's assent
to superseding her son on the throne of Spain. Indeed it
looked likely that he would not be able to hold what his
ancestor had won by the sword. Old Cardinal Adrian—
to be renowned later for his severity when Pope— proved
entirely ineffective in Spain, as well as unpopular like all his
fellow Flemings. Urged by the nobles to take strong measures on his arrival in Valencia, he failed to control the
mob, which, in the country, had been sacking churches and
torturing prisoners. Indeed, the only sign of Christian zeal
they showed was to seize Moors, baptize them by force
and then put them to the sword. As one cynic remarked,
thereby many souls were sent to heaven and many Christian pockets were comfortably filled.

Even in Gandia anarchy showed itself. Less than a
month after the Duchess's death a score of the bolder
spirits nailed a defiant call to arms on the church door
(March, 1520). The Duke replied by confiscating their
goods and pronouncing sentence of death on them. The
new Viceroy, Diego Hurtado de Mendoza, who had entered Valencia on May 18 was forced to abandon it after a
pitched battle in the streets, and summoned the nobles to
join him with all available men at Denia.

The Duke, seeing the dangerous state of the country,
sent his mother and sister and children to the comparative
safety of Peñiscola, 88 miles north of Valencia, one of the
few strongholds which still held out for the King. Francis
alone remained in the palace at Gandia which, in July, was

made the rendez-vous for the royalist army. Though its tragedies may leave indelible scars, youth is elastic, and Francis would not have been a boy if he had not thrilled in response to the splendour and panoply of war. The Viceroy was hopelessly outnumbered by the Germania, whose new and able leader, Vicente Periz, had eight thousand well-armed and trained men. But the two thousand infantry and a hundred and fifty horsemen crowded the town, and the palace was full of nobles and their pages and servants. At a council of war held there (July 24) the Viceroy was for prudence and emphasized the need to wait for reinforcements. The Duke of Gandia, outspoken as usual, was all for strong and immediate action and his arguments carried the day.

On the next morning the army marched out of Gandia, drums beating, banners, with their coats of arms, flying. As the Duke's standard-bearer rode out of the gate the staff of the banner which he carried, draped in black crape in sign of the Duke's mourning for his wife, caught on the arch and snapped. A murmur of superstitious horror went up from the people who had crowded to see the troops leave.

Francis was alone in the palace, but for his governor and a handful of servants. From the height of the palace it was possible to listen to drums and bugles, to watch the line of yellow dust which marked the march to the lower mountain slopes a league away, but impossible to distinguish the fortunes of the day. The battle was soon over. Nobles and their mounted followers found it impossible to charge on the rocky ground which was a tangle of scrub, bushes and pitfalls. The gunners, at the first shout of 'St George!' from Periz's men, deserted in a body and rushed down on Gandia to pillage the palace and the Moorish quarter. The Moors in the viceregal army, who had remained faithful, could not be expected to watch their women ravished and murdered, their homes destroyed. They fled too, in pursuit of the undisciplined mob.

Mendoza, left practically without an army, galloped off to Denia, followed by the nobles.

The Moorish quarter of Gandia was filled by the clash of steel, the shrieks of women and children, the groans of old men wounded and dying. The great door of the palace was shaking under the blows of heavy beams which were battering it. There was only just time for the tutor to rush with Francis through the little garden gate by the river, fling him on to a horse, mount behind him and set off full tilt along the sandy track to the sea before the mob had broken in and begun to sack the palace. When Periz appeared and called the men to sharp account a hundred thousand ducats' worth of damage had been done, in destruction and theft of silver, gold and jewelry, a large quantity of it brought from Italy by the second Duke and the most beautiful work of the best Roman jewellers and goldsmiths of the day.

Two miles away, in the little harbour at the mouth of the Serpis, a fishing boat was lying. In it the tutor and his precious charge reached Denia in safety. The little town, climbing a hill crowned by the old Moorish castle, afforded no prospect of safety. Already a Genoese ship in the harbour was crowded with refugees, the Viceroy among them, and on it Francis rejoined his father. The south wind which had risen made a passage to Cartagena impossible, so sail was set north and the broken remains of the royalist army landed at Peñiscola (July 29, 1520).

For what seemed to him a long time Francis had lived in a world of men: his father, harassed, oppressed with anxiety and responsibility; the menservants in their summer livery of scarlet silk; the Moors, turbaned, bearded, armed with scimitars and lances; the Viceroy; nobles old and young, dark, lean, arrogant in their polished helmets and cuirasses, with fine blades from Toledo; prancing horses and fluttering banners bright with many quarterings. All the panoply of war had glowed and glittered in that bright, clear air under the burning sun of midsummer.

Now, at Peñiscola, all was changed. From being, as he felt himself, a man among men, Francis was back among women and children. The high rock of 'the Gibraltar of Valencia' was impregnable, cut off from the mainland but for a narrow spit of sand just above the level of the tide less sea.

Over the piled houses frowned the old castle where Pedro de Luna, the anti-Pope Benedict XIII, and his cardinals had defied the Church for seven years till his death in 1424. Here were gathered, with other refugees, Francis's grandmother, Sister Gabrielle, his aunt, now Abbess of the Gandia convent, his six brothers and sisters. Luisa, his favourite and 'shadow', was in an ecstasy of joy to see her hero again. If she were with him, it mattered nothing to her where she was, and for Francis, perhaps, it was good to be in new and strange surroundings where every corner was not filled with memories of his mother, renewing the aching loneliness of his heart.

Peñiscola, however, was no place for women and children to be in longer than was necessary. The reinforcements from Andalusia arrived. The royal army took the field. The tide turned, as it generally does however just the reasons for revolt. Town after town was recaptured. Vicente Periz, bravest and most able of the Germania leaders, who had captured Jativa (the ancient home of the Borgias) and taken the Viceroy's brother prisoner, was at last driven back into the city of Valencia, overwhelmed by sheer force of numbers and killed fighting in his home in the Calle de Gracia. His dead body was dragged in triumph through the streets and hung on a high gallows in the market-place as a warning to rebels. Jativa and Alcira still held out, under a mysterious new leader, young, brilliant, learned and daring, said by common report to be a natural son of King Ferdinand. Then they too fell. The 'Encubierto' (mystery man) was assassinated, his body burnt, his beautiful head nailed above the Cuarte Gate of Valencia. Once more the royal standard floated

c

from the two Moorish castles, yellow as the hills on which
they perch, and connected with walls to the little town of
Jativa, given by Jaime el Conquistador three hundred
years before to the men of Borja (November, 1520).

It was not till the next year that the Duke of Gandia
reconquered his own estates, to find Gandia partly de-
vastated, the Moorish quarter wrecked, most of the treasures vanished from the palace, even the strong walls and
roof damaged. He himself had not come out of the war
scatheless. He had been wounded by an arrow during a
skirmish in the autumn. The doctors had not been able to
get the barb out of his throat and they expected the wound
to be mortal. The Duke himself attributed his recovery
not to the handiwork of the surgeons, in which he was
certainly right, but to the intercession of the Virgin of the
Pillar at Zaragoza, to whom he had a special devotion.

But long before the end of 1520, before Periz had been
killed, the family gathering at Peñiscola had broken up.
As soon as news of the royalist defeat in July reached
Baza, Doña Maria de Luna, Francis's great-grandmother,
had sent to the Duke to offer a safe asylum to his children,
mother and sister. She was not the only one anxious to
give the children a home. The same offer came from
Zaragoza, from Doña Ana de Gurrea, mother of Duchess
Juana and of the Archbishop of Zaragoza. Francis's
mother, in her will, had made him her heir and appointed
her brother his guardian and tutor. It was therefore obvious that Francis should be sent to Zaragoza and, to
their mutual joy, Luisa was to go with him. The Duke,
unusually diplomatic, decided to placate the dominant old
Doña Maria by sending to Baza his mother and sister.
Land travel was too dangerous in the unsettled state of the
country, so the two parties embarked on board ship, one
bound south to Andalusia, the other north to Catalonia.
Francis was only to see his father again on brief visits to
Gandia years later.

CHAPTER IV

OPENING DOORS

IT WAS a country different from all his memories that Francis saw the morning after his and Luisa's arrival at Zaragoza. The windows of the Archbishop's palace looked across the rushing yellow Ebro and the old Puente de Piedra on to a wide plain the colour of umber, burnt siena, rust and gold, bounded in the far north by violet-blue mountains, snow-capped against the clear sky, so much paler than that of Valencia. They were the Pyrenees, the northern boundary of Spain, shutting off the world whose echoes had hardly reached Gandia, but which was now to become for Francis something more than a vague dream.

If the burnt plain was unlike the green, fruitful *huerta* of Valencia, so did life here, at the court of Don Juan de Aragon, Abbot of Veruela, Monte Aragon and Rueda, and Archbishop of Zaragoza, differ from that at Gandia. Don Juan had succeeded his father, Don Alfonso, in the arch-diocese a few months before. Alfonso, an illegitimate son of Ferdinand of Aragon by Aldonsa Roig, Viscountess of Evol, was appointed Archbishop of Zaragoza by his father's influence at the age of nine (1478). He was ordained priest twenty-three years later and only celebrated Mass once in his life, on the day of his ordination. Lieutenant-general and Viceroy of Aragon, as well as Archbishop, he had, by Doña Ana de Gurrea, four children, Juan and Ferdinand, who both succeeded him as Archbishop, Juana Duchess of Gandia (Francis's mother) and the Duchess of Medina Sidonia.

Doña Ana, after Alfonso's death in February, 1520, continued to live in the archbishop's palace and to control domestic arrangements and finance. The position was an amazing one even for Renaissance times, more Italian, perhaps, than Spanish, and shows how little dishonour was attached by contemporaries to illegitimacy of birth.

Francis was only ten, but precocious and solidly grounded in religion. Perhaps it was the memory of his mother's prayers and a realisation of the anomalous position at the episcopal court that made him hear Mass every morning and regularly make his confession and Communion on great feasts, for it was during this year at Zaragoza that he made his First Communion—unusually young for those days.

The grandmother took Luisa to her heart and into her personal care, but Don Juan, determined that his nephew and ward should not grow up into a country bumpkin, appointed for him a princely household, professors for the humanities and music as well as first-rate masters for arms and horsemanship. The boy's days were full: Latin, French, Italian, mathematics and music, in which he was a specially apt pupil; hours in the tilt-yard and fencing school; rides through the narrow Oriental streets, where the wind is always whipping round the corners and along the river banks, setting dust, dead leaves and rubbish spinning in a devil's dance.

Valencia was now (1521) at peace again, and the Duke was settled at Gandia, which he was hardly to leave again except for an occasional expedition in the neighbourhood. The Communero rebellion in Castille had also been ended by the defeat of the insurgents at Villalar (April 23, 1521) and the execution of their leader Padilla. The mad old Queen Juana, who for eight months had been a puppet in Padilla's hands, was now in closer confinement than ever. Her son's policy of 'masterly inactivity' over the widespread revolt had been undeservedly successful, and on his return to Spain a year later (1522) he was to embark on the course which emasculated the Cortes as his grandparents had broken the power of the nobility.

To Francis, busy at his desk, in the saddle or the ring,

politics were of little interest or importance, but his uncle, with the keen, cynical outlook of the Renaissance states-man, saw that the awkward, slow, fair Flemish Emperor-elect had in him the makings of the greatest layman of his century, while, by inheritance, he ruled not only over a united Spain, but also over the Netherlands, Naples, Sicily and the larger part of the New World. To worship the rising sun is an innate instinct with man, and the Archbishop, with an eye perhaps to his own interest as well as to that of his ward, resolved to place him where a way would be open to imperial favour.

Meanwhile, now that Gandia was again at peace, the Poor Clares were about to return to the convent from which they had been exiled for three years, but before they left Baza, they were anxious that Francis should pay a long promised visit so that they could see him. Old Doña Maria de Luna too wished to see her great-grandson be-fore she died, and with her to wish was to take immediate steps for the fulfilment of her desire. Don Juan, in this, saw eye to eye with the old lady, and Francis, with Luisa, set out south, this time by land since the country was now quiet (1522).

It was a long journey, three hundred odd miles as the crow flies, over endless Sierras, across the valleys of the Atocha and the Tagus, into the Sierra de Cuenca, barren, rocky, fringed with coarse grey scrub and rising here and there to a snow peak. There were interminable plains, grey, ashen, here and there a shallow salt lake, desolate as the Dead Sea, Moorish castles perched on high hills, whose lower slopes of red earth were terraced with vineyards, above them grey fragrant scrub and yellow broom bright-ening the austerity of sharp rocks. And at long last Baza, age-old, climbing to the ruins of the Alcazaba, and, in front of the cathedral where the mosque had stood, the little old cannon which commemorated the capture of the town by Isabella in 1480.

But before Francis had time to take stock of his new

surroundings or to grow impatient with the fondling of aunt and grandmother, he collapsed and lay at death's door. Whether the cause was over-fatigue, change of climate or merely an unusually virulent form of the fever which was then almost universal, doctors and remedies were useless. Old Doña Maria was forced to watch the slow ebbing of her great-grandson's life, her own dominant will for once unavailing. Worse was to follow. An appalling earthquake swept the kingdom of Granada and half Baza was laid in ruins. Francis, still between life and death, was carried in a litter down through crumbling walls, fallen roofs, the groans of half-buried victims and the wails of terrified women.

For six weeks he lay, still in his litter, protected only by a tent, out in the open country, racked with fever, often delirious. The wild, volcanic landscape, dreadful as a scene from Dante's *Inferno*, with its tumbled rocks and ravines like gaping wounds, mingled in the dreams of fever with the memory of a sermon the boy had heard given by his confessor, a Hieronomite friar, during Lent in the convent of Santa Engracia in Zaragoza. The preacher had described the fate of the damned with such vivid detail that Francis had been frozen with a terror which had made an indelible impression on him and which now returned to haunt him.

A good constitution, however, helped no doubt by the prayers of the nuns more than by the primitive medicines of local doctors, pulled the boy through after six long months, and no sooner was the corner turned than the indefatigable old lady was in communication with the Archbishop over Francis's future. They agreed that, unless they took steps, nothing would be done, for the Duke was about to take as his second wife Francisca, daughter of the Viscount of Evol. A golden opportunity now arose to open for Francis the way to the imperial favour. Poor mad Queen Juana, as soon as the Communero rising had been crushed, was more closely confined than ever under the care of the Marquis of Denia. Her only companion, her youngest daughter, Catherine, was three years older than Francis, and the child's life was made a misery to her by her mother's insane horror of people. Catherine was shut away in a little room, her only recreation to look out of the window through which she could see children playing in a lane or good folk going into church. She managed to write to her brother, complaining of her life and of the ill-treatment of her mother by Denia and his wife, and Charles decided that a companion of her own age must be provided for Catherine.

Such an honour was of course eagerly contested. Doña Maria and Don Juan pushed Francis's claim with vigour, emphasized his cousinship with the Emperor and Catherine, his charm, intelligence and education. It apparently occurred to no one that to send a sensitive child, but lately recovered from a long and serious illness, into an atmosphere of insanity and hatred, was hardly a desirable course. Anyhow influence gained the day and the heir of Gandia was appointed, at the age of twelve, page to the Infanta Catherine.

Luisa was to go to her mother's sister, the Duchess of Medina Sidonia, at San Lucar de Barrameda, a small seaport at the mouth of the Guadalquivir, where Magellan and El Cano had started three years before on the first voyage round the world, and where, in 1517, Henry VIII of England had founded the Colegio de San Giorgio, a hospital for English sailors.

The parting from the brother whom she had loved and imitated ever since she could toddle was a heart-breaking affair for the little girl of ten, devout, intensely affectionate and sensitive. It would have been worse could she have foreseen the future and known that she would only once see again in this world the being whom she was to love more than husband or children.

Three years is an eternity to a child, to whom every week

seems a year, every year a century. Time stands still in the shadows, as when no sunshine marks the passing hours on the dial. Shadows indeed were deep in the castle of Tordesillas, looking on to the old bridge, with its ten arches spanning the Duero and its flanking towers. Opposite was the Royal Convent of Poor Clares, founded nearly two hundred years ago by the daughters of Pedro the Cruel. From her windows in the gloomy fortress the mad Queen could see the Gothic building in whose splendid *capilla dorada* her husband's body had lain for so many years, till taken by her son's command to lie in the cathedral of Granada beside those of Ferdinand and Isabella.

Death is to the Spaniard an ever-present and important reality, the inevitable end to life's brief, bright span. The Spaniard has not that strange northern fear of facing reality which makes it almost indecent to mention death in polite society, but in Juana's case, this realism had been twisted by her diseased mentality into something horrible.

Francis heard, before he had been long at Tordesillas, how the Queen had refused to be parted from her husband's dead body, how the jealousy, only too justified during his life, persisted after death so that she would not allow his corpse to spend the night in a convent of nuns, but, deaf to protests, had spent the dark hours with it in the open country. It was strange that these scenes, and the more horrible ones when, morn and night, the coffin was opened so that the widow should kiss and fondle the mouth and feet of the corpse, should not have affected the child born less than four months after the death of Philip the Handsome. Catherine, however, showed signs neither of her mother's unbalanced mind nor of her father's instability. Born and bred in a dreadful atmosphere of jealousy, hate, imprisonment and suspicion, she was capable, content to wait for a marriage which must be her order of release, and meantime, delighted to have the daily comradeship of her cousin, younger than herself but older than his twelve years in brains and manners.

The two children became devoted friends. The Marquis of Denia, grim gaoler with an unenviable task; his wife, hated by their prisoner; the madwoman herself, old and withered at forty, with wild grey hair, burning eyes, her gaunt body unwashed and barely covered by filthy rags—these were shadows which could not wholly darken nor terrify the Infanta and Francis. Sometimes the Queen would shriek from a window to passers telling them to rob and murder. She would sit for days on the stone floor, till the food round her turned putrid. Worst of all, she declined to hear Mass, except under compulsion, and refused the Sacraments. Though her personal violence terrified her servants, at whom she would throw jugs and glasses, she was passionately devoted to her daughter and, oddly enough in one whose jealousy had been uncontrolled in her best days, she apparently had no objection to Francis.

Winter came and went, with bitter winds sweeping down like hawks from the snow passes of the Pyrenees, bringing little flakes of dry snow sharp as needle-points. Summer came and went, its fierce heat scorching the wide treeless Castillean plains to fierier rust and umber, till the river crawled low in its sandy bed and the hot air quivered till things looked no more substantial than a mirage about to dissolve and reveal the hidden reality. *"Nueve meses de invierno, tres de infierno"* (nine months winter and three of hell), the caustic saying held good of Tordesillas as well as of Burgos.

Catherine was now eighteen. The cousins had been inseparable for three years, and when the Infanta's marriage with John III of Portugal was arranged (1525), she was determined that Francis should accompany her to Lisbon. But she reckoned without the Duke. Himself deeply rooted at Gandia, where he was busy producing a second family, he absolutely refused to allow his heir to cross the frontier and disappear into a foreign country which to his stay-at-home mind was as remote as Mexico or Peru.

Catherine set out for Lisbon, Francis for Zaragoza. The unhappy Queen, for another thirty years, dragged out a miserable existence, alone but for memories, shadows and delusions.

Don Juan was charmed with the nephew whom he had last seen as a boy of twelve, now a stripling of fifteen, who had gained poise and experience as the Princess's companion, a diplomacy in his interviews with the mad Juana. The blade was of good steel, thought the Archbishop, well-tempered. It needed now only a final polish and damascene before it could be put to the use for which he destined it. The Emperor's star was at its height. His enemy, Francis I of France, captured at the battle of Pavia (February 24, 1525), was a prisoner in Madrid and was only to be released in March of the next year, two months before Charles married at Seville the Portuguese Infanta, Isabella. Spain was at peace. The royal exchequer was unusually full, since Charles had extracted a liberal subsidy from the Cortes of 1525 in return for breaking off his matrimonial negotiations for the hand of Mary, Henry VIII's sister.

Meanwhile Francis was kept busy. Twice a day he had lessons in philosophy from the celebrated professor of the Montagu College of Paris University, Gaspard de Lax. Language, mathematics and music lessons continued. Other young nobles were provided by his uncle to study special subjects with him and to carry the spirit of keen and friendly rivalry into the fencing-school and the tilt-yard. There were, too, long days with hounds and hawks, out on to the sun-baked banks of the Ebro and the wide plains whose hot umber and siena were broken here and there by the grateful shade of silvery, wavering willows or the dusky black of spired cypresses and heavy pines. As always, Francis found a keen and exquisite joy in hawking, the feel of a good horse under him, the swift, beauti-

ful dash of the hawk upon its prey, sharp and deadly as the
final stroke of the matador's sword.

Two years passed. Francis was seventeen, a man already,
with all the fierce strong passions and the wild blood of
the south and of his ancestry. He was strong, beautiful,
ambitious, clever, fascinating, altogether the Prince
Charming of northern fairy tales. It was inevitable that
female hearts began to flutter, that the pulses of match-
making parents beat faster. Don Juan, though, saw beyond the yellow walls of Zaragoza. There was no need yet
for marriage which, when arranged, must be something
greater than any which could be found outside the imperial court. Yet the Archbishop was not wholly satisfied
with his young ward. Under all his gaiety and charm the
elder man sensed a deep reserve, as the light touch of a
hand reveals the impenetrable chain-armour under silk or
velvet doublet. True, the boy in the last three years had
made acquaintance with death and with worse than death,
insanity in its most repulsive form. Still, youth was elastic
and there was no sign of morbidity in the young man, nor
of any excessive religiosity. There was a danger, though,
his uncle felt, of his developing into a prig. Virtue was not
fashionable at the episcopal court. Chastity was remarkable for its rarity and everywhere luscious fruit waited
only for a touch or a whisper to fall into the slender hands
of the young prince. An ambitious man, to go far, must
know the world through experience, hinted Don Juan.
The first step in knowledge and experience was obviously
a woman. Noble fellow-students laughed and teased
Francis for his reserve and control. Servants murmured
suggestions and arrangements. The serpent in this Eden
was hydra-headed. It is not from the enemy without that
comes the real danger, but from the traitor in the citadel
who, unnoticed and unsuspected, steals to unbolt the gate
and throw open the entrance. All loveliness—music, colour, the scent of a rose, the gold of a summer moon, the
diamond sparkle of frosty stars—all are allied, till there

comes a moment when it seems as if the flood rising from
the depths of a man's being must join with the rising tide
outside and sweep away his last defence.

Francis Borgia was no plaster saint, as his pious biographers have endeavoured to paint him, feet hardly
touching common earth, eyes fixed for ever on a cloudless
heaven. He came of a family whose every member had
been marked for fame, whether good or bad, whose names
are best remembered among all the mighty figures of the
Renaissance. The mixture of Italian and Spanish blood in
his veins was hardly likely to produce a lymphatic blend
of milk and water. The time was that first quarter of the
sixteenth century when Luther's revolt and the Counter-
Reformation in the Church had not yet sounded the death-
knell of Renaissance culture, when men lived, loved,
learned, hated, fought and intrigued with every fibre of
their being, with every drop of their blood, when the new
spirit of enquiry struck at the roots of everything, human
and divine, and the revival of classical culture had veiled
the medieval spirit with a splendid blossoming of art and
philosophy and beauty, as well as reviving the old vices of
the East, of Greece and Rome.

There was a subtle poison in the atmosphere of the
great palace, looking on to the yellow Ebro surging under
the seven-arched bridge, across the plaza to the Moorish
façade of the Séo, with its gay *azulejo* tiles and its horse-
shoe arches. There was temptation everywhere, in the low
doors of old houses, in the sinister, narrow back streets, in
young blood racing after a gallop with huntsman or a keen
bout in a tourney, in the gleam of bronze, the chiselled
coldness of marble, the glow of silk and velvet, the
glitter of jewels, a touch as light as the brushing of a moth's
wing in the summer dusk, in a whisper soft as the murmur
of wind in the pines.

It is easy to see and know such outward things, but to
read a man's soul, to see the agony of blood and tears, is
given only to God. Ribadeneira, Francis's earliest and

best biographer, passes swiftly over his youth. Cienfuegos
says of the struggle: "This cruel battle lasted many days."
He tells us too that more frequent confession and Communion were Francis's chief weapons, these and continual
meditation on the Blood of Christ. Six years earlier the
sermon on hell which had so terrified the boy had been
followed by another on the Passion of Christ which had
made an equally indelible impression. The Passion and the
Precious Blood were always to be a favourite devotion of
Francis.

There were visits to the Blessed Sacrament too, in San
Miguel, fortress-like with its brown walls and soaring
minaret, in San Pablo, with its gay green and white tiles
contrasting with the sombre black of its marble columns,
in the cathedral, Arab outside, splendid Gothic within,
crowned by the great octagonal ciborium built by the
anti-Pope who had died at Peñiscola. Most often of all he
would kneel in the dark little chapel of the age-old Virgen
del Pilar, where hung the silver head and collar which his
father had offered in thanks for the cure of his throat
wound.

Never again was Francis to know such agony, such a
weariness of war. It is the first decisive victory over self
which marks a man for greatness, as the first mastering of
a wild and refractory horse is the most difficult and the
most necessary. Once the will, by the grace of God, has
checked and dominated the passions, they are never again
so violent and so urgent. Francis bore the scars of this
battle always. He had won a self-control which was endur-
ing, which, strengthened by an iron will and an innate
reserve, was never to fail him through the rest of his life.

The Archbishop decided that the time was ripe for his
nephew's entrance into the great world. All smiled on the
Emperor. His son and heir, Philip, Prince of the Asturias,
had been born at Valladolid on May 21, 1527. The public
rejoicings over his birth were in full swing when news
came of the sack of Rome by the imperial troops under

the Constable of Bourbon. The Pope, Clement VII, was now a prisoner of the Emperor as Francis of France had been. In fact the only cloud on the imperial horizon was the chronic one, want of money. The Cortes of Castille (1527) refused to vote supplies to be spent on war against the Pope. The great Italian banking centres, Genoa, Florence and Venice were enemies, so could not be approached for loans, but Charles had the bright idea of mortgaging Spanish interests in the Moluccas to Portugal and financial disaster was temporarily averted.

Don Juan felt that the psychological moment had come, but it was first necessary for Francis to visit his father, and late in 1527 or early in 1528 he left Zaragoza for Gandia. He could hardly be expected to revel in the beauty of the *huerta*, or the plain provincialism of his father, too fully occupied in managing his estates and breeding a second family to have time for news of the great world. Here, where every turn and corner of the newly repaired palace was fragrant to Francis with memories of his mother, it was dreadful to see in her place a stepmother with whom he had nothing in common and who, later, was to force him into a long and expensive lawsuit. After four years of marriage she already had three children, and before the Duke's death in 1543, was to have seven more. The Duke, by his marriage contract with her, was driven to despoil Doña Juana's children in favour of his second family. He destined all Francis's sisters to the cloister. Maria, Anna and Isabella were put into the Poor Clares' convent in Gandia, the youngest still hardly able to toddle. Luisa was marked in his will for the same fate: "It is my wish that she also shall become a nun." It was easier and cheaper than arranging suitable marriages.

The Duke had refused his permission for his heir to accompany the Infanta to Portugal. Francis began to wonder if the Archbishop's plans would also be turned down. His father had no liking or admiration for a ruler whom he had never seen and whom, in common with the majority of Spaniards, he regarded as more than half a foreigner. The Emperor had certainly not shown to advantage in his first visit to Spain, in the way he had evaded his responsibilities during the revolt of 1521 and in his ungrateful dismissal of the great Cardinal Ximenes. His order to the Viceroy to "hang all you can" and Mendoza's reply that he was "a soldier, not a hangman" were still fresh in Valencian memories.

However, Francis won the day. Perhaps out on the grey mountain slopes, good horses under them, good hounds and hawks at heel and on wrist, father and son found an agreement which had been impossible in the palace, under the stepmother's suspicious eye and disturbed by the screams of the noisy children. In the elaborate and ceremonious letter from the Duke (February 8, 1528) begging permission for Francis and, later, his younger brothers, to enter the Emperor's service, the stately polish bears the mark of Francis rather than that of his bluff father.

Once again the young man left Gandia without regret and rode north to win his spurs in the world, for which the intensive training of the last eight years had been a preparation.

CHAPTER V

PRINCE CHARMING

IT WAS spring (May, 1528), the best of the year when even the austere plains of Castille softened their sharply burnt outlines with the tender green of young corn and the brilliant yellow-green of fresh budded vineleaves. If the nights were pleasantly cool the sunshine of the lengthening days was hot and bright. Life for Francis Borgia was at that moment which nothing can equal, the thrill of anticipation that, in ambition or in love, so far exceeds the satisfaction of fulfilment. "Good was it in that dawn to be alive, but to be young was very heaven." The uncle, who had sent Francis to Tordesillas with a splendid escort, had resolved that his arrival at the imperial court in Valladolid should be truly princely.

Alcalá de Henares was reached on the way from Gandia, the little town whose university, founded by Cardinal Ximenes a quarter of a century before, was already famous. News ran round that young Borgia was on his way to court. Women came out on to the balconies, at sound of hoofs and the jingle of bridles and spurs, for they had heard from Zaragoza of the prodigy who was impervious to feminine wiles. Students on their way to the Paraninfo stopped to admire the long train of servants ablaze in their scarlet livery, to discuss the points of the beautiful Andalusian horses, with the slim, swift lines of Arab blood. Francis, splendid too in brocade doublet, small, stiff ruff, loose short coat with sable collar, and high boots of red Moroccan leather, was kept busy controlling his thoroughbred black, nervous from crowds and noise. He rode bareheaded, hat in hand, acknowledging with smiles and bows the greetings from balconies and street, "superb yet charming," says Cienfuegos. Indeed it was this mixture of charming courtesy and proud, austere reserve which made him so fascinating to woman, who has always hankered after forbidden fruit. At a corner of the long Calle Mayor the triumphal progress was brought to a momentary halt. One of the university professors who happened to be passing has told the incident. A mob of idlers had been attracted by the not uncommon sight of the Inquisition familiars with a prisoner they had arrested. They were in their work-a-day black and white habits, for this was no important event—merely taking to custody a poor student of the university, over thirty, so older than most. He was grotesquely dressed, bareheaded, barefooted but for rude, home-made sandals; and the long, shapeless garment of sacking had been crudely dyed a dark colour and was tied at the waist by a hempen cord.

Except for the odd dress it was an ordinary enough sight, nothing to make the gorgeous young man rein in his black horse and sit motionless as if transfixed at one glance from the dark, burning eyes under the high, domed forehead. We are not even told if Francis asked who the prisoner was, nor does St Ignatius of Loyola, who mentions the incident in his autobiography, say a word of his first meeting with Francis Borgia.

"Charles V and the Empress Isabella received Francis de Borgia rather as a relation than as a subject," says Père Suau. This was not to be wondered at, for in spite of Charles's habitual reserve, he had reason to be grateful to his young cousin for the three years at Tordesillas, and regardless of his ten years' seniority, he soon took Francis into a friendship and an intimacy hitherto unknown in his court.

Francis was accustomed to splendour at his uncle's court at Zaragoza, but he was to find in the Emperor's household a pomp and ceremony entirely new to Spain and very different from the democratic and easy-going traditions of Castille and Aragon, where nobles had always
d

considered themselves little, if any, below the king in position and dignity. Charles had learnt wisdom since, ten years ago, he had roused Spanish wrath and hate by his Flemish household, his all-powerful minister, Chièvre, and the futile rule of Adrian of Utrecht, who had been no more successful during his brief Pontificate as Adrian VI than in his attempt to quell the Germania rising in Valencia. But the spirit of the court was that Burgundian magnificence, hedging the person of the ruler with an inviolable barrier of etiquette, which the Emperor had inherited from his paternal grandmother, Mary of Burgundy, wife of the Emperor Maximilian I, whom Charles had succeeded. In the barrier with which he surrounded himself there was, too, an instinct of self-preservation. Slow in the uptake, shy and awkward as a young man, conscientiously afraid of doing the wrong thing, he had an innate dislike of swift decision or of intimacies which might involve him in difficulties. As Aleander, the Papal Legate at the Diet of Worms, shrewdly remarked: "This prince seems to me well endowed with sense and prudence far beyond his years, and to have much more in the back of his head than he shows in his face."

Charles could not but be conscious of his unpopularity in Spain, where little of his time was to be passed, and of Spanish resentment at his continual demands for money to be spent on wars abroad. It was then all the more pleasant for him to welcome a younger cousin, free from such prejudices, eager to make his way, reserved and discreet beyond his years, but with all the qualities of body and mind to win success in society and diplomacy. So there was laid at Valladolid, this spring of 1528, the foundations of a friendship which was to last till Charles's death twenty-eight years later.

The Emperor was now twenty-eight, but looked older, as we see him in Titian's splendid portrait in the Prado. His face is rather grim and lined, overweighted with care, handsome enough with his yellow hair and beard and fair

skin, in spite of the ugly protruding Hapsburg jaw. His
large white mastiff, beside him, gazes adoringly up at him.
The short, full coat of gold and white brocade, with a
heavy sable collar, opens over a tunic of cloth of gold.
The close breeches are of elaborately tucked lawn, banded
with gold. The silk stockings and shoes are white too.

Near it in the Prado hangs the Titian of the Empress.
It is perhaps a little idealised, or rather the genius of the
great painter has infused the slim, small body and the pale
face with the beauty of the pure, brave spirit. The masses
of braided auburn hair seem to overweight the small head,
as the slender lines of the body are concealed by the gorgeous yet sober richness of the mulberry brocade gown,
thick with gold embroidery. The slashed sleeves and
square décolletage open over fine rucked lawn bound
with gold, and the skirt shows an underskirt of cloth of
gold. The ropes of pearl are looped by a huge square
brooch of jewels, and the pearl ear-rings have the same
soft pallor as the delicate face. The expression of Isabella
is one of gentle serenity, of perfect poise which has no
need of self-assertion or of pride.

One fancies that it was this serenity, this peace, which
made Francis feel for the Empress a love which lasted beyond her death and his leaving the world. Historians, who
too often think it necessary to drag in some sentimental
romance, have endowed Francis's affection for Isabella
with a wholly untrue romance. He was devoted to her—
who that knew her could fail to be?—her able servant, her
faithful friend, and her husband's best friend and cousin.

He often came into contact, too, with her favourite
ladies-in-waiting, Eleonor and Juana de Castro. These
two sisters, of noble Portuguese birth, had been play-
fellows of the Infanta at Lisbon and had accompanied her
when she came to Seville to become Empress. Neither was
calculated at first to attract the attention of a brilliant and
ambitious young courtier. They were quiet, retiring, un-
obtrusively devout. Eleonor dressed soberly, with few

jewels. She was not beautiful, with her dark brown hair, dark, serious eyes under long eyebrows which slanted downwards toward the temples, a long nose, a small mouth and round chin, a reddish colour on her olive cheeks.

There was no doubt at court as to who was the handsomest in the imperial house. Francis, now eighteen, was tall, slim, graceful, with a body trained to the finest pitch by the 'arms and horses' to which his mother had urged him. His hair was thick and dark, his face a long oval, with a warm glow on the smooth skin, as rare among sunbrowned Spaniards as was the brilliance of his clear greyhazel eyes. The high-bridged Borgia nose with its fine-cut nostrils was not large enough to spoil the symmetry of the face. The hands were exceptionally beautiful, strong but with long, tapering fingers. Add to these his easy pride of bearing, his charm of manner, his princely rank, his intelligence, wealth, ambition and prospects. It is little wonder that he was popular, admired and liked by men as well as run after by women.

He was acknowledged to be the best horseman at court, though courtiers considered it politic to add 'in Moorish style', allowing the Emperor precedence with the heavy Flemish chargers which were in such contrast with the swift grace of the Arab breed of Andalusia. His reputation was equally good in the stately intricacies of branle, the peacock symbolism of the pavane. He was in demand as a partner, but none of his vis-à-vis could truthfully claim to have penetrated the steel reserve which underlay the charm and sympathy of manner. Pre-eminent too in the tilt-yard, where men no longer crashed together in the heavy armour of old days but glittered in steel so delicately modelled and so thickly damascened with gold that it made a tourney a thing of balanced beauty rather than brute force.

Francis served a Master who had said: "I am come that ye might have life and that ye might have it more abundantly," and life brimmed with beauty and joy. There was the beauty of jewels, silks and brocades, of armour that was a dream materialized by skilful fingers of Flemish and German artists, of blades inlaid with a lacey fineness of gold by Moorish workmen in the dark streets of Toledo, the beauty of galloping horses, of hawks, the little silver bells on their jesses jingling as their hoods were torn off and they were free to shoot up into a light so dazzling that they became invisible. There was the thrill of the bull-fights, the scarlet of swirling capes and spilling blood, the skill and courage of men, the angry strength of mighty bulls, the red-soaked, trampled sand, all under a sun and sky so brilliant that shapes and colours were burnt on eye and mind as enamel is fired on to metal. There was the delicate skill of carving in the little triangular window from which Prince Philip had been shown at birth to the crowd, deliriously delighted to have again a prince born on Spanish soil. There was the plateresque wealth of ornament on the façade of San Pablo opposite the palace, of San Gregorio, a few yards down the street, the austere splendour of the towering Gothic arches of San Benito, enshrining that marvellous, crowded high-altar by Ber-ruguete, which is to religious sculpture what Chartres cathedral is to Gothic architecture.

There was also the training in politics and diplomacy, the outlook with the Emperor on all those lands in Europe which acknowledged his suzerainty, the Netherlands, Burgundy, Germany, Austria, Naples, Sicily, colonies and forts in North Africa, and the illimitable vistas of the New World.

In May, 1528, as Francis was on his way to Valladolid, Fernando Cortes had landed at Palos (ninety miles north-west of Cadiz), where Columbus had also landed thirty-five years before after the discovery of the New World. There the great conqueror of Mexico met a young man at the beginning of his career as a conquistador, Francesco Pizarro, who had returned to Spain to beg help in the an-nexation of Peru. After a visit to the castle of the Duke of

Medina Sidonia, where Luisa was living with her aunt and uncle, Cortes was received by the Emperor at Toledo. The man who had added a new empire to the territory of Charles came, says the contemporary historian, "not so much as a subject as with the pomp and glory of an independent monarch." The pale, grave man in the mid-forties, richly but plainly dressed, his few jewels of fabulous value, rode one of the Arab stallions given him by Medina Sidonia; but the sight which excited the interest of the crowd in the steep, twisting Toledan streets, as well as that of the court waiting up in the Alcazar, was the sight of the conquered Aztec and Tlascalan chiefs, among them a son of the Emperor Montezuma himself. Their proud, bitter faces, their lank, black hair, their robes of fine hair dyed with cochineal and gaily embroidered, or of feathers of every hue pasted on to fine cotton, their glittering ornaments of huge emeralds and intricate goldwork, all were unique, unforgettable.

There was an exhibition in the Alcazar of strange flowers and animals, bright feathered birds, gold dust, big roughcut emeralds and amethysts; but what pleased and amused ladies and courtiers most were the antics of Mexican acrobats, jugglers and dancers brought over as presents to Pope Clement VII. He, with true Medicean enjoyment of novelty and art, fully appreciated the gifts.

Cortes was high in favour. He appeared with the Emperor on all public occasions, was visited by him when sick and was given the title of Marquis of Oaxaca, when Charles was at Barcelona, about to embark for Italy to be crowned at Bologna by the Pope (July, 1529).

A year had passed and in that short time much had happened to Francis. His friendship with Charles was deeper and more intimate than ever. "Those who were not eyewitnesses would find it difficult to believe the favour which the Emperor showed him in his household and the affection with which he treated him" (Vasquez). It was not only by Charles and the Empress that Francis was liked. Popular with the ladies of the court, it was hardly to be supposed that the self-control won with so much blood and prayer could be maintained without a struggle. Till age or death have chilled desire the passions are never wholly dead. There was only one road of safety for a young man of hot southern blood and strong passion, that of marriage, and already Francis had penetrated the quiet, dignified reserve of Eleonor de Castro and knew that she was the woman for him. Often with the Queen in a homely familiarity unknown to the rest of the court, the two knew each other first through the Empress to whom both were devoted, then without intermediary.

Eleonor had been inseparable from the Queen. She had attended her before the birth of Philip. It was probably she who begged the Empress, during her travail, to break her stoical silence and relieve her agony by cries and groans, and had received the answer: "I may die, but I will never cry out."

Charles, busy with imperial diplomacy, was unconscious of the love affair between his favourite and that of his wife till, just before he sailed for Genoa, his wife begged him to permit Eleonor's marriage. "Certainly, choose for her the husband you wish." But when Francis Borgia was named, Charles was taken aback. Aragonese and Valencian susceptibilities were always being ruffled. He was sure the Duke of Gandia would never allow his heir to marry a foreigner. In short there were a hundred good reasons against the match. He might have known that woman is proof against reason. Isabella insisted, quietly but determinedly. The Emperor's secretary was told to pick a messenger, the Emperor wrote with his own hand putting forward the suggestion, his own, the Empress's and Francis's desire that the marriage should take place. The expected refusal came back from Gandia, but blunter in style than the court could believe possible. It is difficult not to believe that Charles used with his wife the old retort: "I told you so."

Francis, courtier and diplomat, pondered the rudeness

of his father's letter. When his heir was old enough for marriage, the Duke had written, he was able to find an appropriate match for him in the kingdom of Valencia, though he thanked his Majesty for his kind intentions. Matters seemed at a deadlock, but Francis found the solution. He knew his father's hatred of being moved, his absorption by his estates, second family and local affairs. If Caesar would let the secretary, Francisco de Cobos, write commanding the Duke's attendance at court to discuss the marriage, terror of such an uprooting would make the old man consent to anything. The ruse was completely successful. So long as he was left peacefully at home, wrote the Duke, the Emperor might arrange any marriage he liked for Francis. It was Francis's first essay in diplomacy and the management of men, and it was a triumph.

The pill was well sugared in the marriage contract. The Emperor added a dowry of over seven thousand pounds to what Eleonor already possessed, offered a commandership of Calatrava, with a good income and lands near Toledo, "not far from Valencia," to any son whom the Duke might nominate.

The marriage contract was duly drawn up and signed at Barcelona, July 26, 1529. The Duke had made over to Francis half the barony of Lombay. The Emperor elevated it into a marquisate; a special honour, for only once before had a grandee's eldest son received such a title. A greater honour still was in store. Francis was named by the Emperor his Huntsman-in-Chief, by the Empress her Master of Horse, and the young bride became the Mistress of the royal household.

Charles had gone. Isabella was left as regent. "The marquis of Lombay, in this strict, almost conventual court, held a privileged situation which his youth (he was not yet twenty) hardly seemed to authorize. The rigid etiquette of the imperial household did not exist for him. Day and night he had free entry into all the rooms and no criticism ever tarnished a reputation above suspicion" (Suau).

CHAPTER VI

CHEQUERED DAYS

IT WAS unusual for a bridegroom of nineteen to be left in supreme authority over the Empress's household during the Emperor's absence from Spain. Human nature being what it is, it was even more strange that the appointment should rouse none of the customary malice and gossip. No doubt the Castillean nobles were thankful that the honour had fallen to the son of a grandee of Spain, not to one of the hated Flemish, but more than that was needed to silence envious tongues. The Marquis of Lombay had indeed all the gifts with which a romantic novelist endows his hero; but youth, good looks, high birth, wealth, social popularity and preeminence in sport are more likely to arouse envy than to dispel it. Only that indefinable and irresistible something which we call personal fascination can do that, and this invaluable but dangerous gift the Marquis had in generous measure.

So far he had been merely the courtier *in excelsis*. Now he was to show a capacity for organization and a power over men which were to prove the rightness of the Emperor's judgement. During the next ten years daily life in the Lombay household varied little, whether at Valladolid, Madrid, Barcelona, Segovia or Toledo. It was only sharply broken by the Provençal campaign of 1536. The young husband was as intimate with the Empress as his wife had always been. It astonished the court that he had the entry into her private apartments at any time, but it was even more astonishing that, when Eleonor's first child was born (1530), the Empress repaid the services rendered herself at Prince Philip's birth, by attending to the young mother like a sister or a servant. Not content with this, when the boy was baptized Carlos after the absent Emperor, the

Empress and Philip (now three) stood as godmother and godfather.

The little Prince had conceived a violent childish passion for the baby's father and screamed with rage when torn from his arms or his side. It was the Marquis who had to help to hold him on his pony in his first public ride, of which his governor wrote an account to the Emperor from Toledo (1531): "The streets were so full of people crowding to see him that it was difficult to get through them. Everyone was chattering and laughing and His Highness very proud at finding himself on horseback." A little later that same year the solemn ceremony took place when the four-year-old Prince discarded his childish smock and petticoats and was clothed by his beloved Marquis in his first little doublet and breeches. In September, 1531, the court moved to Medina del Campo and there, in the great, square, yellow castle which was one of the favourite homes of Isabella the Catholic, the Lombays' second child was born, a girl called Isabella after her godmother, the Empress.

These moves of the court meant an endless amount of organising for the imperial Master of the Horse. As well as the usual overseeing of the huge and complicated personnel and accounts, there was arranging not only for billets for everyone, from the Empress and her ladies downwards, but also, during the halts by the way, the provision of food and drink, unless by good luck there happened to be a monastery or convent at hand. The sixteenth century was an age of continual movement, of travel in which the highest form of comfort was a swinging litter carried by men or mules, for coaches had hardly yet appeared in Spain, while the servants in charge of baggage and provisions tramped or bumped in springless ox-carts along roads which were no more than sandy tracks strewn with rocks or, in wet weather, running torrents.

News came at last, at the end of 1532, that the Emperor had concluded at Bologna a treaty of peace with the second Medici Pope, Clement VII, who had crowned him as head of the Holy Roman Empire three years before.

The Empress and court were at Barcelona awaiting the Emperor's return before the end of March, but it was a month later (April 22, 1533) that the sails of Doria's ships were sighted from Mount Juich and that Charles landed after nearly four years abroad.

Ceremonies and celebrations crowded the next eight weeks. The old palace of the Counts of Barcelona and the Kings of Aragon could not hold the nobles of the imperial suite, their wives and followers. The alterations and additions of Antonio de Carbonell had left intact the little *patio* whose entrance faces the wide flight of steps up to the west façade of St Eulalia's cathedral. It was gay with uniforms and liveries, the velvet and satin of men's short cloaks and doublets, the flash of damascened helmets and carved Italian cuirasses, with the sheen of women's hair, veiled and jewelled, the cobweb fineness of lace ruffs, the sweep of wide, heavy, stiffened skirts of brocade and cloth of gold. The clank of swords and jingle of spurs, the swish of silk and tap of high heels made a varied accompaniment to a ceaseless flow of talk which, heard from the cathedral steps, was muted to the murmur of flies on a drowsy summer afternoon.

Receptions, balls, tourneys, bull-fights, there was something to please all tastes. The Empress was at them all, her usual fair gravity warmed to deeper beauty by joy at reunion with her husband. Francis was no less glad to be relieved of sole responsibility and to welcome the cousin who, he knew, returned his own ardent affection with a friendship none the less strong for the ten years' difference in their ages. The relations between the Empress, Eleonor and himself had been perfect in their way; but a man needs a man's companionship as well as a woman's affection, and the *parti carré* was fuller and more complete than the three had been.

Where the Emperor went, the Marquis of Lombay

must go. All the Empress did her *camarera mayor* must do too. There were few free moments when Eleonor could escape to kneel alone in the silence and shadows of the Gothic arches of the cathedral, while down below yellow candles winked in the darkness of the crypt round the tomb of the martyred Eulalia. In the cloisters too, through the Puerto de San Severo, brooded a peace and stillness impossible to attain in the hurry and crowds of court. Here the only sounds were the splash of cool water falling into the stone basin where white swans watched the reflection of their own beauty, the soft rustle of tall palms whose leaves shone with the burnished brilliance of metal. Here it was easy to pray, to sink into the depths of contemplation when, as between human lover and beloved, there was no more need of words, and even thought was drowned in the union of the soul with God.

Then, like the crash of thunder from a blue sky, happiness and gaiety were shattered. The Empress went down with fever, went down into the shadow of death from which poor medical skill proved powerless to bring her back. Barcelona became a city of prayer and penitence. Public prayers were ordered (June 29–July 2) when all else had failed. Francis was the only intimate (except the Emperor's confessor) allowed within the wall of reserve which Charles, as a young man, had built to shelter his own awkwardness and indecision and which had become second nature with him.

Not only did Francis share his cousin's anxiety, he had his own. Eleonor's third child was due in a few weeks. The whirl of festivities had been trying enough under the circumstances for one never too strong, but untiring service and ceaseless watching by what looked like being the deathbed of her dearest friend was a far worse strain on body and mind. Only her high courage and serene selflessness enabled her to carry on till at last the corner was turned and the precious life out of danger.

Public rejoicing expressed itself in a big pilgrimage to

Montserrat, where it was customary for young Catalan couples to go on their marriage to beg our Lady's blessing on their unborn children. So far as we know, it was the first time Francis had ridden over the Lobregat and up the steep track under the rocky peaks with their air of strange and unearthly enchantment. He had been born under the girdle of St Francis, had had his first lessons in the spiritual life from the Poor Clares. After his first child's birth he, his wife and their little son had been associated by the Dominicans at Avila with all the privileges of their order. He had known the Black Monks of St Benedict in their great church and cloister in Valladolid, but this was his first taste of Benedictine hospitality.

Here, in this sharp, clear air, high above the hustle of the world and the strife of tongues, grateful after the agonising anxiety of the last weeks, was the peace which, circled by the Crown of Thorns, the world can neither give nor take away. Here, perhaps, he heard from one of the monks the story of the little, lame Basque nobleman who, laying sword and shield on her altar, had spent the night in vigil before the Lady of Heaven, devoting himself, all he was and would be, to her service and that of her divine Son. But, if he heard the story, he did not know that it was the same Ignatius of Loyola whom he had seen in Alcalá de Henares dragged away to the Inquisition, a man whose searching look had pierced his soul with a sharp, swift thrust.

The Empress made such a quick recovery that she was able to leave Barcelona on July 17 for Monzon, where the Emperor had gone to open a session of the Aragonese Cortes which dragged on till December. At Bellpuig, ninety-four miles from Barcelona, Eleonor could go no further. She had to remain in the little country town dominated by the old castle and the Franciscan friary till she recovered enough strength after the birth of her second son, Juan, to join her husband at Monzon.

Hardly was the Court back in Castille than the Marquis

went down with an attack of fever from which he lay dangerously ill for several months. Though only twenty-three and active in mind and body he had suddenly become enormously stout, a sad and unromantic fate for the former Adonis. Not only was this a trial to personal vanity but it was a severe handicap in the long-drawn fight for recovery. There was no room as yet in the palace for the Lombay household so Charles had settled it in an adjoining house and he with the Empress continually went along the covered connecting passage to visit the invalid. Charles spent long hours by the sick-bed discussing affairs of state as well as more intimate and personal matters. But there were times when the fever ran so high that delirium confused past and present, when only Eleonor's cool touch and soft voice brought a moment's peace.

Francis was a child again, lying out in those wild, tumbled landscapes which, with their infernal unreality, had again filled with terror the memory haunted by the friar's grim word-painting of hell and damnation. There was a jangle of bells from the harness of a mule passing with a load of wine-skins. Was it the tinkle of bells as a pet hawk shook its hooded head or the far-off sound of a bell which had called back the Duke and his boy from their gallop along the grey slopes above Gandia? An interval of consciousness and he knew this for the bell which heralded the coming of his confessor bringing what might well be the Viaticum.

The fever had left him, weak indeed and helpless in body but clear in mind. It was a chance for spiritual stocktaking, for a backward look over five years of such married happiness as is given to few. He had been a good Catholic, recipient of many favours, from the Pope himself as well as from religious orders. Clement VII, six months after the Marquis's marriage, had dowered him, his wife and their descendants to be, with many privileges, including the precious one of the use of a portable altar so that Mass could be celebrated daily even on one of those weary journeys from one royal palace to another. He had always made his confession and Communion regularly at all the great feasts, sometimes oftener. His wife shared his special devotion to the Precious Blood and Passion of Christ. The Rosary and the Little Office of our Lady were said daily. Marriage had enabled him to keep the victory over passion which he had won so hardly at Zaragoza eight years ago. Yet now he began to feel the truth of the words: "Lord, I am an unprofitable servant, I have done that which was my duty."

The hours of enforced idleness, so interminable during convalescence to one active and energetic, were used, as Ignatius of Loyola had used them thirteen years ago after his wound at Pamplona, in spiritual reading, the lives and legends of saints, and most of all the New Testament. When, unable to sit a horse, but carried out in his litter, the Gospels and St Paul's Epistles were still in Francis's hands, one would like to think he used one of those magnificent Bibles from the Alcalá de Henares press founded by Cardinal Ximenes.

Recovery was slow, but his doctor, Villabolos, promised a date by which it should be complete, and jokingly demanded in return a fine piece of silver plate from the dresser. On the destined day pulse and temperature were normal. The prophecy was apparently verified, but the honest doctor, shaking his head, said to the patient: "*Amicus Plato, magis amica veritas*" (which to a Spaniard gives a play upon the word *plata*, and may be translated: "I love silver but I love truth more"). "You are not well yet." His reward for truthfulness was two pieces of silver instead of one.

The Marquis, though not yet well, had to begin the weary trail from Valladolid to Toledo and back to Avila and Valladolid (1534). All this year and the spring of 1535 Charles and Francis were as inseparable as their wives. Charles developed a sudden passion for mathematics, which he considered essential for war and sieges. Caesar

could not so far demean himself as to take lessons like a
common schoolboy, so to the Marquis's other tasks was
added that of a mathematical lesson every morning from
the imperial cosmographer and an hour every evening
handing on his newly acquired knowledge to the Emperor. No doubt he was extremely thankful when, after six
months, the imperial appetite was sated, and he firmly
quenched a dawning desire to start on astrology.

More urgent matters began to engross Charles's attention. Kheyd-ed-Din, the second of the Barbarossa brothers,
had succeeded on the death of his brother Uruj to the
leadership of the sea-wolves of the Mediterranean. 'With a
brain of ice and a heart of fire', not only was he the terror
of Christian coasts from the Adriatic to the Atlantic, but,
diplomatic enough to realise the value of Turkish protection, he had done homage to the great Sultan Suleyman
for his kingdom of Algiers, whence he watched with cold
and cynical eye the quarrels and jealousies of Christian
princes.

The Duke of Gandia had been called out in 1532 to
repel a threatened landing of corsairs. Now again (1534)
he received from his son warning of the advisability of
evacuating the Poor Clare convent, where his mother was
Abbess. This time the invasion did not materialize, but
the Emperor's crusading zeal was fanned to flame by a
successful descent of Barbarossa on the Neapolitan coast,
and he resolved to smoke out the hornets' nest.

The parting was terrible for Eleonor, left with the Empress at Madrid. She and Francis had never before been
separated for more than a short time, by more than a short
distance. When men go to war it is the women who suffer
the misery of waiting and anxiety without any of the com-
pensations of splendid panoply, hot blood and desire for
glory. She was a good mother indeed, and had now four
children, for her third son, Alvaro, had been born in 1534
and her second daughter, Juana, was to be born this year.
But before all she was wife, and when Madrid was left

empty of nobles and troops, life for her was even more empty.

At last Francis was to arm in the age-old conflict of his ancestors against the Crescent, and he meant to do them credit. At the grand review of the army outside the Perpignan Gate of Barcelona (May 14, 1535) the Marquis of Lombay and his friend and relation, George de Mello, were remarkable among all the nobles for the beauty of their armour, their horses and equipment and the number and fineness of their followers, mounted and foot. The Emperor was no less gorgeous. He rode bareheaded, golden baton in hand, his pages carrying helmet, cuirass, lance and sword.

The fleet already crowded the sweep of the harbour from the high fort of Montjuich to *Tibi Dabo:* the twenty-two galleys of the great Genoese admiral, Andrea Doria, the twenty Portuguese sail, commanded by Don Luis, brother of King John III, husband of the Emperor's sister Catherine. On the high poop of Doria's flagship the Marquis stood beside the Emperor to review the fleet. Above them fluttered the twenty-four huge banners of silk, embroidered with the double-headed Austrian eagle, the castle of Castille, the lion of Leon, the arrows of Aragon, the Genoese red cross of St George. And the Galera Bastarda, the Emperor's own ship, was such a blaze of gilded bronze, painted carvings, gold plate, Venetian glass, silk and velvet that it would have been a meet setting for Cleopatra.

The feast of Corpus Christi (May 27) was kept with great solemnity: Pontifical High Mass in the old church of Santa Maria del Mar, in whose dimness, under the high soaring arches, sailors were wont to hear Mass and leave votive offerings for their safe return; then a procession through the narrow streets whose dark, tall houses had blazed into the rich colour of rugs and tapestries. The Emperor, with Don Luis, the Dukes of Alba and Calabria, carried the canopy over the Host, and, before dawn next

e

day, galloped inland to Montserrat to make his confession and receive Communion before the fleet sailed on the thirtieth.

Then, on the very eve of departure, the Marquis's hopes and ambition were dashed. He was told to return to his duties in the Empress's household. Why? Because he was still liable to attacks of fever? Because for some undisclosed reason he was more needed at home than abroad? Because Charles wished, if anything should happen to himself, that the Empress should have the comfort and support of Francis's presence, his help in bringing up her son?

George de Mello was gone with the fleet. Francis's other great friend, Garcilaso de la Vega, was gone too, from Naples, where he had been in the service of the Viceroy since he had been out of favour with the Emperor for one of his wild, romantic adventures. But the Marquis of Lombay rode back to Madrid, to the household of women and children and old men, hurt, angry, bitterly disappointed. There is a refreshingly human note of bad temper in the grumbles of a letter from Madrid two months later. "I arrived here ill, victim of such bad luck that I have not had a day's health. None of all the prescribed syrups and purges have done me any good. I am a little better but my digestion is ruined . . . I cannot leave my room and all my children have fever too. The heat is appalling."

To be disillusioned and disgusted, racked with fever, burdened with excessive fat, and to endure the heat of midsummer in Madrid, was indeed enough to try the patience of a saint, and Francis Borgia was as yet no saint. No doubt Eleonor had need of all her competence and serenity.

George de Mello returned to Madrid with news of the glorious capture of Tunis in August and the peace treaty with the Bey in September. Garcilaso had been covered with wounds and glory and was now consoling his convalescence in Naples with one of his impassioned love affairs. But the turn of the year brought new hopes of glory. As the Emperor was enjoying a triumphal reception in Rome after his victory over the infidel, the most Christian King of France sent his troops pouring into Piedmont and war again began (April, 1536).

This time the Marquis was not to be cheated. He was writing to Juan de Garcia, his agent in Valencia, ordering horses and swords. He returned a roan who did not satisfy him and was in a great hurry for the new mount, "for, without him, I cannot manage either to hunt or to get out riding . . . He must be strong and young, with smooth paces and a good mouth, with these it does not matter so much if he is not graceful, high nor very fast." Alas, a weight-carrier was now needed for the increasing stoutness which had engulfed the slim grace of the young Adonis.

At Valencia, before embarking for Italy, Francis was to meet his father, whom he had not seen for eight years. He wrote to Juan Garcia forbidding the ceremonious reception planned by local nobles and civic dignitaries. "As it is Holy Week I do not wish them to miss the ceremonies and I know from bitter experience that, in such receptions, both those who receive and those who are received suffer equally." A homely note about food: "We are greedy for fresh fish after the vile food we have had on the way" (April 8, 1536).

The Marquis of Lombay, with George de Mello, Ruy Gomez (later Prince of Eboli), and a troop raised at his own expense, rejoined the Emperor in Lombardy, where he found Garcilaso de la Vega, recovered from his wounds both of body and heart and in command of a *tercio* of three thousand Spanish veterans.

It was a magnificent army which climbed over the Cola de Tenda, down to Nice and over the French frontier, more than five thousand cavalry and nearly forty-four thousand Spanish, German and Italian infantry. The Emperor rode fully armed, as in Titian's portrait of him at Mühlberg. So did his suite. The August sun of Provence blazed on helmet and cuirass, on brassards, greaves and gauntlets till their steel felt hot to the touch. Then—humiliating note amid all 'the pulse of war and passion of wonder'—the Emperor noticed Francis literally streaming, the sweat pouring off him under the weight of armour. He was bidden take it off, to keep on only helmet and shoulder pieces. No Spaniard could be expected to stomach such a slight to his vanity, to be made ridiculous in public. Francis disregarded the order. It was repeated and, hotter than ever with anger, he had to obey.

The French, for once, had adopted Fabian tactics, and the country lay bare and waste as if a swarm of locusts had passed over it, while Montmorency waited, strongly entrenched, at Avignon and the King at Valence. Aix was captured without a blow, but famine and fever fought on the French side. The imperial troops were dying like flies, among them Leyva who had served Charles so long and so well in Italy. News came that the French army in Italy was attacking Charles's protectorate of Genoa. The splendour of war had given place to lean scarecrows of corpses putrefying in the sun. An unsuccessful attempt was made to save the face of honour by taking Marseilles, then the retreat began.

Garcilaso de la Vega, a special favourite of the Emperor, to whom he had taught Castillean, protected the rearguard with his *tercio*, and Francis was with him. A little round tower near Fréjus, held by only fifty men, was a thorn in the side of the retreating army. It had to be taken. Bareheaded and without armour the soldier-poet was first up the scaling-ladder. Swept down by an avalanche of stones, he was rescued from the moat and carried into safety by his friend, who accompanied him to Nice and never left him during his eighteen days of agony, cheering and helping him "with all the tenderness of a friend and the good offices of a Christian" (Cienfuegos).

It was Francis who told him that his wounds were mortal, fetched the priest when the end was near, closed the dark eyes that had reflected so much gaiety and beauty, saw the laughing face of the great lover and adventurer marbled into the aloof austerity of death. It was the first deep grief of Francis's life since his mother's death, the loss of the friend whose magic had lain not only in his poetry but in a personality which combined the fascinations of the medieval troubadour and the Elizabethan buccaneer.

The Marquis arrived early in December, 1536, to warn the Empress of her husband's return and to tell the tragic news of the Provençal disaster. It was bad enough to be the bearer of ill tidings, to feel in his own heart an emptiness which no other friend could fill. But Francis had barely time to enjoy reunion with his wife, to see the six-months-old Fernando, when he collapsed with a virulent germ that was rampant in Segovia. An abcess formed in his throat so that he could neither speak nor swallow, and once again his life was despaired of.

Since his last serious illness he had lived always prepared for death. Now it felt as if, but for his wife and children, it would be a welcome release from the agony, the misery of a thirst which could not be quenched. It was a fresh reminder, if one had been needed, of his special devotion to the Cross of Christ, of that parched torture which had drawn from the dying human lips the cry: "I thirst."

The failure of the imperial adventure, the decimation of that great army, the long-drawn suffering of the friend who had died in his arms,—as memory's pictures passed before his mind's eye a veil seemed drawn which dimmed the brilliant hues, the glowing splendour of worldly glory. In Italy, in France, he had first perceived the web of European politics not as a dim, tapestried background to the Emperor's figure, but as a moral problem, a ceaseless warfare in which living men and women, nations and peoples struggled blindly towards the light. Truth and right were all that mattered. The eternal was the only touchstone to

try, the only scales to weigh temporal things. The pride
and splendour of court and war, the joy of fine horses and
hawks, gilt armour and Toledo blades, jewels and gold
and velvet, all faded. Only the things of the spirit remained, vivid and vital.

He was alone with God, alone but for his wife who
went step by step with him along the thorny path. When
he knew he was to live he resolved to serve God still more
generously and courageously, to make his confession and
Communion every month, to test and try all decisions, all
action by the Will of God.

CHAPTER VII

1539

IT WAS the spring of 1539. Once more the four friends
were together at Toledo. Charles had returned in the
preceding July from another visit to Italy and a meeting
in France with his old enemy, Francis I. Pope Paul III had
himself travelled to Nice to bring about peace by his personal influence, and at last a ten years' truce had been
signed.

The world was at peace. There was peace too in the
palace of the Count of Fuensalida where the Emperor and
Empress, the Marquis and his wife were living, for the
new Alcazar was not yet finished. As always the fly in the
ointment was want of money. Charles prepared a great
reception for the Castillean Cortes, but his trouble was
wasted. The nobles were willing to spill their blood on the
field of honour but not to open their purses. The merchants, clergy and farmers were sick to death of wars
abroad which drained the country of men and money.
Charles dissolved the Cortes and did not convoke them
again.

On one occasion he got some unexpected home truths
from a peasant who did not recognise his ruler in the
dusty huntsman who, separated from his fellows, begged
to be allowed to put the stag he had just killed on to the
cart returning from market empty but for some fire-wood.
Asked his opinion of the Emperor, the old man gave it in
no uncertain terms. "The worst king we have ever had,
always rushing off to Italy, Germany or Flanders, leaving
his wife and children, taking all the money from Spain. As
if the money from the Indies was not enough to conquer a
thousand worlds, he must still grind down us poor country folk till we're destroyed with new taxes and tributes.

If only it would please God to let him be king of Spain alone he'd be the strongest king in the world !"

The Emperor had indeed got more than he asked for, but he took it in good part and no doubt laughed over it with Francis afterwards, perhaps with a suspicion that Francis was rather of the old man's opinion.

There were many expeditions, out over the splendid old Puente de Alcantara, past the hermitage of Saint Barbara, up into the tumbled, rusty hill whose twisted trees and low scrub harboured such a wealth of game. It was at falconry that the Marquis specially excelled. He had sight as keen as his hawks and a knowledge of birds, their habits, flights and songs. His biographer, Denis Vasquez, tells how once, travelling through Castille with Francis, he was amazed when his companion stopped to watch birds flying so high as to be invisible to ordinary sight and, questioned, knew all about their lives and the different hawks to use for catching them.

At other times Charles and his cousin would climb from the Plaza de San Tomé up the crooked narrow streets, tiresomely steep for Francis and his unwieldy fat, past the cathedral, up still to the Alcazar, where the Cid had lived as Alcaide of the newly reconquered city. There alterations and additions were in full swing as they were in the Great Mosque of Cordoba and in the red courts of the Alhambra. And in the evenings the two husbands and wives would sit in the *patio* of the Fuensalida palace, looking away over the encircling Tagus, hidden by rocks, westward, where red and dun sand, the emerald of young corn and the silvery grey of olives were turned to molten gold by the sunset. There was shelter here from the teasing wind which came dancing round corners all day but, like a sleepy child, grew quiet as the sun went down. It was late April and the nights were pleasantly cool, full of the perfume of the first roses, flowering already in the warm crevices and the first tentative notes of the nightingales. Sometimes fragments of a serenade would float up, broken by piled roofs and walls. Sometimes Francis would sing, in that clear, true voice of his which so pleased the Emperor's sensitive ear, some of his own compositions, grave and liturgical, age-old marches to which pilgrims went to Compostella, or gay, lilting airs of Coplas sung by man and woman as they danced the *jota* or the *passacaille*.

"My fluttering heart alighted on thy breast,
    Thou hast cut its wings so it can no more escape,
But must nest for ever in thy heart."

As the low deep notes sank into silence Eleonor's eyes would meet her husband's. She knew that he sang to her and for her, since after ten years of marriage and the birth of eight children, they were still lovers.

The light of candles, whose flames burned steadily in the still air, fell on Charles's yellow hair and beard, on the auburn of Isabella's heavy plaits, caught a milky sheen in the pearls threaded in Eleonor's dark hair and on her velvet gown, shone on Francis's smooth face, his eagle nose, dark hair and beard and brilliant grey eyes, gleamed on velvet and brocade, glittered on cloth of gold, on Mexican emeralds and polished sword hilts.

Isabella would rise, wearily, for she was near the birth of her child. Eleonor must go with her. But at last came the hour, to Eleonor the best of the day, when she and Francis were alone at last, undisturbed by children, household cares, statecraft or regulation of the imperial households.

There were ten years of marriage to look back on, a union which had been an ideal Christian marriage. Life had always been peaceful and well ordered in the household. Mass heard, husband and wife separated to their different duties, he knowing that he could happily leave all care and responsibility in the home in her competent hands. Always grave and graciously dignified, Eleonor would oversee nursery and large staff at home before she went to her duties in the Empress's palace. Needless to say it was one of her greatest joys that her husband should

have grown as devoted to her friend as she was herself.
Childhood, girlhood, marriage, the birth of children, each
as they came tightened the bonds of affection between
Isabella and Eleonor. The intimacy which existed, both
during Charles's frequent absences and during his visits to
Spain, between the young Marquis and the young Empress was never twisted by the most venomous tongues
into more than the natural and devoted affection on his
part for such a lovely and gentle lady and on hers for her
friend's husband and her husband's cousin.

Francis and Eleonor were one in thought, in practice,
in outlook, as they were in religion. It is rare to find such
union, not only of body but also of mind and soul. There
was nothing extravagant or eccentric in their religion,
though after Francis's two serious illnesses he advanced
rapidly along the spiritual way. Unluckily his biographers
have been more anxious to paint him as a saint and an
ascetic than to show him as model Christian husband,
father and master. It is only by a hint here, a sentence
there, that a glimpse of home life is caught. There is a
letter, for instance, written by Eleonor to Sister Gabrielle,
Francis's grandmother, at the Gandia convent when he
was away in Provence.

"I have nothing to tell you except of my agony of loneliness which, since you are mother to us all, I know you
will share . . . I beg you to write to me often. I shall indeed
be grateful for your letters, for they are my only consolation . . . Also please pray, and ask all to pray, about my
confinement, which takes place this month and here,
where I am all alone" (May 4, 1536).

Ten years of marriage had given Francis and Eleonor
eight children: Carlos, born 1530, a year after their wedding, Isabel (1532), Juan (1533), Alvaro (1534), Juana
(1535), Fernando (1536), Dorotea (1537), and Alonso,
who was to be their last, born at Toledo the preceding
year. It was a big family to provide for, as each boy grew
up and had to be placed in a position worthy of his rank

and fitting marriages to be arranged for the girls. Like his
father, Francis had always been generous in alms, and he
could look for no financial help now or in the future from
Gandia, where the Duke, not content with his first family
of seven, had by his second wife five sons and five daughters. Francis's three sisters, Maria, Ana and Isabel, were in
the convent at Gandia under their Abbess grandmother.
His pet, Luisa, had been adopted and dowered by her
aunt, the Duchess of Medina Sidonia, and next year (1540)
was to marry Martin de Gurrea, Count of Ribargoza, later
Duke of Villahermosa. In spite of her father's and her own
wish that she too should enter the Poor Clares, her aunt,
the Archbishop of Zaragoza and Francis himself, decided
that her true vocation was, like that of Eleonor, wife and
mother. She, like her brother, was to prove that holiness
is not confined to the cloister.

All was peace and happiness at Toledo these spring days
of 1539, as is so often the way in human life before a mortal
blow. Towards the end of April the Empress was stricken
with fever, as she had been six years before at Barcelona.
Again fêtes gave place to penitential processions. Heaven
was stormed with prayers for her recovery. The cathedral
chapter, for seven days in succession, visited all the principal churches in the city, even allowed the famous Virgen
del Sagrario, contrary to all custom, to be carrried in procession from the cathedral to San Juan de los Reyes, which
Ferdinand and Isabella had built for their burial-place,
where the walls of the empty church are still ornamented
with their initials. Covered with jewels that gleamed in the
candlelight, the precious statue was borne down the
twisting maze of streets, where the tall Moorish houses
made a cool shady gloom. There was hardly room for the
bishop in his purple cope, for the canons, glowing like
gigantic fuschias in their crimson and purple, for the long
straggling procession of black-robed hidalgos and veiled
ladies, the poor, ragged folk that followed. The air was
filled with solemn chanting. Bare shoulders were streaked

with blood under scourges. Bare feet were cut and bruised on the rough cobble stones.

It was in vain. The Empress gave birth to a dead child and herself died on May 1, 1539. She had exacted a promise from Eleonor, who had never left her, that no hands but hers should touch her dead body. No one but her lifelong friend, who had cheered and tended her at the birth of her children, must wash and lay out the wasted body and prepare it for the leaden coffin in which it would make its last journey.

Charles, leaving his broken heart in her coffin, fled from Toledo to hide himself in the nearby Hieronomite friary of Sisla after entrusting to Francis all the last arrangements.

The cathedral chapter accompanied the bier to the Puente de Alcantara, and there the Marquis took charge (May 2). Day after day for a fortnight the long *cortège* wound its slow way south, stopping each night at some monastery, convent or castle. There was the Cardinal of Burgos, the group of bishops and prelates on their mules, nobles and gentlemen in deep mourning, the Marchioness of Lombay, her sister Juana, Countess of Faro, and the ladies-in-waiting in litters, the heavy coffin, draped in brocade, its litter trailing black velvet.

The Marquis of Lombay rode alone on his big, black horse, a stately figure, still and erect as if cast in bronze, with the light hands and sure seat that had won him first place in horsemanship at the court. He was as sombre as his mount, black from head to foot, pale face framed in the small stiff ruff and shaded by the velvet hat, long cloak, fringed gloves and high boots of soft Cordoban leather yellow with dust, the only relief the glint of sunshine on gilt sword-hilt and spurs.

He rode alone, but for his thoughts. His wife had her sister and the ladies. She had too the consolation of having done with her own hands the last rites for the beloved body. Sorrow is easier for women. Words and tears wash

away some of its deeper hue. Mercifully, as a man is at first
unconscious that he has received a mortal wound, so one
struck by a blow that pierces heart and soul is at first too
numbed to feel deeply. Across the surface of consciousness, like gnats dancing above water, vague thoughts
flutter and are forgotten. Francis's world had crashed.The
future was a blank. He and Eleonor had no longer position
nor appointment. There were the eight children, the eldest
only nine, to be educated and provided for. Nothing
could be hoped for from Gandia. The Emperor would
soon leave Spain, where nothing now kept him. Francis
saw no chance of glory or wealth abroad. He was no
soldier. He had seen the terrible side of war in Provence,
had seen his friend die in agony, men falling like beasts
under famine and pestilence. He knew his power lay in
organisation and administration, but he could see no
work ahead for him to do.

His work, his job in life, had gone, but something far
greater had gone too. A gracious and lovely friend with
whom he had lived on terms of closest intimacy for eleven
years, a soul in whom he could see only the reflection of
goodness and beauty, a gentle dignity worthy of her rank
as the greatest lady in Europe. With her death something
in him had died too. It was the third and sharpest blow to
sever the tangle of worldly glory and allure.

The Toledo mountains, the wide valley of the Guad-
iana, the steep passes of the Sierra Morena, Jaen, with its
relic of the Holy Face, lay behind. Day after day the sun of
a southern May beat down on the black procession, that
left behind it a trail of dust like yellow smoke. The Marquis rode, head bowed, eyes down, seeing not the sandy,
stony track under his horse's hoofs, but the face of the
dead Empress under the brilliant auburn hair, only a little
paler in the light of the tall yellow candles than he had
often seen it in life. As he knelt there he had felt a sense
of intrusion, as though he saw her, as Eleonor had often
seen her, sunk in deep sleep. Yet her serenity had been no

longer sweetly full of human sympathy, but rather a remote and aloof austerity.

He lifted his head. Before him were the snow-peaks of the Sierra Nevada, remote, aloof, austere under the burning sky. And, glowing red above the darkness of pine and cypress, the towers of the Alhambra.

From the entrance to Granada, through the Elvira Gate, all the way to the cathedral, the houses, like the women, were veiled in black. It was the evening of May 16 when the long journey's end was reached and the coffin placed in the chapel of the Kings, where Ferdinand and Isabella lie side by side on Fancelli's marble tomb, guarding the heart of the kingdom they conquered for Christ.

The next morning, Saturday, the Cardinal of Burgos sang the Requiem Mass followed by the Office for the Dead, in the presence of all who had come from Toledo and the ecclesiastical and civic dignitaries of Granada. It was evening again when all assembled for the last solemn rite. The warmth and brightness outside glowed through the windows of the Capilla Real on to Felipe Vigarni's carved *retablo*, kneeling Boabdil handing the keys of the conquered city to the Catholic sovereigns, friars baptising unwilling Moors.

The coffin, enclosed in another of lead, was carried with difficulty down the few steps into the crypt. Here all was dank and cold and gloomy, the cardinal's scarlet, the prelates' purple dimmed in the faint flicker of waxen candles, men and women's black merging into the shadows. Only the splendid pall of brocade caught the light and glowed in the darkness.

It was the duty of the Marquis of Lombay to uncover the face of the corpse and to swear, before the others, to its identification before giving it into the charge of the chapter, represented by the new bishop of Almeria, Don Miguel Muñoz. The scene has been immortalized a hundred times, as in Carbonero's famous painting in the

Prado, in the stained-glass window at Loyola. The true
drama was not outward but invisible.

Francis came forward. The heavy pall was pulled back,
the outer case opened. The face of the Empress (probably
under a sheet of glass) was hidden by a cloth. He uncover-
ed it and revealed an unrecognisable seething mass of corruption. Others recoiled in horror from sight and stench.
There were cries and sobs from the women. The iron self-
control which Francis had won so hardly at Zaragoza
stood him in good stead now. He pronounced the words
of the oath clearly and steadily. Though not a trace remained of the beauty he had known and loved so well, it
was impossible that the coffin could contain any body but
that of the Empress.

The ceremony was over. Isabella lay beside the plain lead
coffins which are those of the great *Reyes Catholicos*, and
the body of the beautiful, futile, worthless Philip of Burgundy, whose poor mad widow still wept for him in her
prison of Tordesillas. Francis returned to the palace where
they were quartered and, without seeing even his wife,
went straight to his room and shut himself in. Breaking-
point had been reached. There are times when not even
the best loved human heart can company the soul, when it
must be alone with God.

The drama of the scene has fascinated pen as well as
brush, yet perhaps Suau, with his deep historical knowledge and his keen insight into the human soul, is right
when he places the moment of Francis's 'conversion' on
May 1 rather than on May 17. In the spiritual Journal
found among the Jesuit archives in Rome it is May 1, the
anniversary of the Empress's death which Francis notes
year by year, Perhaps, too, in such things, there is no one
particular 'moment'. The spirit which operates out of
time can fuse on the eternal plane two events into one.
Francis Borgia was already a good, a more than good,
Catholic. From now on he set his feet on the path of
sanctity.

It was not by chance that Blessed John of Avila, the Apostle of Andalusia, was chosen to preach in the cathedral on the Sunday morning. His sermon, says Suau, "seemed to Francis the echo of his own thoughts": the vanity of all human hopes and ambitions, sudden death that cuts the thread of life and breaks off the spinning of ridiculous dreams, the building of "castles of wind" (Ribadeneira). That afternoon Francis summoned the preacher, laid bare his soul, was directed along the way of purgation and warned against the special dangers of court life, ambition, envy and self-indulgence.

Back at Toledo the change in the Marquis of Lombay was shown openly in one incident. Francis, naturally hot-tempered and arrogant, had quarrelled with the Admiral of Castille. When he returned from Granada he sent to ask him to arrange a meeting. Don Fernando Enriquez appointed a spot for the duel he expected, but when his adversary appeared he was confounded to see him kneel at his feet and make humble apologies. The Admiral, dumb with amazement, lifted Francis from his knees. The two remained staunch friends, and Don Fernando loved to tell the story of pride humiliated by holiness.

Ribadeneira relates how, back in Toledo, Francis received a letter from his aunt, Sister Francis (his grandmother had died two years before). She wrote to tell him of a dream she had had in which she saw him reaching Granada, hands upstretched to God, Who lifted and drew him nearer.

The Emperor would remain alone with Francis for hours. To him only could he speak freely and fully of his broken heart and empty life. But Charles was not given only to vain words. He saw, as his cousin himself had done, that both Eleonor and her sister Juana, as well as Francis himself, were left without position or prospects, yet how much gratitude he owed them for their devoted service to the wife whom he had so often been forced to leave. On June 26, 1539, the Emperor announced the appointment of the Marquis of Lombay as his lieutenant-general and Viceroy of Catalonia, a post hitherto reserved as one of the highest dignities in his gift, for older men who would afterwards serve as Viceroys in Naples and Sicily.

CHAPTER VIII

HIS EXCELLENCY THE VICEROY

THE journey from Toledo in the scorching mid-summer heat had been lengthened by a *détour* to Gandia, where a duty visit of a few days was paid before the viceregal procession set out for Barcelona. It was a long and cumbrous train: the Marquis and his wife, their eight children (the youngest only a year old), the little girls' governess, Isabella de Rodriguez, Eleonor's sister, Juana de Castro, almost a second self, nurses, waiting women, thirty guards, huntsmen, falconers, a mob of servants, horses, hounds, hawks, mules for litters, oxen for baggage waggons.

Most of the hundred and twenty miles to the Catalan frontier were familiar to Francis: Carthaginian and Roman Sagunto, perched precariously on a steep spur of the Peñas de Pajatito, Villa Real and Castellon, with their brilliantly tiled church cupolas, on the right a distant view of Peñiscola, bringing memories of the small boy of nineteen years ago amid the crowd of refugees, a series of small brown towns, whose flat roofs clambered hillsides to cluster round domed yellow churches or square Moorish castles. Then the country began to change. Olive and almond and peach trees grew rarer, oranges paler and lemons a still more vivid golden green. Every now and then there opened on the right a wide view of the Mediterranean, like ruffled peacock-blue satin shot with violet and powdered with diamond dust.

The frontier was passed and in the cathedral of Tortosa the new Viceroy took the solemn oath to observe the Fueros of Catalonia and to do his duty. The oath, taken in the dim cool gloom of the cathedral that blazing August day (August 14, 1539) was in this case no mere empty form.

The word 'duty' is the keynote of all Borgia's voluminous correspondence of the next three and a half years, as it was of his conduct. He was undertaking his duties in no light spirit, in no justifiable pride at such unprecedented hon-our, but fully aware of the heavy burden of responsibility and of the apparently insuperable difficulties which lay before him. The Emperor's instructions filled twenty-eight pages and these, Caesar said, were only the "most urgent." Fuller details would follow in due course. The first essential was the restoration of order and authority, by the appointment of an entirely new set of magistrates, by personal attention to military discipline, the reconcilia-tion of enemy factions, the extermination of traffic in arms, the tightening and speeding up of justice.

All this was scarcely cheering, and on arrival in Barce-lona (August 23), Francis found that affairs were even worse than he had realised. The cleansing of the Augean stable too, he soon saw, was to be impeded not only by the inevitable lack of funds but by ceaseless opposition both from nobles accustomed to consider nothing but their own pride and quarrels, and also by deputies and officials who equally hated to pay for improvements or to allow anyone but their sacred selves to suggest them. Francis was never one to allow grass to grow under his feet. Like all efficient people he knew that to do a thing well and quickly it was generally necessary to do it one-self. He had hardly entered Tortosa when he ordered the instant arrest of six of the most notorious brigands. "Truly," he wrote, "the brigands of this city alone would keep a Viceroy and whole Council of State hard at work." Four days after his state entry into Barcelona he wrote to the Emperor that he had already studied the *dossiers* of robbers and rebels as far north as the French frontier at Perpignan. "One way or another I hope, with the help of God, to serve your Majesty well and to punish these ruffians. Never losing sight of this business and pushing it forward I am certain that, in the end, I shall pay them out . . . As for justice, highwaymen wander about here in companies of fifty or sixty gunmen and slingers."

He found the execution of justice the more difficult because of the opposition of the Council, some of whose members were in league with the brigands, while others were frankly terrorized by fear of reprisals from castles in the neighbourhood of Barcelona held by such well-known rebel leaders as Semanat and the two brothers Pujadas. The ceaseless war against robbery and rapine continued during his whole term of office. Justice was impeded not only by the fear and corruption of officials but by the bishop himself who, when he could not protect malefactors from arrest, saved them from just sentence by giving them the right of sanctuary.

The relations between this gentleman and the Viceroy were made the more difficult because the Viceregal household, instead of being assigned a home of its own, had been billeted in quarters actually belonging to the bishop, a house at the corner of the street leading to the Plaza Nueva. Francis does not mince matters in a letter to the Emperor's secretary, Cobos, describing how the bishop, Don Juan de Carbona, had snatched and sheltered from justice and sentence passed a notorious brigand, Gaspar de Lordat. Blunt truths about this ecclesiastic were more than justified. Auxiliary bishop of Barcelona since 1520 and titular since 1531, he did not receive orders till 1541 and died five years later after celebrating his first and only Mass, a matter in which Francis's grandfather had created a precedent. "No wonder the people are rebels when those who should put out the fire fan it instead. If his Majesty wrote to the Bishop that he ought to be consecrated and employ the time he fritters away at the gaming-table in performing the duties of his office, H. M. would unburden his conscience already overloaded by nominating such a bishop . . . I wish you to realise, by the care I take for his well-being, that I am no enemy of the Bishop. I am willing to pay him rent for the house in which I live on condition that his house is made a home for God."

This apparently hopeless struggle with violence, robbery, murder, rebellion and all forms of open lawlessness was to continue all through the Marquis's three and a half years in Catalonia. Truces which, by his efforts, were periodically proclaimed between rival factions and hereditary enemies (those for example between Semanat and the Pujadas in the spring and summer of 1541), were only brief breathing-spaces. The capture of rebel strongholds (like that near Barcelona taken on the Eve of the Epiphany, 1541) were only momentary checks to the evil. The execution of highwaymen continued, and legend related that, on one occasion, all the city gallows being insufficient, numbers of temporary ones had to be erected to accommodate the crowd of dangling corpses.

Francis shows no signs of the weak and tearful sentimentality with which some of his biographers have ornamented him. He knew the Catalans, their age-old passion for independence and their dislike of control, now aggravated by the supine incapacity of his predecessors. He knew too the need for swift and inexorable justice, the fatality of delay and indecision. "As the people enjoy shedding blood, they will feel nothing short of bloody punishment," he writes, and again: "This country needs justice rather than mercy." There was no false sentimentality about evil-doers. Telling of a criminal who had died from a hunger strike in prison he remarks, "As he executed himself instead of leaving us to do the job, all was ended well." "Now I am off to hunt and do God's justice." And a grim wish about some refugee robber or murderer, "God grant he fall into my hands!"

These, and many more like them, are his own words, and give the lie direct to the portrait of the tearful, undecided sentimentalist which, if it had been true, would only have shown a weakling incapable of fulfilling the duties of his office. Justice, ruthless and inexorable, was indeed a vital necessity if any semblance of order were to be restored to the state, as the surgeon's swift knife may be necessary to preserve the life of the body. Francis Borgia was not only a sixteenth-century Spaniard and a realist, he was a statesman with a keen vision unclouded by side issues. Seeing the end so clearly himself he could scarcely be expected to have much sympathy with those who, from corruption or stupidity, could or would not see the end for the means, the wood for the trees.

There was so much to be done, so little time to do it, and worse still the maddening lack of money, so that the obstinate opposition of petty blockheads incapable of seeing beyond their dislike of unbuttoning their pockets and their distrust of any proposition that originated outside their own little cliques was indeed to pile Pelion on Ossa.

Time—it seemed to Borgia that by the time a thing had been decided on—long before that slow decision had crawled into action—the time was already past. The walls of the city, begun by his last predecessor but one, Don Fabrice of Portugal, were still unfinished. The capital of Catalonia, the eastern key of Spain, till the discovery of America the richest and most famous port of the world, lay open to attack not only to the sea-wolves of the Mediterranean but to Spain's chronic enemy, Francis I of France, or to the fleets of Genoa, Venice and the Turk. Walls, though their completion was at last begun in June, 1540, were not enough. Ships were equally necessary. Docks and shipyards must be set working at top speed. The pines and oaks of the Catalan mountains, the best wood in the world for ships, must be felled and transported. Labour was not wanting, voluntary and forced, but money was. It was the first time that Francis Borgia had come up against that most degrading and irritating mortification, lack of money and the continual need for demanding it. So far life had been (except for the Provençal campaign, his two serious illnesses and the Empress's death) easy and successful. He had been universally popular, never straitened for the means to do things splendidly. Now he must often have felt that not "filthy lucre," as St. Paul calls it, but the lack of it, was "the root of all evil."

The Viceroyalty had appeared a dazzling, enviable proof of imperial favour and he had come resolved to prove himself worthy of Charles's belief in him. Within a week of his arrival in Barcelona he was writing to the Emperor: "I find in Catalonia an equal lack of corn and justice, and no money even to buy food." "I have to pay out of my own pocket even the guards assigned to me and at this rate my own money will not last long, considering the high price of everything here." His own large household, the splendid entertainments entailed by his position, extra troops needed for perpetual brigand hunts, not only the cost of these had to come out of his own pocket, but often the only way to get such work done as walls and ship-building was for him to stand the expense. His salary was totally inadequate. Beside it he had only the income granted on his marriage and the negligible revenues from his marquisate, all paid irregularly, if at all. Charles, as usual more generous in theory and on paper than in fact, had promised the Commandership of Huelano when his cousin had become a Knight of Sant' Iago. Months later not a penny of this money had been paid. Pious critics who have been shocked and pained at Francis's often repeated and insistent demands for money do not seem to realise that silence would have been ridiculous, if not reprehensible, in a man with a wife, eight children and a numerous household to support and provide for, with a great position to keep up (or royal authority would suffer), having himself continually to pay for public services which should have been financed from imperial or local funds. They forget too that he was the son of the Duke who had so firmly silenced criticism on the high percentage of alms-giving in his budget. In a fragment of the Viceregal expenses among the papers at Osuna Father Suau has found, in one month, fifty-two items marked: '*Lismona*' (alms). "Besides these the other expenses are negligible" (Suau).

Little wonder then that—a new and unpalatable experience—the Marquis's letters to Cobos have to repeat again and again the plea for money. He urges the prompt payment of Sant' Iago revenues long overdue, of a legacy left by the Empress to the Marchioness, for the assignation of vacant abbeys or even bishoprics, "for I have plenty of sons."

It was obvious that the Viceroyalty, far from being a bed of roses, was a thicket of thorns and nettles; yet some of the Catalans themselves, realising the necessity of a firm grasp of the nettle, wrote sincere, if somewhat grudging, praise of Francis and his justice. Indeed if thieves and murderers had reason to know that to fall into his hands meant the gallows or the galleys, other prisoners and poor folk saw another side to the man of steel. He set to work with equal energy on prison reform and the unnecessary severity of certain punishments, such as the loss of a right hand, and consequent incapacitation, for comparatively light offences. Men died of hunger not alone in prison but in those barren stretches between mountains and sea where only Catalans, said their own proverb, could "wring bread from stones." There was lack of corn, as he wrote, lack of money in the treasury to buy it. All the same, corn was brought by sea from France and the worst horrors of famine averted.

It was a period of universal distress and financial depression. Barcelona, whose Consulado del Mar had been the universal maritime code three centuries before, whose ships had traded from the Baltic to Alexandria, had now sunk to comparative insignificance. The trade centre, switched westward to Seville by the discovery of America, left Catalan merchants and ships high and dry. The fictitious period of prosperity and high prices caused by the huge influx of gold was inevitably succeeded by a slump. Men are seldom able to disentangle the true causes of national and financial decline, and Catalans, nobles, merchants and peasants, laid the blame for their present poverty on Castillean supremacy and the Emperor's Flemish favourites.

Borgia himself, in his heart, had perhaps some sympathy with this point of view. Valencian as he was, his first speech had been that harsh Limousin which is a dialect of Catalan. His interests and ideas, if not Catalan, were limited to Spain. He would have been more than man if it had not seemed unjust to him that Charles, who was drenching the battle-fields of Europe with Spanish blood and draining Spanish exchequers dry for his other dominions, could not even pay his viceregal salary nor spare fifty soldiers for the vital task of restoring and keeping order here.

Whatever Francis may have felt, even written to the Emperor himself and to Cobos, nothing of this criticism appeared in public. He was there as the Emperor's representative. Nothing should be spared to make him fulfil this duty to the utmost of his powers. Neither personal effort and sacrifice, neither the use of personal charm nor the splendour of royal and noble blood should be grudged. Mercy was shown as well as inexorable justice. If civic or official susceptibilities were ruffled by work being pushed through at unaccustomed speed, they were soothed and flattered by tactful appreciation. Old feuds were healed. Old quarrels were made up.

Entertainments at the viceregal palace were of regal magnificence. He himself made a splendid figure in the great white satin mantle of a Knight Commander of Sant' Iago, with its blood-red Crosses, the too ample figure hidden by the heavy folds, the keen, handsome face, with the deep-set grey eyes, framed in ruff of frosty lace. And the Vicereine, small and slight beside her big husband, rubies and the famous Borgia diamonds holding her lace at breast and waist, her great skirt of gold brocade and velvet mantle of ruby red, had a gracious charm that won women's hearts as well as men's. These big functions, when the palace was crowded with grandees, nobles, *ricos hombres*, deputies, councillors, merchants, admirals and their wives, when halls and rooms were full of high chatter or the half-heard notes of Flemish musicians, were all part of "the service of your Majesty," of "my duty"; and perhaps only Francis and Eleanor, and Juana her sister, knew how thankful the two leading actors felt when at last the curtain was rung down and the stage empty and silent. Service, duty, conscience were satisfied.

CHAPTER IX

THE THINGS THAT ARE CAESAR'S

IT WAS difficult afterwards to see those three and a half years in chronological perspective, so full had been the days, so crowded the weeks and months. Before the background of continual activity against crime and in the furtherance of military and naval defence, events here and there were alone clear in outline. There was the episode in December, 1539, when Gaspar Lordat had been sheltered and saved by the bishop from execution. There was the angry storm aroused by the Viceroy stopping the Carnival celebrations of 1540 because of mourning for the Empress, barely nine months dead. There was another storm in July, because the Marquis had forbidden the decree exporting horses from Catalonia to be evaded even for the Viceroy of Sardinia, brother of the Duke of Cardona, who wrote angry complaints to the Emperor. A third in October, when the sacred prestige of the nobility was infringed in the person of a Baron de la Roca, who, after open insults to the Viceroy, had added worse ones to the Emperor. He was imprisoned in chains; "as he had spoken like a madman I treated him as such," was Francis's answer to expostulations. Francis, at that moment, was involved in worse worries even than usual. The Cardinal de Tavera, Regent in Spain during the Emperor's absence, wrote telling the Viceroy to visit Perpignan and the frontier to see that preparations against a possible French invasion were adequate. Francis's answer was clear and blunt as usual. "If my presence at Perpignan were necessary I should leave at once, for your Eminence can be assured that in all that concerns His Majesty's service I shall never be found negligent. Also, for a man of my habits, it is much more difficult to sit through long Council meetings than to ride about the country, seeing that my life has been spent in such exercises." He then enumerates the reasons against his leaving Barcelona: the imminent threat of a Moorish landing near Tortosa, the recrudescence of brigandage, at that moment quiescent, the lack of men and money. "If I announce that I am going to inspect the fortifications I shall make myself ridiculous, since without money I can neither repair nor increase them... Your Eminence knows that when His Majesty was good enough to appoint me to my present position, I explained to him that it was necessary for me to be supplied with a company of soldiers or some cavalry at his expense for expeditions. Answer, I was only wanted to remain in Barcelona. Hardly arrived, I am told to embark on a campaign against crime in the country. I repeat my need of a company. Answer, in that case stay where you are. In the end I should like to understand one thing, why when I wish to remain I am ordered to go ... I expend all my energies, I spend all my fortune, I risk my life whenever necessary. I should at least like to retain my honour ... If after all this, after having heard my arguments, your Eminence still orders me to go, for reasons which you know and I do not, I will leave immediately. I will never delay in anything relating to His Majesty's service" (September 22, 1540).

The orders were renewed. The Marquis put his affairs in order, spent nine consecutive hours in audiences, attended the funeral services for his brother Henry, who had just died at Viterbo nine months after his elevation to a Cardinalate, and left Barcelona, October 20, 1541. The evils which he had foreseen came to pass. In his absence of two months there were renewed outbreaks of violent crime throughout Catalonia, and truces which he had with difficulty made between rival factions were broken.

There was something, though, which touched him more keenly than public affairs and that was the state of

Eleonor's health. She had not recovered from a miscarriage a little time before, but though she was obviously unfit to travel, she refused to be left behind. None of them were in any delusion as to the dangerous nature of the expedition on which Francis was starting, with no stronger escort than a handful of guards. Physical pain and misery are not to be weighed against mental suffering. The agony of loneliness and anxiety which she had endured while Francis was at the Provençal campaign had left an indelible scar on Eleonor. Never again would she be parted from him so long as weak and weary flesh could still be whipped to action by love and will. She would not be denied. Perhaps the change of air would do her good. The west wind, cool from the snow of the Pyrenees, would be a welcome relief after the nerve-racking, dreary gloom of Barcelona, when grey clouds brooded over the city and the south wind loaded the heavy air with languor. Besides, Juana would be there, to make arrangements and see that all went on smoothly.

Vicarious suffering is perhaps harder to bear than personal, and the six days' journey north were no easier for Francis on his smooth-stepping Arab than for Eleonor, bumping and jolting over rough tracks in her mule-borne litter. The distant mountains on the left were shrouded in grey mist. The cobalt of the nearer hills was patched with the purple of flying cloud shadows. The wide valleys were warm with the umber of stubble fields and the metallic green of beech copses was inlaid with gold and copper. Gerona was passed, its river fringed with tall shuttered houses, its yellow cathedral crowning the hill. Brown towns succeeded one another, clinging round high ochre churches, alike as figures merging into one another in a dream. The sea crept up on the right, long rollers sullen under the stormy grey sky. Bells clanged the Angelus harshly from their open, square towers. Snow peaks began to frown down on ravaged terraces of vines, rocky inlets of the sea and ruined castles. And at long last Perpignan, rest and quiet for Eleonor's worn-out body, but for Francis work, work and still more work.

The Cardinal had been right about the necessity of the Marquis visiting the frontier. Unfortunately there are generally two sides to every question, though Francis was not by nature quick to perceive the other side. Those who see opposing facets are seldom those who get things done in the world.

There was the whole frontier to be inspected, half a dozen posts to be repaired and made capable of defence. Every detail, as usual, had to be personally decided on and overseen. Perpignan itself was worst of all. "It is tragic to see this great town half destroyed," Francis wrote to Charles. "There are as many houses deserted as inhabited. The famous weavers have fled to France, and if they stay there, industry here will be ruined." Murderers and rebels were executed and justice done, but the Viceroy, moved by the utter misery of the inhabitants, induced the Emperor to grant an amnesty to all remaining rebels, which he proclaimed before leaving for Barcelona on December 15. He was anxious to be back. His work at headquarters, as he had foreseen, was undone. "What Roussillon has gained, Barcelona has lost," he wrote bitterly, "the truces which I made with such difficulty have been smashed. My year's work has been destroyed in three days. There have been eleven murders at Taragona during my absence, to say nothing of robbery and other crimes. Unless his Majesty allows me to return without delay he must face the ruin of this kingdom."

It was not only for public reasons that he wished to be back. Eleonor's health, far from improving, as had been hoped, had grown worse. The bitter winds which brought the snow whirling down from the Pyrenees, the cold fog billowing in from the sea, rain and frost; far from bracing, these lowered the all too small reserve of physical strength. It was therefore with a feeling of special thanksgiving that home was reached in time to keep Christmas Day with the children, quietly but happily.

Another year had passed, ending in disappointment, unpopularity and apparent failure. Greatness entails loneliness. Francis had never been one to broadcast the precious gift of friendship indiscriminately. Garcilaso de la Vega was dead. The Empress was dead. Ruy Gomez was in Germany with the Emperor, who was fully engaged there and in Flanders, trying to stay the rising tide of Protestantism and to quell the revolt of Ghent. Spain had never been Charles's main interest. He felt himself a foreigner there, speaking a foreign language, and since his wife's death Spain in his eyes seemed to have shrunk to the level of a remote province of his world-wide empire, useful chiefly as a means of supplying money which, as fast as raised, went into Fugger or Genoese pockets. On the other hand Francis's outlook at the moment was bounded by Catalan frontiers. The low rocky mountains, the barren plains which only ceaseless work made to provide a bare subsistence for the hardy peasants; the small nobles, rough, arrogant, rebellious, in their fortified castles, many little better than robber strongholds; the *ricos hombres* (the greater nobles), richer, more polished, in their Barcelona palaces, but just as arrogant, individualist and quarrelsome; merchants, discontented because Indian gold instead of pouring riches into their safes, had deflected trade and sent up prices; the poor and miserable, harder hit, many starving, almost or quite destitute from shortage of wheat and exorbitant taxes—all this was enough to keep a man busy, to leave little time for the study of intricate German politics or the more intricate incongruities of Lutheran heresy. And beyond the grey winter sea that could be seen from the high perched tower of Montjuich lay the perennial menace of Islam, the danger of an attack in which Moorish corsairs or Turkish galleys would be helped, openly or secretly, by his most Christian Majesty, Francis I of France. Two years ago Kheyr-ed-Din and his

fleet had smashed Andrea Doria's hard-earned fame at
Prevesa. The greatest of all future corsair leaders, Dragut,
was now a slave in the galley of Doria's nephew, but sea-
wolves still terrorized the coasts from Gibraltar to Marseilles, from Genoa to Naples, Corfu and Corinth. Suleyman the Magnificent, greatest of all the Turks, as Dragut
of pirates, at the zenith of his power, was preparing for a
fresh land campaign against Charles and his brother Ferdinand, while the Turkish fleet was to continue invincible
till Charles's as yet unborn son won the laurels of Lepanto.

No wonder the Viceroy pushed on work on walls and
ships, sometimes at Council meetings—as interminable as
such affairs generally are—forgot diplomacy and swept
away petty personalities and ridiculous objections. St
Paul's advice to suffer fools gladly is never an easy one to
follow. Francis, conscious of his own capacities, anxious
only to use them, as in duty bound, 'in his Majesty's service', was also a Spanish grandee, naturally hot-tempered,
arrogant and impatient, not likely meekly to suffer the opposition of short-sighted, narrow-minded and mercenary
officials and merchants.

Mercifully, though, life was not all council meetings.
There was the episode of Epiphany Eve, 1541, of which
Francis sent the Emperor a racy account. Two famous
criminals, arrested by a Viceregal officer, were rescued by
a robber band which also captured the officer and took
refuge in a castle near Barcelona, where they refused to
surrender, and attracted the rival factions of Semanat and
Pujada. The Viceroy mounted and rode out, ordering the
city gates to be closed. "I was summoned because, without me, nothing would be done. I pressed on, for the sun
had already set and I wished to arrive before dark. I arrived after the Angelus and seeing that nothing, not even
my presence, would prevent them from firing, I invested
the fort." After some hours the besieged offered surrender
on certain conditions. Unconditional surrender was demanded, as they might have foreseen. "At last they gave

up their guns and opened the gates. I entered, disarmed
them, arrested the lot and returned to Barcelona at three
in the morning. On the way back I met the Council march-
ing with two thousand men and four pieces of artillery to
demolish the tower" (February 10, 1541).

Francis was always happier in the saddle than in the
Council chamber, but unluckily once in the recesses of the
rocky hills which were the refuge of the brigands, even
cat-footed Andalusian horses had to be left behind, for the
hunt to continue on foot deep in ravines or climbing
through pines and ilexes of the inaccessible slopes. It was
not as hot here as in that Provençal August which had
drenched Francis in sweat, but all the same it was no joke
scrambling over rocks and through tangles of brambles
and thorns in helmet and cuirass, armed with sword and
lance and overweighted with flesh. "I promise you I badly
need a rest after all this run through the mountains, on
foot and fully armed, just after dinner too, which these
ruffians have made me do. You can guess what a business
that is for me with my big belly!" (To Cobos, March 14,
1542).

In the late spring of 1541 occurred an incident which
shook Barcelona society to its foundations, and seemed
like promoting an outbreak of civil war. A grand tourna-
ment had been arranged for May 3, and the Viceroy was
to act as judge. Just as he was starting, word was brought
that a baldacchino of brocade had been erected over the
seats of the Duke and Duchess of Cardona. Such a sign of
royalty had always been forbidden by preceding Viceroys
and by the Councillors. It was tantamount to an insult not
only to the Viceroy but, as he represented the Emperor,
to the imperial authority itself. An order was sent that the
baldacchino was to be dismantled. It was disobeyed. The
Marquis of Lombay refused to attend, commanded the
postponement of the tourney. The Count of Modica
interviewed and insulted him, returned to the Duke of
Cardona, insisted that the entertainment should take place,
g

with the remark that his servants were ready to stab any officers who should try and prevent it. Sure enough next day they attacked two boys and wounded one of the Vice-regal servants who came to their help. The Count himself put another *hors de combat* and then had the effrontery to attend a big ball and dinner that evening. The Marquis and his friends were waiting at the door of the great hall while the Duchesses and ladies entered to take their place at the banquet. The Count, though warned of the arrangement, began to push his way in among the women and not only insulted the Marquis but put his hand to his dagger. He was persuaded to go home where he plotted revolt while Lombay calmly took his place at the head of the table. The next day the Count was arrested and imprisoned. The nobility, which had viewed brigand hunts with indifference and occasionally condescended to join in the sport, were now amazed and furious to see one of their sacred selves treated like a common criminal. The hornets' nest was stirred to fury. Representations of the Viceroy's insupportable behaviour were made to the Council of Castille. Complaints were forwarded to the Emperor. Forged letters attributed to the Viceroy were circulated in the city. Angry deputations of the Count's relations and friends waited on him.

"Neither now nor in the past have I acted from passion," he wrote after a detailed account of the affair to Charles and Cobos, "nor will I so act in the future, so help me God. They have given and still give me the greatest reason to be furious, humanly speaking, but God is so good that, though such is not my nature, I have been able to hide and shall continue to hide, all personal feelings" (To Cobos June 12, 1541). "I trust that, in spite of all, I have more friends than enemies, for I do justice to all, listen readily to anyone, treat all with honour and attention. I spend all my fortune in so doing, though I can do little in that way. Though overwhelmed with injuries and mortifications I do my best to rescue everyone from lawsuits and quarrels.

I do evil to none. I do to all what good I can. The knowledge of that satisfies me" (June 24, 1541).

The result of this effort to preserve order and justice was what might have been expected. Cobos, after the manner of ministers, washed his hands of the matter. Charles, unwilling to be bothered with what he probably considered a storm in a tea-cup, lent an ear to the appeal of the Count of Modica and begged the Viceroy to let the matter rest.

"I learn that your Majesty had deigned to pardon the Count," Francis wrote to Charles, "the Marquesa and I were delighted to hear it . . . Nothing could more increase our desire to serve you. This pardon granted to the Count is one of the greatest favours which the Marquesa and I have received from your Majesty."

One might be tempted to read into the words a savage sarcasm or piercing irony. That they were genuine and sincere is proof of how far Francis had already advanced along the way of purgation. The spirit which had brought him to his knees before his old enemy on his return from the Empress's burial at Toledo had grown and deepened in a wonderful way during these last two years of hard and thankless work, of unpopularity, opposition and treachery. He showed now and was ever to show that no feeling of injury rankled because his attempts to serve the Emperor had been disowned and condemned by that Emperor himself. 'Duty', 'his Majesty's service' and 'conscience' continued to the end of his term of office Francis's motto and inspiration. "Render to Caesar the things which are Caesar's" was a command he obeyed to the spending of his last ounce of energy, the last ducat of his diminished fortune.

The autumn brought an adventure which wiped out all personal jealousies, united all Spain, as always, against the power of Islam, enabled the Marquis of Lombay to use all his talent for organisation to the full. The Emperor resolved to repeat the successful expedition to Tunis of

1535, to complete the conquest of Algiers and stamp out the nest of Barbarossa's corsairs. He wrote affectionate letters to the Marquis and Eleonor from Mallorca where he had landed in October to find his camp equipage ready and his squadron fully fitted out, thanks to the promptness and efficiency of his cousin. "My Cousin," he wrote to the Marquesa, "I am delighted to hear that the Duke, your father-in-law, is to serve in our expedition. I know that the Marquis too would only be too glad to come if his duties did not prevent him." As for the old Duke, if twelve years ago the thought of a journey to court had filled him with horror, it was hardly surprising that the idea of an expedition to Africa threw him into a fever which prevented him from leaving Spain.

High hopes and ambitions were dashed in spite of the public prayers ordered by the Viceroy in all the churches and monasteries of Barcelona. That year the Crescent was at its zenith. Suleyman had inflicted a crushing defeat on Ferdinand in Hungary (July 30, 1541), and by the end of November Charles had landed at Cartagena, having with difficulty re-embarked the remains of his army in the few shattered galleys that were all that was left of Doria's fleet by terrible tempests.

The letter Borgia wrote to Charles was in the finest Spanish tradition of courage, common-sense and resignation to the Will of God, as indeed the Emperor's own behaviour under disaster had been. "Courage, my children," he had calmly said to the terrified troops on seeing the destruction of the fleet. "Wood and nails lost, no more. Very soon, at midnight, the monks all through Spain will be rising to pray for us."

"All that could be done, humanly speaking, was done," wrote Francis (November 22). "We all remain still more your Majesty's devoted servants, more resolved than ever to consecrate to your service our lives, our persons and our possessions . . . Only ships and wood are lost and your Majesty has enough of them in this principality alone to fit out twenty more squadrons. I have already had pines and oaks cut down so as to be ready to carry out your Majesty's orders ... Since God moulds everything to His glory and the good of souls, and your Majesty desires only that, I am sure you will give thanks, as we all do, to God."

A week earlier a sterner note had been struck in a letter to Cobos.

"In truth one can only daily expect worse misfortunes if the reform of the Church is not carried out, as it must be, and if each one does not chase from his conscience and his home the enemies of the soul. It is these who give victory to the Turks and defeat to us, so that we are compelled to surrender to the forces of evil."

Indeed the slackness and disorder of many religious houses in Catalonia was a continual grief and scandal to Francis, as was the life of the bishop, but any attempt at thorough reform was impossible to a layman, who, moreover, had already more on his hands than man could cope with. That something had been attempted is shown in a letter to St Ignatius five years later (1546). "The convents of nuns at Barcelona, Gerona and other places are so disorderly that to impose perfection on them in one blow would be most imprudent. One might make a beginning by forbidding their running in and out and other such offences against God and by forcing them to keep the letter of their rule. Disobedience must be punished ... The wound is so wide-spread it must be cauterized ... When I left Catalonia the reform was well started. The Cardinal of Seville had charged the Inquisitor (now Bishop of Lerida) with it. He and I were resolved, if necessary, to die in the attempt ... I believe, little as I wish to, that if a vote were taken through the city the majority would be against us, though right and justice were clearly on our side."

The Epiphany came. Another year (1542) had begun, with a sense of expectancy and change. The Cortes of the three kingdoms of Catalonia, Aragon and Valencia were to meet at Monzon in the summer to swear allegiance to Philip, now fifteen, as heir to the throne and, needless to say, to be asked for money. The Marquis's three-year term of office would end in the summer, and though the old Duke of Cardona and his faction and the more obscurantist of the councillors were eager for a change, many others thought "better the devil you know than the devil you don't know." Certainly the poor and peasants uttered a heart-felt prayer for his continuance in office. He was a familiar figure to nobles and great merchants and officials at the splendid entertainments which did not dishonour Borgian hospitality, tall, stout, imposing in the silks, brocades, velvets and jewels to wear which he had been dispensed from the rule forbidding Knights of Sant' Iago to don anything but plain coarse wool. He was a familiar figure in the Consulado del Mar, his face occasionally flushed with the attempt to restrain his words of anger and impatience or with pleasure when some plan for defence or employment was passed with unexpected quickness. He was familiar too with soldiers and dockyard workers, with the peasants who, as they straightened their aching backs from hoeing the stony ground, would receive a cheery greeting. Often, in spite of meetings and city business, they saw the big figure ride past, helmed and armed, with his thirty guards and some civic troops when the brigand hunt was up, mounted on his pet Arab, dressed in leather jerkin and high boots of Cordoban leather, bells on the jesses of the hooded hawks jingling, or hounds baying if the chase were the order of the day.

Something of the spirit of Francis of Assisi, under whose cord he had been almost miraculously brought to birth, inspired this Francis in his dealings with animals. Often impatient with the stupidity of men, there was no end to his patience with animals. The fresh-caught hawks, wild, fierce, terrified in their dark room and blinding hoods, first learnt to feed from his hand, at sound of his gentle voice to perch on the leather gauntlet at his wrist. His long, sensitive fingers had no rival in 'imping' broken wing-feathers, in tending wounds. He was seldom seen about without his pet greyhound stalking gravely beside him, or, unless the journey was too rough and long, mounted on his favourite Arab. The knowledge of birds which Vasquez describes was not limited to hawking, though this was his special hobby. In *The Practice of Christian Works* written during these three years, he shows a keen detailed observation of Nature rather unusual in his compatriots and contemporaries.

The session of the Cortes, which lasted till late September, 1542, was as stormy as the last years in Catalonia. The atmosphere can be guessed from hints in Francis's letters. He describes a later battle-royal of his own with the Council, "One might imagine oneself with the Estates at Monzon !" And "I am in the middle of a business almost as uncomfortable as the end of the Cortes !" But Monzon to Francis was a place of re-union with his father, his uncle, the Archbishop of Zaragoza and the Emperor. The two cousins had not met since just after the Empress's death three years before. Inevitably it renewed for both a wound over which Time had begun to draw a veil. But the party, Charles felt, was incomplete. Eleonor, who this time had remained in Barcelona, was summoned and arrived in Monzon in mid-June. She was received with extraordinary marks of respect and affection, surprising to those younger members of the court who saw little in the small, slight, black-clad figure to justify such esteem.

While Francis was renewing acquaintance with the fair, slender boy of fifteen who had been invested by him in his first doublet and breeches, the Emperor was discussing future plans with Eleonor. In spite of protest from the opposing factions, the Marquis had been re-elected Viceroy for another term of three years. This, Charles confided to the Marquesa, was merely a temporary arrangement. Philip, the only son and heir, was now ready for marriage and negotiations were on foot for his alliance with the Infanta Maria of Portugal, daughter of John III and Charles's sister Catherine, whose page and playmate Francis had been at Tordesillas. It was the Emperor's desire, or rather his command, that Francis and Eleonor should take charge of the young couple's household as they had of the Empress's, he as Grand Majordomo, she as chief lady-in-waiting.

Naturally there was some gossip about these long and intimate talks. One great lady, puzzled because Eleonor was neither smart nor beautiful, asked curiously why she dressed so plainly. "Why should I dress more richly than my husband?" was the quiet reply. It was no longer necessary for Francis to go splendidly clad and jewelled, since the Emperor, as whose representative he had shown such state, was now there in person.

Charles arrived in Barcelona (October 10) where, after a great reception and his acceptance of twelve new cannon named after the twelve apostles, he was followed a month later by Philip. The young prince, good-looking in a heavy, fair way, in spite of the Hapsburg jaw, was scarcely likely to win all hearts with his reserved, almost sullen manner and usual silence, but he bore himself well enough as he swore in the cathedral of Barcelona to observe liberty and justice in Catalonia, as he had already sworn at Zaragoza to observe those of Aragon. Perhaps Francis succeeded in breaking down some of the excessive reserve, and re-kindling some of the old attraction. It was only common sense to wish to stand well with the prince with whom his relations would necessarily be so intimate. He himself had renewed his oath as Viceroy early in December, a few days after the Emperor, the Prince, the Duke of Gandia and the court moved on to Valencia.

If Francis and Eleonor hoped for a quiet and happy Christmas and Epiphany with Juana and the children now that pomp and entertainments were over, they were disappointed. Ever since that time at Perpignan, two years ago, a dark shadow of anxiety had been in Francis's mind. Garcilaso de la Vega's death, much more that of the Empress, had stabbed him with the <u>intransience</u> of all earthly things. *transience* The memory of that terrible corruption, which only a few days before had been the serene and lovely temple of a serene and lovely spirit, was stamped ineffaceably on mind and soul. It had been rendered more poignant by the realization of Eleonor's delicacy, the weakness of body which no heroic efforts could wholly conceal from loving eyes. Her life was but one frail thread, yet on it hung, and had hung, all his human happiness and security, a frail thread, yet so inextricably intertwined with his own that he could hardly fancy life without her.

This time, though, it was he and not she who lay in bed racked with fever all through Christmastide, and was left so weak that not till well into February was he able to crawl out to inspect the fortifications. The body might be too weak to walk or to mount a horse, but mind and will were strong as ever. Councillors and nobles, summoned day after day to the Viceregal bedside, and Cobos, who received letters with outspoken criticism of civic meanness and dilatoriness, found no sign of irresolution in the fever patient. "By dint of battling and promising to help with the expenses out of my own purse, I have persuaded them to carry on the work on moats and walls. As the execution of this will be in my hands I hope that things may be pushed on" (To the Emperor, January 9, 1543).

While the Viceroy was still laid up, an experiment took place in the harbour to test an invention of one Blasco de Goray, in which a ship of two hundred tons was driven by two wheels propelled by steam. There was a successful exhibition before members of the Consulado del Mar, but the treasurer, who had a spite against the inventor, drew up an adverse report and no more was heard of the unfortunate Goray. It is strange to think that, if Francis had not been incapacitated by illness, steam-power at sea might have developed two and a half centuries before it did. That Francis was an enthusiastic amateur of ship-building is seen, to quote but one instance, in the account he wrote to the Emperor of the launching of a small galley in whose laying down he had taken a personal interest. "Yesterday morning (13 July, 1541) she was launched. Impossible to do it sooner because of the bad weather. The wind having gone down the evening before, I got up at three o'clock yesterday morning and rushed to the Arsenal where Don Bernardino was waiting for me. As soon as I arrived she was launched and it was a good thing I had got up so early, for hardly had the ship taken the water, than torrents of rain, such as I have never seen, came down on Barcelona."

This month of January, 1543, came news which was to change the whole of Francis's life. Hardly had the Duke of Gandia got home after the royal festivities in Valencia than he went down with fever. He died on January 7, but though aware that his stepmother and her brood of locust children were in possession, Francis remained in Barcelona for over three months, till preparations were completed against the threatened invasion of French and Moors. Not till April 18, 1541, did he set out, with Eleonor, Juana, the eight children, his favourite George de Mello and their household. He had no idea of resigning his post. He had written to Charles demanding leave of absence on January 14. "It will be necessary for me to go down and arrange various business, but the service of your Majesty would suffer here, so I have not dared to ask a holiday till my presence here is less necessary." There is nothing here of the pious joy in renouncing the world which has sometimes been attributed to him. Nor, it must be confessed, any foreshadowing of the note which he himself was to make in his diary, April 18, 1564: "Thanksgiving and gratitude for my departure from Catalonia, which took place twenty-one years ago to-day." Things bear very different aspects when seen close by and in distant perspective from some remote mountain top.

Francis Borgia had been hated, maligned, insulted during his term of office. Posterity has seen his work in truer proportions. His bust is among those of the six best lieutenant-generals of Catalonia which ornament the façade of the palace of the governors in Barcelona.

CHAPTER X

"THE PRACTICE OF CHRISTIAN WORKS"

THE sixteenth century is perhaps the one in all human history when life was most keen and full. The man who buried his talent was the one who earned the terrible condemnation: "Wicked and slothful servant, depart into outer darkness, where is weeping and gnashing of teeth." It was a sentence never merited by Francis Borgia. His talents, and they were many, were used to the full, not as with so many of his contemporaries only to increase their own capacity for pleasure of body and mind, but to do to the utmost of his power the 'duty' and 'service of his Majesty' which he so continually repeated as the inspiration of his work and public life. "Render unto Caesar the things which are Caesar's." The command was obeyed in the fullest degree. But this unceasing battle against crime, treachery, opposition and malice would not have been possible without inner peace and inspiration.

It is probable that to be the wife of a man of genius is the most difficult vocation in the world. It was one which Eleonor fulfilled perfectly. She had every virtue of the valiant woman in the Bible. "Far and from the uttermost coasts is the price of her." Ribadeneira describes her as "gifted with great courage, discretion, true grace, very devout, modest, peaceful, compassionate, eager to do good to all." Perfect wife, perfect mother, perfect mistress of her household and hostess to her guests, the words of Suau about her sister might have been written of her. "Never pushing herself forward, always holy and devout, she deserves to be better known yet, from her very obscurity exhales a poignant charm." It is only possible to see glimpses of her now and then, as one may catch the

fleeting reflection of passing loveliness in some old mirror whose dim, green gloom hints at a beauty it cannot
reveal. Her husband knew that when he returned, dusty,
scarred in mind and feelings from the strife of his public
life, he would find that perfect peace at home which falls
to the lot of so few, to a love and sympathy, to a quiet
wisdom and understanding rare indeed in stormy human
relationships.

Francis and Eleonor no longer lived together as husband and wife, whether because the state of her health had
caused the decision, or his new spiritual orientation. That
they had taken a vow of chastity is disproved, as Suau
points out, by her will of 1536 in which, after providing
for her children she adds "and any other children which
God may be pleased to give me." But the snapping
of one strand of the triple cord which bound them, only
united Eleonor and her husband more closely in mind
and spirit. She followed, if she did not sometimes lead
him, on the strait and thorny way along which he had advanced so far in the last four years.

Two influences had come into his life since his arrival
in Barcelona as Viceroy which, in their different ways,
were deeply to affect his spiritual life. A humble Franciscan friar, who had fled from his home in Estremadura
after a murder by his brother, soon after his arrival in
Barcelona had a vivid dream of a man whom God designed for greatness in the Church. During the Carnival festivities he recognised the figure of his dream in a rider in a
procession and was amazed to hear that it was the Viceroy.
The fame of the lay-brother, whose visions and austerities
were a prolific subject of religious gossip, reached Francis's
ears. The friar was presented to him by a visitor of the
order and acquired an extraordinary ascendancy over
him. With papal permission Francis took Texeda with
him to Gandia, and while there Texeda was ordained
priest. Francis had spent his earliest years in the atmosphere of Franciscan devotion so specially strong in the

convent of the Poor Clares where both his grandmother and aunt had been Abbess. In Texeda's mysticism and austerity there was something ruthless which struck an answering note in Francis Borgia.

Francis was now thirty-three, in the prime of manhood. The fight against physical passion at Zaragoza sixteen years ago had resulted in victory, but passion, though dominated and controlled, cannot be held to be dead till the body itself is corruption. Francis had in his veins not milk and water but the fierce hot blood of Italy, Valencia and Aragon. It is not easy for such a man to live in the world the life of a cloistered monk as regards chastity, a world moreover in which, owing to the duties of his position, it is impossible to avoid temptation and the occasions of sin. When his mother lay dying Francis had had some childish perception of the value of sacrifice. Now, as a man, he realized it far more deeply. Against the passions of lust, anger and hatred measures as stern as those against criminals were necessary.

The scourge, which the small boy's hands had tried to wield, was now locked away after it had been used to blood in the war between flesh and spirit. Now too was a hair-shirt put on whenever duty necessitated his appearance at social functions where women were all too ready to forget excessive flesh in admiration for the handsome face, and beautiful hands and voice, to say nothing of royal blood and princely rank. So, all the time, under lace and velvet and jewels, or fine gilded chased cuirass, the perpetual irritation of delicate skin and sensitive flesh were there to remind Francis of the unending war. "So fight I, yet not vainly as one that beateth the air." Folly? Yes. "To the Greeks foolishness and to the Jews a stumbling block," the divine folly of "Christ and Him crucified."

When the Viceroy returned from the frontier at Christmas, 1540, Barcelona was still full of the wonderful preach-

ing of a young Basque religious who had landed there
in October 1539 on his way from Rome to Madrid, but it
was not till eight or nine months later (August or September, 1541), when he was busy with preparations for the
disastrous Algiers expedition, that he himself came into
personal contact with a member of the new order which
had been authorized by Paul III's famous Bull of the preceding September *Regimini Militantis Ecclesiae* (September
27, 1540). Peter Faber, one of the original seven who had
taken the first vows at Montmartre, wrote to St Ignatius
from Montserrat after his brief sojourn at Barcelona to tell
him that the principal people in Catalonia had been informed of the aims of the Society, so it is certain that he
had seen the Viceroy and that, on his return to Barcelona
the next spring (March, 1542), he was greeted as an old
friend. "We have been lodged by the care of the Marquis
of Lombay, who is devoted to us," wrote Faber to Ignatius in Rome, "so is his wife."

Francis could hardly have failed to give a sympathetic
hearing to one so radiant with 'the beauty of holiness' as
the Savoyard shepherd who was just four years younger
than himself but, unlike him, had spent a life of wandering since he had taken his degree and been ordained priest
in Paris. As Francis listened, with Eleonor, to the gentle
voice, with its foreign accent, watched the tired, serene
face, with the large eyes and hollow cheeks, the strife and
turmoil about him were silenced, illimitable horizons
opened before his eyes. From that day of the Assumption,
1534, when Peter Faber, the only priest among them, had
celebrated Mass for his five Spanish companions and one
Portuguese, the Company of Jesus had spread from Rome
through Italy, France, Germany, Spain and Portugal. As
Araoz, a relative of Ignatius of Loyola, had been the first
Jesuit to set foot in Spain, on his first visit to Barcelona
(1539), so Francis Xavier, Basque nobleman like Ignatius
himself, had been the first to enter north Spain only two
years before. Perhaps Faber told how Xavier, after Igna-

tius his best beloved, had just missed him at Parma and was now half the world away, the first missionary Jesuit to sail for India.

Faber was gone, but his memory remained, so did the memory of his master, small, slight, lame, in rough grey cloak and hat. He had been a familiar figure among the sailors in Santa Maria del Mar praying for a lucky voyage, and among their wives, sisters and mothers, praying too in the shadows of the high, austere Gothic arches for the safe return of their loved ones or the repose of their souls. Francis remembered the story the black monks had told him at Montserrat of this same Ignatius of Loyola, who had kept vigil before his Lady's altar. Perhaps too he remembered that encounter in the dusty street of Alcalá de Henares and the long, steady glance so full of a meaning still undisclosed.

He was at Monzon for the Cortes when Araoz came back to Barcelona (1542), but Eleonor attended the sermons in Santa Maria del Mar and the cathedral, sermons that struck straight to heart and soul not by the fine arts of oratory but by the burning zeal and love which set fire to all who listened. Eleonor, when she joined her husband at Monzon, gave him such an account of the almost miraculous effect of the mission that, when Araoz was ordered to return to Rome, Francis wrote to Ignatius urging him not to cut short such good work. "I assure you that, if you take him away, I shall consider his departure a great misfortune for the city . . . To snatch him away would be to compromise all he has done . . . I beg you for the love of God to leave him . . . The service of God and the good of Barcelona demand it" (July 18, 1542). Ignatius, however, was under obedience to the Pope, and Araoz with his companion sailed on October 26, five days after the departure of the Emperor and Philip for Valencia.

Under his direction the Bishop of Barcelona, the Duke of Cardona, the Admiral of Naples and many others, had made the Spiritual Exercises. It is hardly possible that

Francis should have done so, for in the fortnight between his return from Monzon with the Emperor and the day of Araoz's departure, he was continually occupied with attendance on Charles and, later, Philip. But he had already heard their outline from Faber, and to his mind as to his spirit there was something that struck an answering note in their uncompromising denunciation of sin, their delineation of the ceaseless war between good and evil, their passionate devotion (which he had always shared) to the sufferings and death of Christ, and the resolve, in so far as was possible, to imitate His sacrifice. "It is my wish, desire and deliberate intention, provided it be to Thy greater service and praise, to imitate Thee in bearing all injuries, all reproach, all poverty, actual as well as spiritual, if Thy most sacred Majesty shall wish to choose and receive me to such a state" (*Spiritual Exercises*).

Already, during his Viceroyalty, he had begun to put the ideal into practice. True, the time which some of his biographers allege him to have devoted to prayer every day was impossible for one who was compelled to devote such a large proportion of his day to Council meetings, consultations with the Consulado del Mar, correspondence, superintendence of work in docks and fortifications, to say nothing of brigand hunts and the passing of judgments. Nieremberg's account of the day, then, must be taken with some reservation. "The first thing he did on retiring was to say the Rosary very devoutly, meditating on its Mysteries in their due order." (He was bound as a Knight of Sant' Iago to say daily fifteen Mysteries of the Rosary, an obligation which he observed faithfully.) "Then an examination of conscience, reminding himself of the hourly occupations of the day and begging pardon for faults. He noted these to be confessed later, promising penance and amendment. This was his usual time for the discipline which he used frequently ... Before sleeping he recommended himself to his guardian angel and asked him to watch over him to keep him in all purity ... He

h

told his angel also what he desired, so that while he slept, his angel might pray for him." This special devotion to his guardian angel is shown too in his *Practice of Christian Works*, a little manual whose combination of fervent love and practical common-sense mirror his personality as no secondhand reminiscences can do. "Our angel," he says, "we ought to carry a singular devotion towards him as to a most particular benefactor of ours. For we are more bound to him than to any other next to God and our Lady." His advice to the Christian how to arrange the day so as not to waste time, "for there is nothing in this world so precious as the time that God has given us," is the surest guide to the order of his own day.

Dressing himself, Nieremberg tells us, so that no page nor servant should know of the hair shirt, he went always to Eleonor's room on his way to Mass in the house chapel, where he frequently received Holy Communion, as well as making it publicly in the cathedral every month, a thing so rare then that it occasioned gossip and even disapproval. "If we give every day to our body to eat, nourishing, entertaining and strengthening thereof, is it not reason that our soul, that hath also great need of nourriture and new strength, should be entertained with his heavenly food at least once a month?" (*Christian Works*) After Mass came the business of the day, audiences, conferences, arguments and interviews with obstructive councillors and quarrelsome nobles, not always smooth and conciliatory on Francis's part. There were many occasions —he allows it himself—when his hot temper broke bounds, when he impatiently rode rough-shod over opposition which seemed to him petty or malicious. Time was too short and precious to be wasted. Opportunity, once missed, so seldom returns.

"As soon as any good work is concerned and approved by the judgment of reason and so admitted and accepted of the will . . . it must diligently and without delay be put into practice and execution. For if we neglect to do good when we may and are able, great damage will return unto us thereby, and better had it been not to have made any purpose thereof at all than afterwards not to fulfil or neglect the same . . . All our works are to be done in God and referred to His glory, for so they will be permanent and stable for ever. So all things must be done, and done by all, whether kings, nobles, tradesmen or peasants, for the glory of God and inspired by the example of Christ . . . When you pray, hear Mass, sit at table . . . in business that concerns our own profit or our neighbours' . . . when at your going to bed you put off your clothes . . . crave of Him that by the pain which He felt when, being to be crucified, He was stripped of His clothes He may strip us of our evil habits of mind and conditions that, naked of earthly things, we may embrace the Cross."

The need for ceaseless self-control is emphasized. "Every one of us ought to keep an even hand over himself in governing his body in eating, drinking, in repose and in sleep, in his demeanour and carriage, in his functions, offices and travails." (Francis's own rule now reflected the influence of Texeda. In Advent, 1541, he had observed the Franciscan fast, of one meal a day and that only of vegetables, and declaring that it suited him perfectly, he had kept to the régime in the Lents of the succeeding years, though his table was always so laden with good things to eat and drink that only the most observant of guests noticed their host's own abstinence.) The burden of greatness and power is touched on. "Marvel is it that any dare take that charge upon him which Christ Himself refused, unless he peradventure take it for his Cross and undergo it for the love of Christ." (The influence of the *Spiritual Exercises* is seen in the practical advice how to advance in virtue by practising one virtue till that is perfected and checking progress by daily or twice daily examination of conscience. There is a special devotion to our Lady.) "We must often contemplate this beautiful mirror and looking-glass without stain of sin, shining in all manner of virtues."

Finally, "Matter faileth me not but time," so "We shall get over the stormy and dangerous sea of this miserable life and, in the end, through God's mercy, arrive to the safe port of heaven."

CHAPTER XI

EXILE

ONCE more summer was beginning, and the sun blazed from the arch of sapphire above the Earthly Paradise. The Serpis crawled lazily, a thin yellow snake nearly lost in its wide bed of brown stones. The little sunk garden was cool and green under the waving fans of the palms. The oranges were ripening and a few sprays of blossom still mixed their scent with that of red and white and yellow roses. The little round stones were damp and cool underfoot and the only sound in the sleepy afternoons was the splash of the fountain.

Eleonor lay where Francis's mother had so often lain in the months before his birth. She was glad of silence and solitude, tired mind and body thankful to be away from the stress and turmoil, the coming and going, the noise and crowds of Barcelona. The rustle of palm leaves and the splash of water reminded her of the greatest peace she had known in the Catalan capital, that of the cathedral cloisters. Memories of the Empress, her quiet beauty aglow with joy at reunion with her husband, memories of the days four years ago at Toledo, when the four friends had sat in happy silence, broken only by snatches of distant music or a nightingale tuning for his first love-song— strange how in stillness, when the soul is not troubled by earthly happenings, it mirrors then and now, past and present in one reflection.

With Francis too it was as if scenes of long ago were re-enacted now. The Duke of Gandia and his son rode out with gay clatter of prancing hoofs, the jingle of bit and spurs, the tinkle of little silver bells on jesses, sharp claws clutched tight on gauntlets of morocco leather, and little feathers on falcons' hoods aflutter.

Water gleamed between the tall stems and long, blade-like leaves of the sugar-canes, and the squares of autumn-sown corn were tinged with yellow as pale as the lemons. The hedges of truncated cypresses sheltering the gold-green of young vine leaves contrasted with the grey-green of olive and mulberry trees. The white *barracas*, under their steep thatched roofs, were full of the stale, sour smell of millions of silkworms, crawling everywhere, over mulberry leaves and green branches, spinning yellow cocoons that the women's quick, dark fingers would wind off into gossamer threads of golden silk. As always there were arguments and quarrels, to be settled by the Duke or referred to the *Tribunal de las Aguas* in Valencia next Thursday. Improvements were needed in the old-fashioned handmills whose wooden rollers flattened the striped yellow joints of the cane and squeezed out the juice to be boiled down into syrup and molasses. From late November till mid-January five hundred and fifty men and two hundred mules would be working full time in the ducal factories, which brought a yearly income of a thousand ducats from the export of molasses to Flanders alone.

Everything was the same as twenty years ago, except that now it was Francis the Duke who listened, advised and decided, and Carlos, his thirteen-year-old son, who fidgeted and ached to be off to the rocky slopes, grey with olives and low fragrant scrub, where at last hawks or hounds could be unhooded or unleashed and the real business of the day begun.

Sometimes, in the most exciting moment, through the hot, still air or fitfully down the gusts of south wind, came the distant tinkle of a bell which meant that a priest was on his way to some deathbed with the Blessed Sacrament and the holy oils. Back would gallop Francis on his big black, Carlos, perhaps a little reluctant, after him, to dismount and follow bareheaded. Carlos related long years afterwards how: "The Duke my father would stop suddenly and, after listening, cry out 'The bell !' speaking of that

which rang in the city before the Viaticum was taken out.
We might be a league or several away, in the valley of
Alfandech or on the plains of the Torro de Xaraco. But he
insisted that he heard it and was astonished that we young
ones had hearing less keen than his. Wheeling his horse he
would turn back to Gandia, followed by us. We found he
was always right."

Francis had only asked for leave from his duties and was
anxious to settle the business at Gandia as quickly as possible so that he and Eleonor should be ready to take up
their new posts, he as Majordomo to Prince Philip, she as
Camarera Mayor to his wife. Their diplomas of appointment had reached them at Gandia at the end of April,
1543. Eleonor's sister Juana, as well as two of the girls,
Isabel and Juana, were also appointed to the royal household. All were to be lodged in the palace with the young
couple, and Duke and Duchess were to receive a yearly
salary of four thousand ducats.

Affection as well as ambition made the prospect an al-
luring one. The small boy who had cherished such a fervent devotion to the handsome young Marquis had grown
into a fair, slender, delicate youth. He did greater credit to
the Salamanca professor who had taught him the humanities, Latin, French and Italian than to his other tutor who
failed to make him anything but an awkward and timor-
ous horseman and swordsman. Francis had renewed the
old friendship with the prince at Monzon and Barcelona
and knew that the Emperor intended, when quitting
Spain again, to leave his son as regent. Charles had drawn
up copious instructions for the young regent and had appointed a council, of Cardinal de Tavera, the Duke of Alba
and Francisco de Cobos to advise him. Francis was friends
with all three, and his post, as well as giving him Philip's
ear, offered ample scope for his energy and powers of
organisation. It is almost certain that the Emperor had
already mentioned to his cousin, in strictest confidence,
his intention of abdicating as soon as possible and ending

his days in a cloister. He had expressed the highest praise
and gratitude in the form confirming the appointment of
the new majordomo, and all signs pointed to the Duke of
Gandia being chief minister when Philip assumed sover-
eignty.

Meanwhile there was more than enough to do. The
threat of invasion by Barbarossa and his corsairs was still
imminent. The city walls and moat of Gandia, like most
of the east coast towns, needed repairing and completing.
Sixty pieces of artillery were mounted on them. The
palace itself had been neglected and wanted a lot done.
The old state must be kept up, in spite of huge debts left
by the late Duke. The armoury was brought up to a
standard when fifty men-at-arms and six hundred infantry
could be equipped from it. The great stables on the left of
the main entrance were the Duke's special hobby. Forty
of the finest horses in Spain were housed there and the
Gandia stud was considered the best in the country. One
hundred and thirty gentlemen and pages were in the ducal
household. Innumerable servants in the gorgeous scarlet
livery comprised house-men, grooms, falconers, kennel-
men and the usual tribe of old retainers and hangers-on.
The family circle itself embraced the Duke and Duchess,
their eight children, Eleonor's sister Juana, Isabel de
Rodriguez, the girls' governess (to whom Eleonor left a
special legacy in her will) and Francis's favourite cousin,
George de Mello.

The city itself was a problem. Only thirty of the hundred and twenty poorer families were old Christians. The
rest were Moors, on whom Christianity had been forced
at the sword's point and on whose faith little reliance
could be placed. The same was the case with the large
number of Maranos (convert Jews) throughout the duchy.
According to the old saying *"Quien tiene Moro tiene oro"*
(who owns a Moor owns gold), Francis should have been
vastly rich. An actual goldmine too was discovered on his
estate in December, 1545, but it justified his scepticism,

"I am afraid my gold mine will end in alchemy!" Sugar factories, though, were more satisfactory than goldmines and supplied the larger part of his annual revenues of forty-two thousand ducats from Valencian properties.

Unfortunately the old Duke, a bad administrator, burdened with a greedy second wife and her large brood, boundlessly generous in his charities, had left things in a hopeless muddle. It was chiefly to try and clear this up that Francis had begged for a month's leave at Gandia, where he had no intention of staying longer than necessary.

The dowager Duchess had done well for herself under her husband's will. By it she got back the whole of the dowry she had brought as well as the half of its amount which the Duke had added (nearly three thousand pounds equivalent to four or five times its present value), and heavy charges were laid on the estate for her ten children. Her eldest son, Pedro-Galceran, whom she put forward for the Grandmastership of Montesa, was defeated in the election but obtained the appointment, thanks to Francis who used his influence with the Emperor, Philip and the Pope. Doña Francisca's method of showing her gratitude was a demand that the Duke should pay his father's debts, which amounted to twenty-four thousand ducats, out of the already impoverished estate. He did not consider that justice should be sacrificed to generosity by crippling the revenues which were his son's by right of succession, so refused her application. Pedro-Galceran wrote to Philip, begging him to protect against the hard-hearted Francis "this inconsolable widow, burdened with so many children and such poverty." The poor woman also appealed to the Prince "to have pity on my misfortunes and my tears, I have so little help and so many children . . .[signed] the sad widow of Gandia."

The long inventory of silver, jewels, tapestry and furniture which she carried off from the palace is proof that her stepson interpreted his father's will in no mean spirit, but

he was inexorable in the matter of the debts. Not satisfied
with the substantial advantages awarded her in the Valencia court, in 1544 Doña Francisca refused to submit to
arbitration by Philip and the Archbishop of Valencia (St
Thomas of Villanueva) and took the case to Castille,
where it dragged on for another five years.

Meantime, all the summer of 1543, Francis and Eleonor
were waiting their summons to court at Valladolid.
Eleonor felt that she could fulfil, as no one else could, the
pleasant duty of mothering the bride of sixteen, Portuguese like herself and daughter of Francis's cousin and
playmate, Catherine. Philip wrote affectionate letters to
Gandia and Francis's own letters show no desire to leave
the world and bury his talents in obscurity. The legend
which has crystallised the cry in the crypt at Granada,
"Never again, never again will I serve mortal master," is
not verified by the three and a half years' service as Viceroy of Catalonia, and the alleged desire to renounce all
and enter religion is contradicted by Francis's letters from
Gandia and the negotiations over his and his wife's appointment to the charge of the young couple's royal
household. "If this exile is further prolonged, as my sins
deserve it to be," he cried in a letter to St Ignatius (1545),
and to Philip, "Though we are forgotten here it does not
follow that we deserve such treatment from his Majesty
nor your Highness."

Francis Borgia has been hidden in a cloud of inhuman
virtues by hagiographers. He has been labelled by his
detractors as cruel, money-grubbing and ambitious. Truth
lies perhaps not in a *via media* but in the realisation of apparently opposing facets of character. The Duke of Gandia kept up a princely establishment and lived in great
state because he considered this was due to his position
and his retainers. He fought hard to preserve the estate
and inheritance intact for his heir and his heir's future
children. He begged posts and appointments for his four
other sons who, otherwise, were entirely unprovided for.

He arranged suitable matches for his daughters, as was customary, but he did not push them into convents as his father had done with *his* daughters when hardly able to walk or talk.

Such was his outer life, the life of a grandee of Spain, a keen Christian, a good husband, father, master and land-lord. The household was strictly ruled. All were required to hear Mass every morning, to go to confession and Holy Communion once a month in the collegiate church. All could see and admire this, but his inner life was known only to God and himself, to Fray Juan de Texeda and, in a lesser degree, to Eleonor. There was more time here than there had been in Barcelona for prayer, vocal and mental. Austerity increased enormously, fostered by the visionary friar, but that other spiritual influence, so necessary to check undisciplined excess of mortification, was rapidly growing stronger.

The pure and gentle holiness of Peter Faber had left an ineffaceable impression on Francis Borgia. The military spirit, the efficient organization, the hitherto hardly tested strategy of the new order appealed to the keen vision and practical common-sense of the Spanish realist. The spirit behind these externals was to prove for Francis his great-est help along the way of holiness. He had not yet done the Spiritual Exercises, with which Antonio Araoz had ob-tained such marvellous results in Barcelona, but he was already practising them, "preparing and disposing the soul to remove from herself all disorderly attachments and, after their removal, to seek and find the divine Will, in the planning of life to the salvation of the soul."

His will was already subordinated to the Will of God, but the way marked out for him to serve God seemed to be not in withdrawal from the world, but by using, in the world, his great powers and opportunities for the good of others and the greater glory of God.

Suddenly fell a bolt from the blue, news that John III and his Queen absolutely refused their consent to the

Duke and Duchess of Gandia being in charge of their daughter's household. The only reason given, a paltry and ridiculous one if true, was that their Majesties had been slighted because the Emperor had not consulted them before making arrangements. A rumour spread that it was because the Duchess had been a friend of the Cardinal Bishop of Visieu who had, very foolishly, circulated a story that John III was illegitimate because his father had not obtained a dispensation before marrying his sister-in-law, Maria of Aragon, Charles V's aunt.

Francis and Eleonor wrote at once to Lisbon, he being prudent enough to send his letter to Cobos, who approved and forwarded it. The Emperor had left Spain to which he only returned after his abdication thirteen years later. Incredibly insulting replies were received from the Queen and her brother-in-law, Don Luis, with whom Francis had made friends at Barcelona eight years before. Queen Catherine, after a long and pompous list of her own titles and dignities ended her letter to Eleonor: "I have seen your letter to me and the Infante, my brother, has told me what you wrote to him. As there is no more to be said and the Infante will communicate with you on the matter I leave it to him" (Cintra, August 30, 1543).

"Remember you are Portuguese," wrote Don Luis to Eleonor. "Impossible for you to enter the service of the Princess in such a manner . . . When your letters arrived I wondered how you could think that such an arrangement could succeed or how you dared to think of entering the Princess's household when you knew their Majesties' displeasure . . . Do not imagine you will ever enter sword in hand when the friendly consent of their Majesties is necessary."

Such language, in an age of ceremonious courtesy, from royalty to a grandee who was also a cousin, or to his wife, was almost unbelievable. But so the deadlock continued through the autumn and winter of 1543, the spring of 1544. Charles V, who had concluded one of his frequent peaces with France after another two years of war, was now in Germany trying to force agreement on the Protestants and to restore the unity of religious belief in the empire. He wrote in no uncertain terms confirming his appointment of the Duke and Duchess as heads of the royal household. Philip wrote frequent and affectionate letters to Gandia, assuring the Duke of his keen desire to welcome him at court. His marriage to the Infanta Maria at Salamanca (November 15, 1543) left his determination unaltered, but his bride, with the unshakable obstinacy of a stupid and narrow nature, refused to allow the Duke and Duchess near her. When it was known, early in the New Year of 1545, that she was pregnant, it was thought best not to force an impossible position till after the birth of the heir.

"Though this business has been most unpleasant," wrote Eleonor to the Emperor, "I would endure it in your Majesty's service but, after the Princess's letters, I judge it would be hopeless. Thanks to God and your Majesty, I am not destitute though the Queen is so furious with me that, if she could, she would deprive me of all my money as she has done to the Cardinal of Visieu" (October 2, 1543).

Francis was unconsciously prophetic. "Their opposition is very harmful, for it prevents the Princess from being looked after as your Majesty wishes her to be . . . As things now are I get nothing but insults and humiliations whether I go or stay."

Indeed if Eleonor had been in charge things would have gone very differently for the young couple. The Princess gave birth to the future Don Carlos on July 8, 1545. Four days later the Duchess of Alba and Doña Maria de Mendoza, who were in charge of mother and child, went out to enjoy an *auto-da-fé*. When they returned the princess was dead. If Eleonor had been at the head of the household the invalid would certainly not have been left to the care of ignorant and incompetent servant-maids.

"What still further deepens our grief is the thought of your Highness's despair," wrote Francis to Philip, "but I hope that, as a Catholic, you know how to accept the Will of God and so to deserve a great increase of grace. When our Lord visits us and we receive humbly and with resignation what His pitiful hand deals out to us, in a way we force Him to cherish us in His arms with yet more love and graces" (July 20, 1545). He wrote a couple of months later to Peter Faber who had just returned from Germany to Spain. "As for the Princess's death I have been much comforted to learn from your letter that she made a good end. I wished to serve her soul more than her body so I was anxious for news of that soul. Those alone are great who know their own littleness. The rich are not those with great possessions but those who wish to possess nothing, who know that true honour consists in knowing and glorifying God. So that, come death or long life we may say 'Their heart is ready to hope in the Lord'" (Sept. 20).

Already later in the same year negotiations were on foot for Philip's marriage with Maria, daughter of Emmanuel of Portugal and Charles's sister Eleonor, now Queen of Francis I of France. Araoz wrote to Ignatius, "The prince is to marry the French princess and it is thought certain that the Duke and Duchess of Gandia will go to court to take up the same posts as before. The Duke has told me that he wishes to go only to make known the Company of Jesus at court, not for his own interest nor for ambition for he no longer feels anything but disgust for honours" (December 11, 1545).

So two and a half years had passed at Gandia, years of hope deferred, apparent disgrace, litigation, and (greatest of all trials) anxiety about the Duchess's health. She had never been strong since that miscarriage in 1540. The good which it was hoped she would gain from the quiet life at Gandia was more than undone by the shock to her of the Portuguese King's and Queen's attitude towards

her husband and herself. Such savage and unreasonable
words and deeds from her own sovereigns and Francis's
childhood friend dealt what was to prove a mortal blow to
one already delicate, highly strung, gentle and affectionate. It is so much harder to bear and forgive injuries to one
we love than to forget those offered to ourselves. That
Eleonor bore no malice nor hatred for the Portuguese
treatment of her husband shows that she, as well as he,
was far advanced in holiness.

She was ill on and off all 1544. "I must give you news
of the Duchess," Francis wrote to Cobos. "A few days
ago she was so bad that we were afraid we should lose her.
Our Lord has restored her a little. She is now able to dress
herself and lie out of doors . . . I am taking her to the
mountains, away from Gandia, which is too near the sea.
I hope God will cure her and that the Prince will tell us to
come. While waiting we are getting ready so as to start as
soon as God has given the Duchess the strength we want
for her" (November 17, 1544).

Three weeks later he reported that the change had done
good. "She is convalescent but still very weak." The
winter tried her. She was not well enough to travel when
a summons came from Philip. Then it was decided to postpone the arrival of Duke and Duchess till the royal baby
was born.

"Thank God she is better than last year," wrote Francis
of his wife in a letter to St Ignatius. "May our Lord reward you for your prayers for her and me. We recom-
mend ourselves to you the more as our leaving for the
court draws near. They are pressing it on their side, and as
the patient has improved in health we cannot resist" (May
22, 1545).

In six weeks the princess was dead. The proposed
French marriage never materialised. Nine years elapsed
before Philip was married again, to Mary Tudor. The end
of those long months of exile, apparent disgrace, unreasonable opposition and malice seemed at last in sight,

but in the spring of 1546 that hope was finally dashed. Faber, just arrived at Valladolid, was begged by Francis to pray for Eleonor, "for she travels swiftly to death" (March, 1546). Her weakness had increased so rapidly that after each relapse recovery was slower and less complete. Francis was faced by the prospect of losing her who for so long had shared his every thought and wish, of being left with the care of eight children, Carlos, the eldest only fifteen, Alfonso, the youngest just eight. He multiplied his already generous alms to the poor of Gandia, ordered prayers and Masses through the duchy for his wife's cure. When not at her bedside he was on his knees in his little private oratory before the Crucifix which still stood there till the expulsion of the Jesuits in 1932.

One day as he stormed heaven with violence for Eleonor's life his soul was suddenly filled with divine light and in the silence he heard the dying Christ speak. "If thou desirest to keep the Duchess longer on earth, so be it, but see I tell thee plainly that this is not the best for thee."

The answer which Ribadeneira attributes to Francis expresses his absolute resignation. "My Lord and my God, whence is it that Thou leavest in my hands what should be only in Thine? Thou art my creator and my all. Who then am I that Thou shouldst do my will? For I desire nothing but in all things to deny my own will that Thine may be done. Who better than Thou knows what is best for me? From this hour, Lord, I promise that I am no longer mine but Thine, seek not my will but Thine, desire only what Thou desirest. I offer Thee not only the life of the Duchess but that of all my children and my own, all that Thou hast given me, all that I have in this world. I beg of Thee to dispose of all according to Thy holy Will."

The supreme sacrifice was offered and accepted. From that moment Eleonor sank rapidly. She made her confession and received the last Sacraments from the Jesuit father, Andrea Oviedo, who had arrived in Gandia four months before for the foundation of the new Jesuit Col-

lege endowed by the Duke. Eleonor lay in the great bed
in the 'Duchess's room', where Francis had been born,
where his mother had died. She asked that the Passion
should be read aloud to her. Before it was finished the
Crucifix had slipped from her fingers. She was gone
(March 27, 1546).

"What can I tell you of your dear friend but that God
granted her death as He had given her life? She was marvellously mortified in her illness. In her death she was
wonderfully rewarded," wrote Francis to Araoz. "I am
longing for Father Faber. He can only come for a few
days. If he could only spare a few hours I know I am unworthy to enjoy his saintly company" (April 29, 1546).

i

CHAPTER XII

THE NEW ORDER

UNDER the influence of Fray Juan de Texeda, installed for the last three years in the ducal palace, it was natural that Francis's mind, stunned by his bereavement, should turn to the order of his patron saint. The poverty and penance, the mortification, obedience and humility of the Franciscan spirit made a strong appeal to one who had learnt the bitter lesson that "the world can give no more than it has." The rough brown habit, the hempen cord, the bare feet, they had been familiar all his life, yet, when he offered this intention to God, "he found himself dry, his soul lifeless."

The friend and counsellor for whom he had been longing came in May. "We arrived in Valencia Easter Thursday," wrote Peter Faber to Araoz, "and I stayed there all Friday. On Saturday I left for Gandia which I only reached Sunday night. I only spent two whole days there which I devoted partly to our brethren, partly (almost all) to the Duke and partly to the nuns."

The friendship between the great noble and the Savoyard peasant was one of those which only grow to full fruition in the soil of sanctity. Faber had all the qualities needed to console, cheer and strengthen a broken heart. His limpid sincerity, his dazzling purity, his gentleness, burning zeal and charity made him one of Ignatius's dearest sons and, after Ignatius, Francis Xavier's best loved friend. Told when he was designated Patriarch of Ethiopia that this was a death sentence, he answered, "It is not necessary to go on living, it is necessary to obey."

In those two crowded days it was impossible for Faber to give the Duke the Spiritual Exercises. That was left for Father Oviedo to do. But his holiness, his tender sympathy and wise advice did all that could be done humanly speaking to close Francis's wounds and set him on the right path.

The two never met again. Faber left Gandia (May 4, 1546) on his way to Rome, whither he had been summoned by the General to be sent to the Council of Trent as Papal Theologian. He was charged by the Duke with a message announcing his resolve to enter the Society of Jesus. Hardly had he reached Rome when the body, worn with ceaseless travel and work, gave out. "Faber died," (August 2) says Crétineau-Joly, "because all was dead in him except his heart and the Faith."

Francis Borgia's determination to enter the new Order, still comparatively unknown and in many quarters the object of acute dislike, suspicion and calumny, was not a rash impulse undertaken in an unbalanced moment. He had been in constant correspondence with Ignatius Loyola for several years. The first letter is lost which he is said to have written from Barcelona in 1541 asking direction about frequent Communion, but the letters of the following years are published in the *Monumenta*, the Duke's in the five volumes of *Borgiana*, the General's answers in *Epistolae S. Ignatii*.

It was well indeed for Francis that, to counteract the excesses of the friar, he should have had the practical realism, the clear and far-sighted vision which were of the essence of Ignatius's genius. Wise common-sense guided all his religious plans and reforms in the duchy. Sometimes indeed the Jesuit General, with an admirable mixture of diplomacy and decision, entirely altered or vetoed the Duke's schemes.

Francis had always been friendly with the Dominicans. His confessor at Barcelona had been Juan Michol, O. P. Now, distressed at the lack of education among the Morisco children, he had endowed a foundation for ten friars at Lombay and handed it over to the Dominican Provincial (Aug. 1543). One of the first friars was Luis

Bertrand, who was canonised the same day as Francis Borgia. The Duke also increased the endowments of the collegiate church in Gandia, introduced a new splendour and dignity of ritual and himself composed the music for several Masses. "He won a place among the most famous Spanish masters. His musical compositions were so well known that they were sung in many cathedrals . . . They all had for their object divine worship, liturgical singing and organ music" (Cienfuegos).

Francis's organ still stands in the *galería* of the palace at Gandia, with its narrow keyboard and slender, gilded pipes. The ivory notes are yellow with age. The black sharps and flats are worn and chipped. It was one of the first organs to be brought from Flanders and is like that (now in the *Armería* at Madrid) which accompanied Charles V on all his campaigns and went with him to Yuste. The echo of faint, ghostly music still seems to hang in the sunlit air of the long gallery, the harmony drawn from the ivory by those long, fine fingers, the notes of that strong, sweet voice which had satisfied even the fastidious ear of the Emperor but had found their true home in Eleonor's heart. The palace is deserted and desolate, a sad and soulless museum, the doors leading to the enclosure roughly nailed up with coarse boards.

Charles's Flemish musicians had curried favour by composing Masses to his favourite airs, *De la bataille écoutez* and *Baise moi, ma mie*. In Italy choirs sang the profanest music, even substituted lewd words for the liturgical office. It was high time for the reform of church music ordered at Trent. The music of a love-song popular in Spain under the title *Cancion del Duque de Borja* was attributed to Francis but its authenticity is doubtful. The Masses which he composed were scattered in MS. through Spain, in the cathedrals and chapels where they were sung. All have been lost except the one found by a Benedictine from Montserrat among the archives of the Gandia collegiate church, where it has always been sung on the Sundays of Advent and Lent. As well as the Mass (for four voices but without *Gloria* and *Credo*) there are also eight motets in strict contrapuntal style. These last formed a kind of oratorio, a setting to music of the dialogue for the procession of the Blessed Sacrament which took place from the convent of Poor Clares on Easter morning. Magdalene's final cry of joy "Christ is risen !" is repeated three times and the last triumphal outburst of the whole choir in "Alleluia ! Alleluia !" have, Suau points out, "all the brio of the Valencian school."

It was natural that Francis should find consolation in music, the art which, beyond words, unites science with emotion. Like all outward beauty it awoke beloved memories, but like all artists, he found relief in expression and creation. As artist he appreciated Platonic beauty in sight as well as in sound. *The Practice of Christian Works* shows a keen observation and love of nature. "God hath indeed given thee eyes that by beholding the beauty of His creatures thou mightest love him in all and everything and give Him thanks for all." The note is amplified in a passage about "the poor creatures of the earth" which shows a knowledge of nature gained in long days out with hawks and hounds and even in the scrambles after brigands in the Catalonian mountains. Earth, water, fire, air each yield their lessons. So do rocks, deep-rooted trees, growing plants, the perfume of wild flowers, the sweetness of honey. "The silly sheep clotheth you with his skin and fleece and nourisheth you with his flesh. The beasts carry men on their backs and ease them wearied of their labours, and when thou givest thy beast meat think thus how much more meet it is that thou serve them than they thee, since they have never been rebellious or ungrateful to God as thou hast ever been and still art." "Ants, bees, the silly worms and other like creatures" are all conscripted, and there is an amusing description of "the deaf adder that stoppeth her ears." "Let the wisdom of serpents which are said to put one ear close to the ground and stop

the other with their tail that they may not hear the voice
of the enchanter put you in mind of your imprudence who
have not yet learned to stop your ears against the temptation of the devil."

The boys—Carlos now sixteen, the favourite Juan fourteen, Alvaro twelve and Alonso, the baby of the family,
only eight—must have learnt far more than the science of
falconry on those long days out on the *huerta* and the foothills with their father. It was probably now that he practised that small but difficult act of self-discipline which
Vasquez describes, turning away his eyes at the very
moment when the hawk he had flung from his wrist fell
upon its quarry. A petty thing but an exercise of self-control which strengthened the already strong will to restrain
desire.

The rides through the countryside resulted in more
than sport. Like his father he was always being appealed
to for advice and judgment. Unlike his father he realised
that a thorough religious education was the only chance
of keeping for the Faith the children of Moors who, baptised against their will, still practised Islam in secret. He
decided to open a school for these children in Gandia and
confided the project to Araoz (Lent, 1544).

Ignatius, asked for Jesuit masters, advised the Duke
not to confine the school to Moriscos but to found a college open to all. Francis agreed. "The need here is men.
The learned ones lack good will. Those of good will lack
knowledge. So we can only limp along or rather we do
not get on at all . . . I beg your Reverence to advise me by
letter. I know you will not forget me in your prayers. God
grant that I may not always be an unprofitable servant
who eats his bread without having earned it" (May 28,
1545).

"You ask me not to forget you in my prayers and to
keep in touch with you by letters," answered Ignatius.
"As for the first I do so every day . . . Thus, having you in
my mind daily I think will suffice to satisfy your desire for

letters. Those who leave themselves to enter into their
Lord and Creator have mutual communication and consolation . . . I am deeply grateful to the divine goodness
that you receive our Lord frequently . . . Travelling along
this road with this divine help, winning your neighbours
and brethren, you will use the talents which his divine
Majesty has given you" (Nov. 1545).

The personnel of the new college was welcomed to
Gandia in November, that same year, four months before
the Duchess's death. It consisted of two students from
Coimbra university, a young Spaniard, Andrea de Oviedo
(the only priest of the party), and a Frenchman, François
Onfroy, with five scholastics from Rome. "All well, for
they bear God in their souls," said Francis two months
later in a letter to Ignatius thanking him for gifts sent by
him, rosaries for the Duke, the Duchess and her sister.
"Useless to try and tell you the pleasure I have had from
their arrival and from Father Araoz's visit . . . Help me,
your Reverence, to be granted what God Himself desires
for His creatures to experience, continual contemplation,
to which end we were created. I know that I ask much,
that to acquire this grace costs much. But it is only reasonable to ask that fire should warm. So is it reasonable that
man should contemplate, praise and sanctify his Creator"
(January 16, 1546).

After his visit to Gandia Araoz too had written to the
General of "the Duke whose goodness and perfection I
cannot describe. He is so disinterested that he seeks only
the glory of God . . . A soul in which God is marvellously
mirrored."

The prayers for Francis's spiritual advancement were
answered by his wife's death. His last tie with the world,
he felt, was snapped. As Nieremberg somewhat cold-
bloodedly remarks, "He was now freed from the chains of
marriage." He had never been one to delay. He had sent
by Faber news of his resolve to enter the Society of Jesus,
but, afraid that the dying man might not have been able

to deliver his message, he wrote to the General to say that,
after due consideration, he had made before Father
Oviedo (June 2, 1546) a vow to enter the Society "as soon
as I shall have wound up my affairs, which my conscience
bids me do."

Ignatius's answer was a splendid mixture of courtesy,
common-sense, prophetic foresight and holiness. He
thanks God for the Duke's determination to join "this
little company," which will produce "great fruit, first for
your Grace's soul, then for those of innumerable others
who will benefit by such an example . . Now as to the
details which you wish me to decide, when and how you
are to join. Having referred my judgment to God, directly and through the medium of others, it seems best to me
that this step should be taken slowly and prudently, the
better to fulfil all your obligations and for the greater
glory of God . . . You should arrange things so that you
will soon be at liberty to do what you so deeply desire in
the Lord, but tell no one of your decision. To descend to
details. You should arrange suitable marriages for your
daughters as they are now of marriageable age. If possible
.he Marquis should also marry. As for your other sons, it
is not enough merely to leave them under the shadow and
protection of their elder brother, to whom you will be-
queath your estate. You must also supply them with an
income large enough to enable them to live comfortably,
for example in one of the principal universities where they
can continue the studies already begun on such a sound
basis . . . While waiting for all these affairs to be settled I
should like you—I think it will be for God's service—to
study and take your doctor's degree in Gandia university.
You already know enough to begin theological studies.
But great secrecy must be observed, for, at the moment,
the ears of the world are not strong enough to stand so
violent an explosion. By the help of God the time will
soon come when you will be completely free. I shall expect frequent letters from your Grace to keep me in touch

with all that happens. I will write regularly and pray the divine goodness to continue with His favour and grace the mercies begun in your soul" (October 9, 1546).

CHAPTER XIII

"MANY-COLOURED GLASS"

FRANCIS'S was an impatient nature, one, as Araoz wrote to Ignatius, which "needed bit rather than spur." His resolution taken he saw himself already "one foot in the stirrup," dressed in the black habit. As things turned out it was four years before the business of family and estates was concluded and he could leave that exile where he had meant to spend a few weeks and ended by spending seven years.

The last four years at Gandia were full as ever of external activities. He was still, in the world's eyes, the owner of a princely estate, whose financial and social affairs were a whole-time job. The long-drawn-out lawsuit between him and his stepmother ended at last in 1549. "I have good news for you," he said one day when visiting his aunt at the Poor Clares. "The Royal Council have given their verdict against me." "What?" cried the Abbess with truly human surprise, "you call *that* good news?" "Yes, my sons need less than the Duchess, and I always hoped for this." He had done his best for the last six years to preserve his son's inheritance from the greed of his father's widow. Judgment given against him, he welcomed it as the Will of God.

Obedient to Ignatius's advice he spared no trouble in arranging for adequate provision for his four younger sons. He tried to get the governorship of Jativa for Juan, begged from Philip II a benefice for Alvaro, who was to take orders, obtained for his sons from Paul III the Valencian estates left at the death (intestate) of the Duke of Camerino, grandson of Alexander VI. Carlos would be sufficiently provided for by the Gandia and Lombay estates, whose revenues had been substantially increased by the competence and organisation of his father. A large part of the present income was spent in charity, as it had been in the old Duke's time. As well as the Dominican priory and the Jesuit college, a hospital of St Mark had been endowed for ninety-nine sick poor of the duchy and was regularly visited by the Duke and his sons. Naturally his special favourite was the Jesuit foundation, of which the first stone had been laid by Peter Faber the day he left Gandia (August 4, 1546). The ducal thought and generosity were endless. He bought and presented a whole shipload of French and Flemish books. He gave olive orchards, vineyards and other properties. Oviedo wrote an account of the solemn blessing of one large vineyard and orchard, "the first time such a ceremony had taken place in the duchy." There was a procession to the site and chanting in which the Duke and his sons joined with the clergy. Finally Francis flung off his cloak, told the young men to do the same, seized a spade and himself planted several vines, Carlos and his brothers finishing the job.

When Oviedo began a public course of philosophy in the palace (October 1546) it was the first time that Jesuit classes had been opened to outsiders, and so was the inauguration of that Jesuit education to young laymen which spread so rapidly through Europe. Francis himself, in strictest secrecy, was working at theology. "He chose for fellow student Canon Diego Sanchez," Oviedo wrote to the General. "The Duke continues his studies and makes great progress." "Considering his great talents I believe he will become a famous theologian who will greatly enlighten the Church . . . destined to be one of its chief pillars and a help to many."

There is a large tapestry in the Gandia palace of Francis receiving his doctor's degree after passing his examination in theology. The Jesuit library is hung with laurel wreaths in honour of the occasion. Carlos, very smartly dressed and looking rather supercilious, stands in the background with his brothers, surrounded by a canon and various

Jesuits, all appropriately edified. Francis kneeling, holds his doctor's brevet, a page waits with the ring on a cushion and Father Oviedo is about to place the beretta on Francis's bowed head. As Suau pertinently remarks, it would have been hardly diplomatic to allow the founder of the college to fail in his examination, but "the capacity which he showed later in directing the studies of the Order and the enthusiasm with which his preaching was everywhere received, are surer proofs of his learning" (August 20, 1550).

That was four years after Francis had done the Spiritual Exercises under Andrea Oviedo (September, 1546), who had written in cipher to the General: "This is how the Duke made his choice. He did the Exercises in order to make his decision, after having clearly examined all sides. By natural and supernatural reasons he decided in favour of the Company" (Sept. 22, 1546).

No soul can emerge unchanged from the trial of heart and will in the Exercises. Not only did they help Francis Borgia to decide the direction of his life, but soul, mind and will were marked indelibly with their seal. They had not yet been approved by the Pope. It was largely due to Francis's efforts that Paul III gave them his official blessing in the Bull *Pastoralis Officii* (July 31, 1548) and that the first edition of them was published in the same year.

Araoz had been appointed Provincial of the newly founded Spanish Province (1547), when there were as yet only seven Jesuit houses and forty-one Jesuits (eleven of these at Gandia) in Spain. The Duke founded burses for Jesuit students at the university of Alcalá de Henares, gave a thousand ducats to those at Valencia, offered his own house and land at Zaragoza for the foundation of a Jesuit house there, as well as writing to his uncle the Archbishop and his sister Luisa, Countess of Ribargoza, whom he had not seen since they were children together at Baza. He also persuaded the famous Doctor Miguel de Torres to join the Society at Zaragoza. "The Doctor has gone off with a good load of nets," he wrote to Ignatius, "we shall see what his fishing produces!" He helped too in the foundation of the first Jesuit house in Andalusia. There might be "the strictest secrecy" about his future, but it was fairly obvious where his sympathies lay.

All was not plain sailing during these years, however. Francis proposed to found another monastery in Gandia to be under Jesuit direction. Ignatius, realising all the practical difficulties, vetoed the project. There were already as many religious houses as such a small town could support. The number of available Jesuits was limited. It was necessary to leave them free for parish work, as well as teaching and directing. Oviedo had his time and hands more than full enough touring towns, villages and hamlets of the duchy, where religion was at a low ebb and few frequented the sacraments.

Worse difficulties were raised by the undisciplined zeal of Texeda. His religious superiors had refused to allow him to be ordained priest so, much to the scandal of pious folk, he rushed off to Rome, was ordained and returned fuller than ever of visions and excesses. Oviedo, young and ardent, and the Frenchman Onfroy both caught fire from the friar's flaming zeal. Wonderful plans were discussed. The three were to leave the world and lead lives like those of the early Fathers of the desert in the hermitage of St Ana, just outside Gandia. Oviedo even dreamed of celebrating Mass several times a day. Ignatius was quite capable of using whip as well as spur and bridle when a member of his team threatened to get out of hand. Obedience in a religious, he pointed out, came before solitude. "If Father Andrea were in Rome I would cure his exaggerated fervours in another fashion, by forbidding him to say Mass even once a day . . . They risk landing themselves in a worse desert than they dream of if they do not learn humility and obedience."

Francis too came in for his share of rebuke. Though he had tried to curb Oviedo's ill-placed passion for solitude,

he had himself been affected by the friar's frenzy of mortifications and indulged in them to excess. Ignatius, who
knew by experience how immoderate penances and long
hours of intensive prayer weakened not only the body but
also mind and will, wrote to Francis: "When temptations
weaken and die and are replaced by good and holy desires
we no longer need the same arms to conquer our enemies.
Your Grace would be wise to give to study, the management of your estates and to spiritual talk the hours you
now devote to prayer. Wait till your soul is calm and at
peace and ready to do all that our Lord asks of you. It is
a higher virtue to be able to enjoy God in different occupations and in all places than only at prayer in your oratory. As for fasts and abstinences I wish you to increase,
not to lessen, your strength . . . Body and soul alike belong
to their Lord and Creator, Who will demand an account
of them. Health must not be injured for if the body is
weakened the soul cannot act . . . The end of all this fasting will be that your stomach will cease work and no
longer be able to digest the food necessary for health . . .
As for scourgings I advise you to stop those which draw
even a drop of blood" (September 20, 1548). Ten months
later he wrote to tell Araoz, then visiting Gandia, "to appoint a master whom he [Francis] must obey in matters of
health."

Ostensibly in preparation for Carlos's marriage in 1548
Francis gave up the principal suite of rooms on the first
floor, the 'Duchess's Room', where he had been born and
where he had seen his mother and Eleonor lie dead. He
kept for himself a kind of flat tucked away in a corner,
consisting of a study, bedroom and a small oratory. The
bare floor of the bedroom was of square tiles, red pattern-
ed with white. The hard camp bed had for its only cover a
rough woollen rug. The big window, like that of the
study next door (now a chapel) has a wide view away to
the distant mountains. The oratory, eighteen feet by seven,
the traditional measurements of the Holy Sepulchre, is

shaped like a coffin, with sloping roof, and its windows look down into a small courtyard. The miraculous Crucifix stood on the altar, the Cross of wood inlaid with gold, about eighteen inches high, the Figure an Italian bronze of most beautiful workmanship. The white walls are covered with frescoes, between slim carved pillars with delicately gilt foliage capitals. Above a painted balustrade are represented scenes from the Passion, and in front of the Scourging at the Pillar Francis Borgia used to kneel to scourge himself. A small corner of the original floor is visible under glass, below the later mosaic of woods from the Philippines, hard as stone and every shade from pale cream to dark blood-red. The *azulejo* tiles, far older than Francis's day, have a primitive design in blue and white. They are marked with faded patches of rust-red, the blood which fell in those cruel nightly scourgings. Four centuries have passed but those stains remain, an echo of the voice of him who tried for his Lord's sake to wash out in blood not only his own sins but those terrible crimes of his forefathers which have made the name of Borgia one of the most infamous in the world's memory.

The Duke's day was a strenuous one. Every morning, till St Ignatius cut down the time by half, he rose at four o'clock and meditated till eight, when he heard Mass and made his Communion in the chapel of San Miguel, which was followed by another hour of prayer. The long tunic, which he wore as mourning for his wife, was of coarse serge, so shabby that his smarter friends were shocked. The only servant allowed to valet him and to look after his room was Joanico, a little negro page. This was probably to save gossip about the hairshirt and the bloodstained floor. His official almoner dealt with the alms apportioned after the morning inspection of the list of sick and poor in Gandia, but when the Duke went out he carried a fat purse of money to be given away as he walked through the streets. Oviedo calculated that at least fifty thousand ducats were spent in charity in the last six or seven years at Gandia. There were two lessons of theology a day and very often the Duke would stay to dinner with the Jesuit community. "His menu consists of a few vegetables to begin with, a dish of *garbanzo* (dwarf peas) and a scrap of dessert, no fish nor eggs" (Oviedo).

The frugal diet had had some effect. When he had returned in 1543 he had been bluntly described as "the fattest man in Valencia." His servant, who had boasted at Barcelona that his master's belt would hold three men, now had to take it in "a hand's breadth."

There was all the business of household and estate to be attended to. Luckily his sister-in-law, Juana, was there to see to the women servants, but there was a princely staff of men as well, gorgeous in their scarlet livery, silk in summer, velvet in winter. The stable was unequalled, so were kennels and falconry. The chapel was enriched with gold and silver altar vessels, the walls hung with Flemish tapestries and vestments embroidered by workers specially engaged. The music, some of it the Duke's own composition, was executed by Flemish musicians whom he had brought with him from Barcelona. Nothing was neglected that could enhance the splendour and beauty of the *Opus Dei*.

In preparation also for his heir's marriage the Duke restored the whole interior of the palace, which had not been adequately done since its sack by the Germania nearly thirty years before. The great reception hall, known as the *Salón de Coronas* (on the right of the main entrance), has still the dado of *azulejo* tiles, for whose design and manufacture Valencia was unequalled. The panelled ceiling was decorated by Francis with the radiant crowns which also ornament the Borgia apartments in the Vatican, but, as a corrective to this worldly glory, he had painted round the frieze, "None shall be crowned but he who has fought manfully. So run that ye may obtain the prize."

The estates of Gandia and Lombay, property in the city of Valencia, all had to be overseen. In spite of the immense sums given in charity, the Duke's head for business and organization had increased his revenues to a much higher figure and for the last few years the sugar crop had been phenomenal. Often indeed Francis must have sympathised with Texeda and Oviedo in their desire for solitude and silence. All these activities occupied so much time which he would rather have spent in prayer and contemplation. "Life, like a dome of many-coloured glass, stains the white radiance of eternity." Only a great saint can unite the active and contemplative life in their perfection, and Francis Borgia was not yet a great saint. To the world he remained what he had always been, good father and master, charming friend, courteous and generous host, kindly to all his dependants. Yet holiness, even to the casual visitor, was evident. The Bishop of Cartagena wrote after a stay at Gandia, "I have seen a duke, Don Francisco, who is a miracle of a prince and knight, absolutely humble and holy, a true man of God" (1548). There is a quaint note of naïve surprise that a grandee of royal blood should have the appearance of a saint.

"Grace," as Cienfuegos truly remarks, "does not destroy natural charm but increases it." It is odd that the portrait of so attractive a person as Francis Borgia should have been unrecognisably defaced by a tradition of rigid, inhuman, cruel austerity. Suau is indeed right that "few saints have been more disfigured." A specially uncomfortable corner in Purgatory must surely be reserved for the hagiographers who have drawn their heroes as prickly bundles of inhuman virtues or as anæmic plaster figures with tear-streaming eyes fixed fatuously on a cloudless sky.

There was still much for Francis to do before freedom was won. In obedience to the General, the future of five sons and three daughters had to be mapped out. Carlos, Marquis of Lombay, was now eighteen. The first project for his marriage had fallen through, but in November, 1548, his wedding with Doña Maria-Magdalena, daughter

k

of the Count of Oliva, took place and he and his bride took possession of the state rooms which the Duke abandoned to them. Three weeks before, his eldest sister, Isabel, had been betrothed to the Count of Lerma and appointed lady-in-waiting to the poor old mad Queen at Tordesillas. The second girl, Juana, was married at the age of fifteen to the third Marquis of Alcañices (1550) and the same year the Duke made over the Commandership of Reyna to his second son Juan. Carlos and his aunt Juana undertook the charge of the three younger boys, Alvaro, destined for the church, Fernando and Alfonso. The youngest girl, Dorothy, entered the Poor Clares' convent in Gandia where her great-aunt was still Abbess and three of her father's half-sisters nuns.

But before the end of this had been reached a dreaded summons had come calling Francis back to court and the world. The Emperor was at war with the Protestant princes of Germany, whom he had defeated at the battle of Mühlberg (1547). He had tried to please both parties, so had pleased neither, by the Interim, a confession Catholic in spirit but making concessions to Protestants. As usual when in most urgent need of money his thoughts turned to Spain. The Cortes must be summoned and, if possible, induced to bleed the country white to supply the sinews of war for Germany. It would be a difficult task. The young widowed Regent needed fresh and wise counsellors, for the Cardinal de Tavera, Zuñiga and Cobos were all dead. Francis Borgia, wasting time and talents in the backwater of Gandia, was obviously the man for the job, so he was named by the Emperor one of the four intermediaries between the Prince of the Asturias and the Cortes which were to meet at Monzon on July 15, 1549.

Francis obeyed the imperial command. History repeated itself. It was the same story of storm and battle as in old days. In spite of angry and argumentative sessions, two hundred thousand pounds were wrung from the unwilling deputies, largely by Francis's masterly diplomacy, and a personal gift of twenty-five thousand to Philip was added. Once again Francis was a target for abuse and detraction. "I am just leaving for home," he wrote on December 1, "and not before a rest is needed after the many unpleasantnesses of all sorts I have had to put up with here." And to Ignatius (December 28, 1547): "Our Lord has at last deigned to release me from that Babylon, Monzon."

The popular idea was that, once more in favour, the Duke of Gandia would be Philip's minister. But Francis had safeguarded himself against such a contingency. With permission of the General and of the Pope (who, however, did not know to whom leave was granted) he had secretly made to Oviedo his profession according to the form received in cipher from Ignatius. "I Francis Borgia, Duke of Gandia, vile sinner, unworthy of the call of our Lord and of this profession, trusting only in the goodness of the Lord Whom I am about to receive, make the vow of poverty, chastity and obedience according to the Constitution of the Company, using the faculty and dispensation sent me by Father Ignatius, Superior General. I pray the angels and saints in heaven to be my advocates and witnesses. I beg the same favour from Father Master Andrea and from Father Master François Onfroy, from Father Master Saboya and Father Juan Texeda, also present. Made at Gandia, to-day, Feast of St Ignatius, February 1, 1548."

Ignatius's commands had been faithfully obeyed and Francis's responsibilities were over eighteen months later. The future of all his children was assured, the three elder ones were married. Like Peter in prison the hour of his deliverance was at hand, when, at touch of the messenger of God, "the chains fell from off his hands, the iron gate of itself opened and, going out, they passed on."

PART II
UNDER AUTHORITY
(1550-1565)

CHAPTER XIV

OUT OF EGYPT

OF the events of forty years three pictures remained
more vividly memorized than any others, like
mountain peaks which tower flushed by sunrise
while everything else, hills, valleys and rivers are veiled
by drifting mists and shadow. The great 'Duchess's Room'
beside the chapel of San Miguel, the iridescent colours of
its *azulejo* tiles and Moorish pottery, the dim warm richness of the Persian rugs on the tiled floor, the dimmer
hues of the Flemish tapestries on the walls, the tarnished
gold of the brocade curtains on the huge, canopied bed,
the yellow glow of wax candles on the cold beauty of the
dead face, himself as a child of ten, broken-hearted beside
his dead mother, yet already catching a glimpse of the
truth that across all earthly love lies the shadow of the
Cross. That was the first, then the same room twenty-six
years later, himself kneeling beside his dead wife, having
made the supreme sacrifice and knowing it accepted by
God. And that other terrible scene in the vault at Granada
where he had seen human loveliness turn to seething corruption. Mother, wife and friend, they had been the only
women he had loved, and each, in death as in life, had led
him a step nearer to the vision of God.

He thought of those three vows he had taken two and a
half years ago, poverty, chastity and obedience. His own
hidden life had for long been one of poverty and austerity. That hard victory at Zaragoza, the discipline and iron
self-control of later years had kept him from sins of the
flesh. He had never known any woman but Eleonor.
Obedience had been put to a hard test these last four years,
and even now the world was only to know that the Duke
of Gandia was making a pilgrimage to Rome to gain the

Holy Year pardons. He had hoped to travel humbly in the black Jesuit habit, free at last from possessions and responsibilities. Now he would still have to endure pomp and ceremony, those receptions which he had always hated.

The distant mountains which he could see through the tall window were no longer dim shadows beneath the stars. They took on their sharp, familiar shapes under the lightening sky of dawn. He flung back the rough wool cover. The red and white tiles were cold under his bare feet. Over the hairshirt he put on a fine linen shirt, doublet and hose not quite so shabby as those which had shocked the worldlings. He went into the little Oratory which had seen that violence of prayer when, like Jacob and the angel, he had wrestled for Eleonor's life. He knelt for the last time on the tiles stained with his blood, under the painting of Christ at the Pillar, before the bronze figure of Christ on the Cross which had laid the choice of life and death in his hands.

He knelt to receive Communion in San Miguel's chapel, took his frugal breakfast of rough red wine and coarse white bread, made from the grapes and wheat of his own lands. There were goodbyes to be said: the stables, where soft noses were thrust into his hand and soft whinnies answered the master's voice; the falconry, where the young hawks he had tamed and trained flew from their high curved perches to take their portion of raw meat from his hand; the kennels with their familiar smell of straw and meat and dog, and all the while his greyhound, old now, stalked stiffly at his side, dark eyes sombre with the knowledge of separation. There were human goodbyes too, though not to Fray Juan, for he had been sent to tell the Duke's sisters of his departure for Rome, but had died at Valladolid before he had reached Luisa at Pedrola. There were his sister-in-law, Doña Juana de Meneses, an echo of Eleonor, whose life had been interwoven with his for twenty years, and the girls' faithful governess, Isabella de Rodriguez.

There was the young Marquis and his wife. Francis was humorously aware that his visits to them in the rooms he had left for them had somewhat of the air of a schoolmaster visiting his late pupils. Carlos was a successful example of his training, he thought, keen on the estate, on hunting and hawking, and a good Christian. Francis had already been to Valencia to bid farewell to his old friend the Archbishop, Thomas de Villanueva, and to the convent of Poor Clares, where only the Abbess knew the real reason of his journey.

The courtyard was filling with servants in their silk liveries. The air was full of the noise of champing bits, the stamping of impatient hoofs, of last-minute hurry. Francis was at the Jesuit college, beside the city walls which he had repaired, with a wide view from its raised garden over the *huerta*. Father Oviedo was coming to Rome, with the Provincial, Antonio Araoz, six other Jesuit priests and one lay brother. The Duke embraced all the Jesuits who were to stay behind in the college. Then, shutting the door of the Rector's room, he flung himself at the feet of Father Barma, the new superior, kissed them, much to the good man's embarrassment, and put him in charge of his children, for whom he had provided in a will signed five days before.

"This departure has caused great edification," wrote the Rector to the General, "and the sight of the joy and delight shown by the Lord Duke in leaving Egypt and in his farewells to his children, his vassals, his lands. We are indeed ashamed when we compare our renunciation of the world and his, our cowardice and his courage, our meanness and his generosity " (Oct. 5, 1550).

The streets were crowded to witness the Duke's departure (August 31, 1550). However carefully a secret is kept some suspicion of it blows abroad. "The well-to-do are much grieved at the Duke's going," Father Saboya wrote to Rome. "The poor declare that he is going to Rome to be made cardinal or General of the Company of Jesus!" Carlos had the gate walled up by which his father left the city. A long cavalcade followed him, his favourite son Juan, now seventeen, the nine Jesuits, a majordomo, masters of the bedchamber and stable, an official to go a-head and arrange board and lodging, nearly twenty pages, grooms and valets.

A little way north along the road to Valencia stands a stone cross which has replaced the old broken one originally erected to mark the spot of St Francis Borgia's farewell to Gandia. It was there that he reined in his horse and turned to look back for the last time. On his right hand hills, rocks, olives and low scrub were all a dusty grey. On his left, beyond the smiling *huerta*, the Mediterranean made a glittering line on the horizon. Little white *barracas* with steep thatched roofs, fresh-ploughed fields where corn had been cut and carried only a few weeks before, vines heavy with great bunches of green and purple grapes, green swordblade leaves and little grey flowers of the sugar-cane, palms high above the mass of mulberry trees, their feathery leaves still and metallic as bronze, all were brilliant and sharp-cut as the colours of an illuminated missal. The southern mountains, under the mid-day August sun, were faintly transparent as tumbled gauze. Gandia, brown city, four-square within its walls, its roofs dominated by the tall yellow arches of the collegiate church and the clifflike pile of the palace, was quivering in the heat, unsubstantial as a painted canvas stirred by a draught.

Bareheaded and motionless the Duke sat in the saddle, then his deep, beautiful voice broke the silence. "When Israel came out of Egypt and the house of Jacob from among a barbarous people, the mountains skipped like rams and the little hills like young sheep . . . The snare is broken and we are delivered."

CHAPTER XV

HOLY YEAR

FRANCIS'S journey overland through France and
northern Italy was fully reported by Father Pedro de
Tablares, one of the nine Jesuits with him.
"The pleasure that the Lord Duke received on the way
from the exercise of the fathers with him compensated for
the mortification of the receptions given in France and
Italy, specially in Parma by the Duke Camerino. On his
arrival in Bologna the Lord Duke went to see the fathers,
who met him with such an affectionate welcome as pleased
his spirit more than anything else. From there we came to
Ferrara, where the reception was still more splendid"
(Cienfuegos).

Ercole d'Este, Duke of Ferrara, son of Lucrezia Borgia,
so Francis's cousin, had sent a deputation to the Italian
frontier to beg him to visit Ferrara. Francis had hesitated.
It would add another sixty miles to his journey to Rome,
where he longed to be with Ignatius. He was sick to death
of ceremonies and pompous receptions. But obedience, at
once the foundation and the keystone of the religious life,
triumphed and he left Bologna, the great university city,
whose streets were crowded with students, a Babel of every
European tongue. The thirty-mile road north-east to Ferrara ran through a fertile, marshy plain, its sugar-canes
and network of water reminiscent of the Valencian *huerta*.
The flat silhouette of the city, broken by four tall towers,
was dark against the golden evening sky. Ercole, with a
crowd of horsemen, was waiting for his cousin at the city
gate. The scarlet Borgia liveries made a welcome splash of
colour against the black gowns of the Jesuits and the
mourning of Francis and Juan. Ceremonial welcome and
speeches over, the cousins rode through the wide streets,

oddly quiet after the noise and bustle of Bologna. The great palace of the d'Este's, grim and fortress-like with its moat, arched portcullis gate and four machicolated towers, seen from outside seemed not unlike a Spanish castle. Inside, though, Francis found himself in a world both new and strange to him. He was accustomed to the stately ceremonial of the Spanish court, the harem-like seclusion of Spanish women. Here their equality with men, the freedom with which they appeared in public, talked, argued ably in favour of their own opinions, was as foreign to him as was their expanse of bare arms and bosoms, their heads bare of all but jewels and curled, dyed, scented hair. Weird astronomical frescoes by Dosso Dossi covered the walls. Nude gods and goddesses gleamed pearl-white against brocade hangings. The table was laden with gold plate, with flagons of iridescent Venetian glass, with enamel from Limoges, eggshell bowls brought overland from China, piled with green and purple grapes set in melting snow. Tall wax candles, lit as the twilight of late October fell, glowed softly on the exquisite work of Benvenuto Cellini, who had stayed here ten years ago on his way to France.

The Duchess, Renée, daughter of Louis XII of France, talked brilliantly. She had that sceptical mind which denies everything, but (most likely to win a reputation for originality) she had declared herself patron and admirer of Calvin. Her daughter, Leonora, was fifteen, delicate, studious and intellectual, to be famous later as the star round which Tasso fluttered and to whom many of his poems were addressed. Juan found a contemporary in Alfonso, the Duke's heir, with whom the ill-fated house was to die out.

The court of Ferrara was one of the most splendid in Italy, with its pageants, its hunting parties and country villas, its dramatic entertainments (Alfonso, Lucrezia Borgia's husband, had built the first permanent theatre in Italy), its patronage of music, painting and poetry and all kinds of learning and culture. What Symonds calls "the hectic bloom and rouged refinement" of Ferrara had all

the beauty and fascination of a sophisticated and ultra-
civilised society at the moment when incipient decay is as
yet hardly visible.

The birth of Italian prose with Boccaccio, the soaking
of Greek thought through every phase of art and intellect,
stimulated by the discovery of such classic masterpieces as
the Laocoon and the Apollo Belvedere, the attitude towards life of that modern Maecenas, Leo X, Julius II's
grandiose dreams of a new Rome which was to spring
from the ashes of the Middle Ages, immortalised by the
genius of Bramante, da Vinci and Michael Angelo, the
less material dreams of humanists and Neo-Platonists like
Pico della Mirandola, all that splendid flowering of the
pagan Italian Renaissance was entirely alien to the mind of
Francis Borgia, because it was outside the limitations of
Christian morality, its only criterion the worship of beauty.
To beauty and power all was sacrificed. *Il Principe* of
Machiavelli and *Il Cortegiano* of Castiglione were the bibles
of the Renaissance. Even the courtesans, as in the golden
age of Athens, reigned as much by their intellectual bril-
liance as by their physical attractions.

Spain, within living man's memory, had achieved freedom and unity. Most of the Italian duchies and republics
had sold their birthright to become vassals of Charles V
or to be absorbed by the greedy nepotism of Farnese and
Caraffa Popes. When freedom is dead, gaiety and art are
no more than the dance of gnats above a putrescent pool.

Already twilight was stealing on the gods of the Renaissance. Francis Borgia belonged to the new era when the
Bride of Christ, so long dragged through brothels and
gutter, should again arise in her full beauty.

He had sung his thankfulness on leaving Gandia. How
much more he must have rejoiced when, shaking the gold-
en dust of Ferrara from his feet, he pushed on to Florence
and south to Rome. His time had not been wasted in his
uncongenial surroundings. He had obtained promises for
the foundation of Jesuit houses from the Archbishop of

Genoa at Bologna, Duke Ercole at Ferrara and Duke Cosimo de Medici at Florence.

Viterbo was reached, "the city of beautiful women and handsome fountains." It might be possible, by an early start to cover the less than fifty miles over the pass and across the Campagna in a day, so slip into Rome after dark and escape another wearisome reception. Letters came, from the Cardinal de Cueva and from the General of the Jesuits, pointing out that to evade a state welcome would be to belittle not only the Duke of Gandia but his cousin the Emperor. With a sigh Francis rode south along the old Roman Via Cassia, through country scarred and cracked with volcanic ravines like those in the inferno of his fevered dreams at Baza. From the summit of L'Imposta Pass, like Moses on Pisgah, he surveyed the Promised Land, west to the glitter of the Tyrrhenian Sea, south over the Campagna, girdled by the Apennines and the Alban hills, where forests of beech and chestnut were a flame of copper and gold. The autumn sun was casting long blue shadows from poplars and cypresses when at last Francis saw, on her seven hills, the huddle of roofs and towers that was Rome (October 23, 1550).

The Jesuit community in their crowded house next to the tumbledown church of Santa Maria della Strada had been busy and excited. The house at the end of the garden, with its own entrance and way into the church, had been done up and furnished for the guests. The fitting up had not been an easy task, for money, as usual, was short, and the General had had to incur a debt of several hundred crowns, in addition to the thousand ducats which the procurator already owed for unavoidable expenses. There was a good deal of excitement, wonder why the Duke of Gandia should have chosen to stay here, instead of accepting invitations to the Vatican, the Cancellaria, a score of other palaces. Hardly any one but Ignatius himself and his invaluable secretary, the young Jewish convert from Burgos, Juan Polanco, knew the truth.

Everyone, however, knew the arrangements for the Duke's welcome to Rome. A troop of mounted Spanish and Italian nobles were to meet him at Storta. Outside the Porta del Popolo there would be a riot of colour, cardinals in their scarlet, the glowing purple of bishops and prelates, the glitter of gilt armour on Ascanio de Colonna, Grand Constable of Naples, the sombre richness of the Spanish ambassador, friars brown and white and black, a peacock iridescence of brocade, cloth of gold, velvet and fur of Roman nobles, young and old. The Pope had sent word that the Duke's proper place was the Borgia apartments in the Vatican, which were ready for him. Julius himself could hardly be torn from the new villa outside the Porta del Popolo, which was his chief hobby.

The speeches must be interminable. The waiting seemed so. At last there was a ripple of excitement coming down the old Via Flaminia to the Piazza Venezia. A clatter of hoofs, a babel of many voices and a crowd of horsemen filled the narrow street. At the door of the Jesuit house stood St Ignatius, surrounded by his community. The Duke of Gandia dismounted, a tall, stout man, with a black cloak over his long mourning tunic, his black cap in his hands, as he towered over the small, slight figure of the General. Father André de Freux, the classical scholar of the house, saluted the distinguished guests in endless, sonorous Latin verses. At last he finished. The Duke bade a courteous farewell to his escort, once more refused all offers of hospitality. The shabby door of the house shut behind him and his hosts. He was alone with Ignatius of Loyola, in the little bare room with a window looking on to the high altar of the church.

Francis threw himself at Ignatius's feet, seized his hands and kissed them. Ignatius, not to be outdone in humility, was on his knees too, trying to prevent his hands being kissed. Like most of life's sublime moments this one had more than a touch of the ridiculous.

There was altogether a good salting of humour in the situation, though at present Francis was unconscious of it. Accustomed to princely state and enormous households, he had no idea of the straits to which the community had been put to provide the lodgings which were to him redolent of holy poverty. He, Juan and their score of servants packed into the newly furnished house, with its tribune opening into the church. His Jesuit travelling-companions were of course housed in community quarters. Oviedo, who had been so severely reprimanded for his wild visions of solitude, was received by the General with special affection.

Francis, at the age of forty, was now to receive a liberal education. He himself had managed men successfully, in spite of fierce impatience and occasional outbursts of hot temper. Now he saw real genius in action. "Up till now," he said, "I looked on Faber as a giant and myself as a child, but, compared to Ignatius, Faber himself was but a child." Hitherto his view had reached little beyond Gandia, Catalonia, Spain. Now he saw in Ignatius's hands the threads connecting "the uttermost parts of the earth" with this little lame man in the little overcrowded house in a back street.

The Society of Jesus, limited ten years ago to sixty members, was already overflowing Europe. On the Feast of the Assumption this year (1550) Francis Xavier, with the Spanish priest Cosme de Torres and the Portuguese Brother, João Fernandez, had landed at Kagoshima and said the first Mass in Japan. There were under him four Jesuits in the Moluccas, two at Malacca, six at Comorin, two at Bassein. In his last letter before leaving Malacca for Japan he had written, "I have almost continually before my eyes and in my mind what I have so often heard our blessed Father Ignatius say, that those who wish to belong to our Company must work hard to conquer themselves." A year ago six Jesuits had sailed with Portuguese colonists to Brazil, where there were now three Jesuit residences.

The conquest and renunciation of self, "not to wish for health rather than sickness, riches rather than poverty, honour rather than ignominy, a long life rather than a short one," this was the spirit of the Exercises and here Francis saw it being lived, by men of different ages, character, and nations, but all inspired by the great leader. He heard the three questions which Ignatius put to each Jesuit priest. "Are you ready to obey in whatever occupation is chosen by you? Do you consider yourself better fitted for one work rather than another? Do you prefer one occupation to another?"

He met Lainez, one of Ignatius's original band of seven who had taken the vows at Montmartre, who had been chosen with the Toledan Alfonso Salmeron as Papal theologian at the Council. Lainez was just back from Tunis where he had been chaplain with the expeditionary force sent against the corsair Dragut. That marvellous Jewish intellect, remote and brilliant as a star, but burning with an all-consuming love of God, was a revelation.

The Burgalese Juan de Polanco, also member of a family of coverted Jews, only three years younger than Lainez, was yet more closely in touch with Ignatius's mind and methods, for, as his secretary, he handled that immense correspondence with all classes and kinds of men round the world.

It is rare indeed for a man to find in life a perfect friend or a perfect lover. Francis Borgia had both. When he had lost Eleonor he had found Ignatius of Loyola. The two men were alike in nationality, noble birth and a court education. Both were capable of deep passion and iron self-control. But there were those differences without which friendship is as insipid as a dish without salt. Ignatius by nature and profession was a soldier. It has been said, perhaps too often, that his Order, his Spiritual Exer-

l

cises and Constitutions all are stamped with the military spirit of fervour and discipline which had conquered Islam in Spain after seven centuries of struggle. "Teach me to be generous, to give and not count the cost, to fight and not heed the wounds, to labour and ask for no reward." There is the summary of the Ignatian inspiration, the passionate love of God and complete renunciation of self which were also the aim of Francis Borgia.

Mean and narrow spirits cannot be expected to see the splendour and beauty of love and sacrifice which burn so fiercely that in them are consumed all smaller affections, all earthly desires. Belloc has finely said that, since we are all cowards at heart, courage is one of the virtues we admire most. Yet, because we are cowards, we shrink before sanctity and, like the rich young man who valued his possessions more than Christ, we go away sorrowful.

There is a tradition that, nine years before, on receiving Francis Borgia's first letter, Ignatius had prophesied that the writer "will enter the Company and come to Rome to govern it." He realized now that, as always, with the hour heaven had sent the man. When he had said farewell to Francis Xavier, his best-loved son, he had known that he should see his face no more in this world. Now another Francis had come to be trained to take up his burden. "This marvellous man," says Astrain of Francis Borgia, "to whom the Company owes so much and who forms with Ignatius and Xavier the glorious trinity of saints whom we venerate in the forefront of the Company and who were, without doubt, the three greatest men then in the world."

The Duke of Gandia's profession was still a secret which few even of the professed fathers in the house knew. His generosity and work for the Society were public property. He promised four thousand ducats for the rebuilding of Santa Maria della Strada, and the first stone was blessed in his presence. Enthusiastic about the idea of founding a house of studies for noble youths, he supplied money to buy a house and site so that the college could be opened in the Via Capitolina in 1551. He was therefore the patron and founder of the original Collegio Romano, though it now bears the name of Gregory XIII. Ignatius refused to accept the sum offered to cover the cost of his hospitality towards the Duke, his son and suite. He would only allow payment of a debt left by the procurator who had just died.

Luckily the General, like most Spaniards, had a sense of humour. It was often needed. The edifying humility of the Duke sometimes took inconvenient forms. On one occasion the General and several fathers were invited to dine with their guest. Francis and Juan, bare-headed, girt with large white aprons, acted as waiters, pouring out water for hand-washing, laying and changing plates, serving drink, all the time on their feet and with bare heads. Dinner over, the Duke intended to go to the kitchen and wash up. On this occasion Ignatius prevented it by a diplomatic ruse. Another time (February 2, 1551), when the whole community were entertained, he was not so successful. After waiting at table the Duke and Juan washed up, the result of this unskilled labour being that Juan broke a dish and had to confess his fault in public!

The fourteen weeks spent in Rome (October 23, 1550–February 4, 1551) were not wholly devoted to Jesuit interests. The pilgrimages and stations of the Holy Year were done. Endless visits had to be paid to Cardinals, ecclesiastics, nobles and the Pope himself. Julius III (Cardinal Monte) had been elected to succeed Paul III in February, 1550. His chief interest in life was his villa near the Porta del Popolo, where an endless succession of architects, painters and gardeners were kept busy by his continually changing ideas. Francis, like the Emperor, loved flowers and gardens, but the lure of the Eternal City for him lay not in art and architecture, nor in the ruins of classic pride and luxury. He visited Cardinal Alessandro Farnese, grandson of Paul III by an early marriage, in his great palace of the Cancellaria, designed by Bramante, decorated by Vasari, but he was more interested in the handsome Cardinal, with his lustrous dark eyes, neat dark hair and beard, subtle mind and wide diplomacy, than in the beauties of his home. He visited the most famous of all the Roman palaces, that of the Sienese banker, Agostino Chigi, crammed with art treasures old and new, the Palazzo Madama (designed by Raphael and given by Paul III to Charles V's natural daughter, Margaret of Austria, now married to Ottavio Farnese, grandson of the late Pope) and a hundred other palaces. They were 'a weariness of the flesh' to him, spoke a language he did not understand. St Peter's, hidden behind a forest of scaffolding, Santa Maria Maggiore, with the dark old Madonna that reminded him of the Virgin of the Pillar at Zaragoza, the black Virgins of Montserrat and Valencia, the Ara Coeli, with its Bambino smothered in priceless jewels, the dilapidated church of the Jesuits, into which he could slip from his guest-house, they were his spiritual home, the sources from which he drew peace and happiness.

Then, while saying Mass on Christmas Day, the General had a seizure. He was not yet sixty, but terrible penances and austerities, ceaseless work and heavy responsibility had worn him out, so that he was not expected to live. It seemed to the community as if the end of the world had come.

Ignatius recovered but felt that he was no longer equal to his task. "I am entirely lacking in the strength necessary to bear the burden of this Society which has been laid on me," he wrote when convalescent, "so I wish the matter to be well considered in our Lord and another chosen who will fill the post of governing the Society better or at least less ill." Lainez was obviously marked out for the next general, but every professed father, with one exception, voted for Ignatius to carry on. The exception was Andrea Oviedo, under orders for Naples. Perhaps his own frustrated desire for solitude and peace made him sympathise with his spiritual father's longing to escape from activity, business and the strife of tongues.

The invalid was up and about again at the beginning of February, 1551, able to attend the farewell dinner on the second and to approve the letter which Francis had written to the Emperor at Augsburg, asking leave to transfer his titles and estates to his son and to enter religion.

"Our Lord knows how keenly I hoped that your Majesty would come to Italy, so that I could have said what I now must write . . . Since the Duchess's death I have considered and weighed my decision, had it prayed for by numerous servants of God. Day by day my desire grew stronger and the darkness of my heart lightened, though I do not deserve to be employed in the Lord's vineyard, specially as I come to it so late and my work so far has only been to root up the young vines planted by others. But the divine Goodness is gentle as an immeasurable and unfathomable ocean and has inspired its servants of the Company of Jesus to admit me into their Order, in which I have for long wished to live and die. Before realising my desire, however, I have fulfilled all the obligations owed by a father to his children" (January 15, 1551). The letter was sent off by one of his gentlemen, and letters were also despatched to the Cardinal of Lorraine and the Bishop of Clermont, begging help of the latter for the foundation of a Jesuit College in Paris and outlining plans for the near future.

"For many reasons I could not make my profession in Rome but I leave tomorrow for the part of Spain bordering on France, called Guipúzcoa. A house of the Company has been recently founded there, and there, far from my own company and my friends, having renounced my possessions, I shall follow my Lord, despoiled of all, and shall devote to God, in this holy institute, all the rest of my life" (February 3, 1551).

He still dreamed of such a life of solitude as had tempted Oviedo and Onfroy, 'the world forgetting, by the world forgot', in that remote corner of the Basque country which, to his Valencian mind, seemed as 'far from friends and home' as if it had been Japan or Brazil.

The day of parting came (February 4). It was twenty-four years since that May day in Alcalá de Henares when Ignatius and Francis had first seen each other and there had passed between them that long, searching look. Now it was one of those bitter days of early Roman spring when the Tramontana pierces like a jagged knife and snow is all the sharper for its rarity. Polanco has left a description of the scene. The Duke "asked a blessing from Father Ignatius, embraced each father with great tenderness. It was snowing and the cold was terrible for the Duke, accustomed to a warm climate. However Saint Ignatius was forced to order him before he would consent to put on his gloves."

There is the picture, the impatient horses, the thirty travellers, including Juan, Araoz, Lainez, who was going as far as Genoa with them, the other Jesuits and servants, the Duke, big and burly, blue with cold even in his fur-trimmed travelling cloak, the General, frail and bowed, leaning on his stick, the great burning eyes the only live thing in the ivory face.

They were gone. The far wing of the house was empty. The community itself seemed strangely quiet. Even Jesuits are human, and life must have felt a little flat and dull now that the excitement of the last three months was over.

CHAPTER XVI

PORT AFTER STORMY SEAS

TWELVE days riding north, through the snowy Apennines down the valley of the Arno to Pisa, Francis on his big black Andalusian horse, young Juan, Antonio Araoz and Diego Lainez on his mule, Lainez, the most brilliant and burning intellect of his day, two years younger than Francis, pale, fragile-looking, with aquiline nose, high forehead, luminous dark eyes, smiling lips and an air of remote, composed serenity. They jogged on, sometimes silent, sometimes talking intermittently. Francis was never tired of hearing about the early days, at Paris, at Venice, at the first tiny house in Rome, of Ignatius, Faber, Xavier and the fiery Bobadilla, who had returned to Rome boasting how he had braved the Emperor's wrath by denouncing the Interim, only to find himself forbidden the house by Ignatius. Araoz could laugh now at the story against himself, how he had arrived in Rome, full of ambitious designs, a fashionable dandy, dressed all in silk, and how, after he had met his kinsman Ignatius and entered the Company, he had been made to preach in poor churches still decked out in his dandy's garb.

It was all deeply interesting to the Duke, but no doubt Juan's eyes and attention often wandered and he was not sorry to see the leaning tower of Pisa in the distance and enjoy a little civilisation at the court of Duke Cosimo, to whom Francis presented Lainez. The Duke offered a galley to take the party by sea to Genoa, but the weather was so bad that Francis rode on and the ship in which Lainez embarked was wrecked.

Francis wrote from Avignon (March 8, 1551) that all were well but very tired and forced to enter Spain by Perpignan instead of by San Sebastian as Henry III of France was on the brink of yet another war with the Emperor.

The ex-Viceroy passed within six miles of Barcelona but refused to enter it, refused too to visit Zaragoza or Pedrola where he would have seen his uncle and his sister Luisa. She had been deeply hurt that she alone of his near relations had not been told of his journey to Rome. It was not till later that she learned how Fray Texeda had died on the way to tell her.

This time Father Emmanuel de Sa had been told to report the journey. He wrote to Rome on the Thursday in Holy Week from Segura. "Thanks be to God we are all well. The Duke and all of us are delighted with the country and its good people. They for their part seem happy and religious. To-morrow, the fourth of April, we shall sleep at Azpeitia and from there go on to Oñate by Vergara."

Francis, who could not spare a day to see his relations, was pushing forward as a thoroughbred strains every nerve and muscle to be first at the winning-post. Yet, for all his hurry, he paused when Azpeitia was reached, a short day's journey from his goal. A mile from Azpeitia, up the wide valley of the Urumea, which rushes along its rocky bed, stands Loyola, steady and strong as the gaunt grey mountains which encircle it. The huge square blocks of the original fortress still form the lower half of its walls. Above them rise two storeys of narrow bricks, a warm rose-brown, their ornamentation of diamond pattern in stone and small delicate tourelles showing that when they were built peace had succeeded war.

Compared to the arrival at Rome it was a small band which rode up the stony track from Azpeitia, Araoz among the Jesuits. It was his aunt, Magdalena de Araoz, who had married Martin, Ignatius's eldest brother, but Martin was dead, so was his son, Beltran, leaving only a widow and her two daughters to receive the guests.

Francis found their two days' stay (Saturday April 5-

Monday 7) all too short. Everything spoke to him of his beloved father and master. Here was the room where Ignatius was born, used unromantically as a stable, the big, heavy-ceilinged room where, crippled from his wound and weary of reading, he had laid down the lives of Christ and the saints and looked within. Long dreams of love and service of "the lady of no ordinary rank" had faded and he asked himself, "What if I did what St Francis and St Dominic did?" In that same room, as he lay awake one night, our Lady and the Holy Child had appeared to him and "never again gave he any consent to fleshly things" (Autobiography of St Ignatius).

Every morning Francis knelt at Mass in the tiny, dark chapel where Ignatius had prayed as child, youth and man, where another Francis, eleven years ago, "the right noble Don Francisco de Jasu y Javier, Master of Arts," had celebrated Mass on his way to Lisbon and the far East. Over the altar hung, and still hangs, the painting of the Madonna given to Doña Magdalena de Araoz by Queen Isabella, a homely, serene Flemish girl dimly seen through the darkening smoke of candle-flames and the faint light from the narrow window.

Azpeitia was left. Vergara lay behind. There was only one more reception to face of all the enthusiastic welcomes which had marked the route. But the hospitality which had pleased Francis most had been that of the kindly, simple, generous countryfolk when he and his party had been unable to reach a town before nightfall. "Even in the mountains," Polanco says, "they supplied their guest with all the comforts of a city."

The valley widened, grew gentler and more fertile. Everywhere fruit-trees were in bloom, rosy clouds of apple, snowdrifts of pear. The earth was the same dun colour as the oxen ploughing, while autumn-sown corn was as emerald as the pastures on the lower mountain slopes. They were a rainbow of wild flowers, yellow king-cups along the water edge, tall purple orchids, little purple blooms like bunches of fairy grapes, others palest mauve, sky and gentian blue. Dead bracken and oak leaves showed patches of autumn copper among the bright green of young beeches and the foam of wild cherry. Crooked grey tree trunks were armoured with pads of bronze moss. Green streams came tumbling down in little water-falls over slate-blue and rust-red rocks. The polished jade of the valley rivers, Olabarrieta, Auntzerreka and Ubao, reflected tall silver poplars and drifting clouds in their still surfaces. Spruce firs made a dark, serrated silhouette on the higher slopes. Below them were golden splashes of flowering gorse, dead trees on whose skeleton arms hung ghostly bunches of grey mistletoe. The high tower of San Miguel showed above the yellow houses and their tiled roofs. It was Oñate, tucked away in a fold of the Aitzgorri Mountains.

Don Iñigo Velez de Guevara, son of the Count of Oñate and parish priest, was waiting at the entrance to the town, with a troop of local notabilities, mounted and in their Sunday best. The streets were packed with a noisy, eager crowd of students and poorer folk, whose cries reminded one onlooker of the Hosannas of Palm Sunday. Francis and his travel-stained little company reached the church of San Miguel, with its domed tower, its long, arched Gothic cloister. Near it was the University, *patio* and chapel splendid with the finest flowering of Spanish Renaissance architecture, founded by a native of the town, the Bishop of Zuarzola, friend of Cardinal Ximenes. The town was very proud of its University, formally established six years ago by the Emperor under the proud title of *Colegio Mayor y Universidad de Santi Spiritu*.

Oñate with its three hundred Basque and Spanish students hurrying to public classes of philosophy, theology, law and canon law, "with universal acceptance by the Basque people" (typical Basque nationalistic touch !), its big Franciscan friary, its market crowded by peasants from the neighbouring country—this was not the silence and solitude for which Francis's tired body and mind had hoped, but Don Luis de Mendoza had arranged for a hermitage of Santa Magdalena, a mile outside the town, to be enlarged enough to hold the Duke and half a dozen religious.

The alterations were not yet finished. A miracle is needed to make builders complete their work to time, and Francis Borgia had not yet begun to work miracles. So he was installed meantime in the house at Oñate which Antonio Araoz's uncle, Don Miguel, rented to the Jesuits, a large pretentious place with two towers and a garden but bare and poorly furnished.

Francis had reached the haven where he would be, but he was not satisfied. No man is ever perfectly satisfied in this world, except for a fleeting moment of ecstasy, whether of body or soul. He was still Duke of Gandia, grandee of Spain, owner of huge estates, master of thousands of servants and tenants. He could do nothing till the Emperor's answer to his letter came. It was possible that this might be a refusal, for Caesar's dislike to the new Order, fanned by Bobadilla's ill-timed zeal against the Interim, was well known. Waiting and suspense were nerve-racking and there was a reaction now that Francis was away from Ignatius's personal influence. The excessive penances of Gandia began again and Araoz encouraged and joined in them.

Don Juan was a young man with his father's capability and he sat down to write to Father Polanco about his father's and the Provincial's ill-advised zeal. "The Duke and Father Provincial eat practically nothing. This is contrary to our Father's will for he wishes his subjects to look after themselves in order to serve our Lord better. These two eat too little and take no trouble to eat what suits them and avoid what upsets them. It is no good warning them for no one has authority to check them . . . And that your Reverence may know that I wrote with the approval of the brethren, they sign with me." Miguel Navarra added a P.S. "I vow that the Duke and the Father do not eat a kid's head between them !" There were five other signatures to the round robin (April 24, 1551).

Juan also enclosed a letter to the General, stressing the fact that "the Duke and Father Provincial are treating themselves very badly. They take no care of their health nor allow others to do so. Nobody can tell them what to do as regards food, sleep, prayer and the rest."

Araoz, too ill to write himself (and no wonder), "wished to know if the Duke should scourge himself to blood." Ignatius answered by ordering moderation to Araoz both in work and penance and putting the Duke under sub-mission to doctor's orders (June 1, 1551). But long before this letter was received much had happened at Oñate. The Emperor's answer came in May. It was all that could have been hoped for, friendly, affectionate, gracious, approving the Duke's plans, asking for prayers, promising favour for the Marquis of Lombay and his brothers. The one note of reserve was in answer to the prayer for his patron-age of the Society. This was only vaguely promised in guarded terms, "by respect for you . . . but if any special case arises it must pass through the usual channels and be considered by the Council."

A lawyer was at once summoned and in his presence, before witnesses, the Duke signed the documents by which he formally renounced his titles, estates and pos-sessions in favour of his eldest son Carlos. A more drama-tic scene followed. His clothes and jewels were handed over to Juan. That young man, far from showing signs of a Jesuit vocation, as his father had hoped, had lost his heart at Loyola to the heiress Doña Lorenza, and one can scarcely fancy him wishing to wear the immense garments of the widower. Jewels, though, are always acceptable. The Borgia diamonds had been famous when Eleonor had worn them, and would look to advantage in the dark

hair and round the slim neck of Lorenza. Francis's hair
was cut and tonsured, his beard shaved off; then, anxious
to fulfil his vow of poverty to the letter, he begged his
outfit from the fathers present. Each contributed something, but with his huge height and girth, it is likely
enough that he cut a ridiculous figure. He had arranged
for the future of all the servants who had followed him
from Gandia to Rome, from Rome here. The old ones
were pensioned off and Juan was charged with providing
them with money for the journey to Gandia where Carlos
would look after them. There was a sad scene of tears and
hand-kissing when their master, looking so oddly unfami-
liar with his clean-shaven face, in his long black habit with
its winged sleeves, came out to say goodbye. He cut it
short, re-entered the house and shut the door on his last
links with the world.

The Bishop of Calahorra was at the Council of Trent,
then holding its third session. In his absence the bishop
auxiliary, Don Juan Gaona, came to Vergara where,
thanks to the dispensation obtained by Ignatius from the
Pope, he conferred minor orders on Francis on the Wed-
nesday in Whit-week and major orders the following days.
Father de Sa reports the elevation to the priesthood (May
23, 1551). "The bishop celebrated the ordination with
great solemnity, in presence of the local clergy and nobility, in the hall of the house where his Grace was accustomed to hear Mass," all "showed themselves most edified at
sight of the duke whom they had known before and
whom they found so changed and become a model of all
the virtues."

Ignatius had written advising Francis to postpone his
first Mass, so as to allow time for the special indulgence to
arrive from Rome, and meantime Luisa was hard at work
making the satin chasuble, covered with exquisite and intricate embroideries, which still hangs in the Casa Santa
at Loyola. Araoz wrote (June 25) to announce its receipt.
"Father Don Francis . . . since his ordination and the re-

nunciation of his possessions is so happy and contented that we must praise God for it . . . He has strictly ordered Don Juan no longer to call him lord or duke. Don Juan obeys and says your Reverence. The vestment proclaims its sender. Oh, if your ladyship could only have heard father and son when they saw it and heard the father complain that it was too rich for so poor a man !"

Trinity Sunday, the day after his ordination, de Sa reports that "his Grace went to Father Araoz's sermon at the Trinitarians. This is the first time he had gone out as one of us, in our usual habit and shoes . . . They are working hard at the Magdalena." It was to be another two months, though, before the hermitage was habitable.

Francis was kept busy with letters, to Ignatius and other fathers in Rome, to the Empress and other notabilities to beg their favour and influence for the Society. He wrote to the Jesuits in Portugal where Simon Rodriguez (who had started for India with Xavier and got no further than Lisbon) was head of the college founded at Coimbra in 1542. He signed himself the last and least of the brethren. "I have been like Esau, a mighty hunter, and chased not only birds, but souls, acting as beater for the devil" (May 29). Ignatius stopped him signing "Francis, sinner," pointing out that this showed singularity rather than humility.

At Rome Francis had been besieged by Cardinals and prelates, princes and nobles. Here it was townsfolk and country people who surrounded and followed him. It was a triumphal procession every time he walked to Mass at Vergara, six or seven miles away. He was asked to give a series of lectures in the university. He gave the Spiritual Exercises to secular priests from far and near. The church of San Pedro in Vergara was crowded to suffocation for his first sermon on June 29. He preached again at Oñate the following month. A man was stabbed in the church of Oñate in mid-July. Francis happened to be the only Jesuit in the house when a summons came. He ran to the church but the wounded man was past speech and he could only give conditional absolution before death. Besides priestly duties he still kept up his waiting at table, going every Friday to give the hospital patients their meal and then serving the Jesuit fathers at dinner.

Ignatius's letter came at the end of July with permission for a Jubilee indulgence to be gained on the usual conditions at Francis's first public Mass, but there was still delay about arranging this so he resolved to say his first Mass privately in the tiny oratory at Loyola (August 1, 1551). It was served by Juan who, with the rest of those present, received Holy Communion. An old painting and a stained glass window at Loyola show Francis in the chasuble worked by Luisa. The chalice which he used was, till the Revolution of 1931, still venerated on the chapel altar.

That very day Francis, under direction from Ignatius, began a tour through Guipúzcoa, preaching a series of sermons in San Sebastian, Villafranca, Rentería, where no doubt he visited the famous Christ of Lezo, Hernari and Tolosa. None of the poor and countryfolk could understand a word of his beautiful and fluent Castillean, nor could he speak a word of the Euskera which is the oldest and most difficult of all European tongues, first used in the Garden of Eden (not by the Serpent) according to those who speak it. Preacher and hearers had often not a word in common, yet the effect of the sermons was electric. Neither then nor later was it obtained by the arts of the orator, nor by great learning and scholarship. "In his talk and sermons," says Ribadeneira, "one saw that the ideas he expressed were freely poured into him by God rather than culled from books." His absolute and simple sincerity, consuming love of God and souls were gifts of the Holy Ghost, like the tongues of fire at Pentecost which enabled the wondering multitude to exclaim, "We have heard him speak in our own tongues the wonderful works of God."

CHAPTER XVII

THE HERMITAGE

LUCKILY Francis was kept busy or his impatience might have got the better of him over the dilatoriness of builders and workmen. The civil authorities of Oñate had handed over the hermitage to him unconditionally. His exertions and six hundred ducats which he spent hurried on the alterations, though the house was a poor enough place when it was at last ready. The church of San Miguel, with its gorgeous plateresque *retablo* and fine tomb of the founder of the University, was crowded to hear Father Francis preach on the Feast of the Nativity of our Lady (September 8, 1551), and later in the day he, Father Ochoa and three lay-brothers moved in, a happy date for what he hoped would be a peaceful and solitary life.

Six days later there was a solemn procession from Oñate with the relics from Rome. Thousands crowded to Santa Magdalena to gain the Jubilee indulgence. "It never stopped day or night," said an eye-witness, "not even a child was left in some of the villages. The Father heard confessions and received crowds of people. He generally celebrates Mass every day. I cannot describe the devotion of the people."

The crowds dwindled at last. The pilgrimage was over and Francis could spend long hours in prayer in the little chapel which he had designed, like his oratory at Gandia, to the traditional measurements of the Holy Sepulchre. He was free from the burden of possessions, free too he hoped from the press of people and external activities which obscures the vision of God as hurrying clouds hide the sun. The desire of the lover is to be alone with and united to the beloved. The most passionate human love beside the love of the human soul for God is a pale, flickering candle-flame before midday summer sunshine. This is the essence of sanctity, love, with its humility, its self-denial, its willingness to suffer, its consuming desire for union with God.

Francis had that humility. His refusal of titles of honour, his plain signature 'Francisco', his eagerness to perform the most menial duties show it. The renunciation of rank, titles, wealth, estates was only the outward sign of that inner renunciation of self which is so much harder. *"Contra te ipsum"* was a saying of Ignatius of Loyola which held no obscurity for Francis Borgia.

The cruel fasts and penances, the terrible scourgings (one hopes there is an exaggeration in the story of one witness who declared he counted eight hundred strokes of the discipline when Francis occupied the next cell), these had a more than physiological reason. The fierce battle of youth at Zaragoza, and probably others at Barcelona, had left lasting scars. "Every man must realise that he is bound by unbreakable chains to a fierce lion always ready to slay and destroy him," Francis said later; "mortification is the royal road to heaven." But there was more than this, a desire to expiate by the suffering of his own flesh, the shedding of his own blood, those wild unbridled fleshly lusts and cruelties of some who had bequeathed him their name and the dangerous heritage of their blood. More yet. There were terrible sins of so-called Christians, all that neo-paganism which seemed to have eaten almost to the heart of the Church. "Would to God that in this city of Worms," Peter Faber had written ten years before, "there were even two or three clerics who were not fornicators or blackened with other infamous crimes." And again, "I wonder that there are not more heretics . . . for all the evil springs from the scandalous lives of the priests." Surely reason enough and more than enough for the greatest cruelty to self, if such suffering could in the smallest degree expiate insults and injuries to the Crucified Christ.

m

Union with God, such is the final stage of the mystical way. St Teresa of Avila, one of the greatest of mystical writers, in her description of the 'Prayer of Quiet', tells how far Francis Borgia had advanced along the road to union when he visited her (1557). "She knew someone whom our Lord often raised to this state [prayer of quiet]. She could not understand it and questioned a great contemplative [Francis] who told her that such a thing was quite possible and indeed had happened to himself" (*Way of Perfection*). "At this time Father Francis, who was Duke of Gandia, came here... He gave both medicine and advice as one who had made great progress himself, for experience is very important in these matters" (*Autobiography*).

The mystic, contrary to common belief, is no mere visionary lost in idle dreams. The greatest mystics, St Teresa, for instance, were eminently practical and competent. The combination of vivid perception of the spiritual world and a keen realisation of the material is a salient characteristic of the Spanish character and certainly of the majority of Spanish saints. Francis, under obedience, always moderated excessive austerity. As superior he was "severe with himself but very charming and gentle to others" (Ribadeneira). He was to realise, too late for the health of his own body, the truth of what Ignatius had written to him at Gandia. "When the body collapses from too great a strain, it should be cured, not only so that the soul may be healthy but that the healthy soul may inhabit a healthy body and so the whole man be readier and better able to serve God."

Indeed a healthy body was needed at Oñate, and Francis, now forty-one, only suffered occasionally from the universal fever and gout. He caused a mixture of scandal and edification by tramping the streets of Oñate with an old bag slung over his shoulder to receive the alms given in kind. On one occasion he came home carrying a pig ! Visitors to 'the holy Duke' met him wheeling a barrow of manure or coming out of the kitchen with his apron wet and greasy from washing up. He even tried his hand at ploughing, but this, no doubt, was more than the Basque peasants could endure.

He was gloriously happy. "We are delighted with the country," de Sa had written, and who would not love the Basque countryside, with its sloping, green, sheep-starred fields, flowery pastures, its mountains skirted with beech and oak and pine woods, their steep summits of copper and slate-blue patched with the flying violet shadows of great white clouds or wreathed in transparent veils of pearly mist, with its air soft and caressing yet keen with the salt tang of the western seas across which Basques have sailed to find new realms for the Church and Spain or to girdle the ungirdled globe?

"In continual prayer he made a habit of finding God in all outward things so that all places became an oratory and all things material for recollection and prayer" (Ribadeneira). Francis had lost none of his knowledge and keen observation of nature. His far sight could spot the tiny black speck, high in the sunlit sky, which was an eagle. It reminded him of the old fable how the eagle, grown aged and feeble, flies into the very eye of the sun till all his feathers are burned away and, fallen to earth, he bathes in cold, clear water and renews his youth, symbol of the sinful soul purged in the fire of God's love and cleansed by the sacrament of penance. Walking along the winding tracks, stony and dusty in summer, torrents in winter, he watched and listened to the birds, the shrill twitter of swallows on their way south for the winter, the slow flapping of stork and heron, the flocks of migrating pigeons bound for the Pyrenees, the high notes of larks, first and last of birds to sing.

He visited the people, as gaily, simply happy as all truly Catholic peoples must be, proudly independent, individualistic and ready to fight in defence of their national *fueros* and liberties, a nationalist spirit which he, half Valencian, half Aragonese, could so well understand. He was at home alike in the *casas solares* of the nobles, the square farms of wood and stone, all with their balconies and carved scutcheons over the arched doors, the huts where the poorest dwelt with their few goats and sheep and fowls. He enjoyed the country *romerías*, stocky brown men in black bérets and blouses, bright neckerchiefs and belts, women with blue and white handkerchiefs over their dark hair, dark blue skirts looped up to show scarlet petticoats, white stockings and white *alpargatas*, like Red Indian mocassins. Fingers cracked and voices broke into song while agile feet skipped and twinkled to the wild, gay music of pipes and drums. He heard from the open window of his cell songs almost as old as Christianity, the beat of marches to which an endless stream of pilgrims had tramped along all the roads of Europe to the shrine of Sant' Iago at Compostella—Sant' Iago, whose knight he had been, splendid in great cloak of white satin sprinkled with blood-red crosses.

He loved the people and they loved him. His confessional was always crowded. How did he understand? A few broken words of Castillean, not even that, could most of them talk. How did they understand? Not a word of Euskera could he speak. But in the mercy of God, there is a language above and beyond words, the language of heart and soul in which the grace of the Spirit makes itself understood.

Yet days of uninterrupted quiet were rare. Francis's vision of solitary peace was to prove no more substantial than the brief, broken dreams of fever. His fame had spread not only through Spain and Portugal, but to Rome France, Germany, Austria. Drama is one of man's most deep-rooted instincts, and there was drama with a universal appeal in the action of this descendant of Pope and kings, Viceroy and grandee, who had given up everything to become a poor religious without even a habit he could call his own. The Order he had chosen too was a new one, almost untried, only just beginning to be known, disliked by the Emperor, hated and slandered by all the narrow old diehards, both cleric and lay.

A stream of visitors began to arrive at Oñate, "to such a degree," wrote Francis in despair, "that my hermitage is turning into a court." The influx was checked for a few weeks when at the end of October, Francis left for Pamplona at the urgent request of the Viceroy, the Duke of Maqueda. He wished to stay with his two companions in a poor house in the Navarrese capital but was compelled to move to the palace. He was kept hard at work during his fortnight's visit, five sermons in the cathedral, endless conferences in all the convents. He was already a fluent preacher, and his utter sincerity, simplicity and burning zeal made a deep impression on his hearers. But there was room for improvement. Two years later a listener wrote to Ignatius from Burgos. "He seems now to have received the real gift of preaching, to have acquired the drama and pathos which were lacking, so that his work is more fruitful . . . He speaks to-day with the greatest ease, without much preparation. He moves people by a single sermon more than do famous preachers in many. All are lost in admiration of a duke who is poor and who preaches. He must be encouraged."

Back over the steep, rough passes of the snowy Pyrenees rode Francis and his companions, to prepare for his first public Mass on November 15. Oñate was too small for such an occasion, so Vergara was decided on and Francis spent the preceding night in the hospital there. The town (even now there are only three thousand inhabitants) was packed with more than ten thousand men, who had to put up where they could that cold wintry night. Early in the morning Francis gave Holy Communion to four hundred people in the church of San Pedro. It was obvious that it was far too small for the multitudes, so a procession was formed and led to the hermitage of

St Anne outside the town, where an altar was hurriedly erected out of doors. Everywhere, as far as eye could see, was a packed mass of men, women and children. Men and boys had clambered on to the roofs and, like Zaccheus, into the trees whose bare boughs were weighed down by their bunches of human fruit. Mass and sermon over, the endless procession returned to San Pedro where Francis communicated more than twelve hundred and fifty people, to enable them to gain the Jubilee indulgence granted by the Pope for his first public Mass. It was not till the afternoon that he got back to the hospital to break his fast.

At the end of November Oñate was invaded by a party of Francis's relations, Carlos, Duke of Gandia, Alvaro, now seventeen, Luisa's husband, the Count of Ribargoza (later Duke of Villahermosa), Don Felipe, Francis's half brother. (He had met his two sons-in-law during his visit to Pamplona, the Marquis of Alcañices, husband of the sixteen-year-old Juana, and the Count of Lerma, whose nineteen-year-old wife Isabella was lady-in-waiting to the mad Queen at Tordesillas.) They attended his Masses, heard him preach and received Communion from his hands. "My father often talked of this incomparable sermon," said Luisa's son, the second Duke of Lerma and minister of Philip III, "and of the deep impression made on him by his visit to Oñate." But Francis, when he bade them farewell and godspeed, begged them to come no more, "not to disturb him again." They brought with them echoes and vibrations from the world he had left and which he wished to forget. Carlos had given his father one piece of good news, that the Duchess, after three years of marriage, was expecting the birth of an heir.

There was an amusing incident when Sansonete, the old servant sent to announce the heir's birth, arrived at Oñate. Before he had time to speak his former master asked him smilingly, "Well, and how is little Francis getting on?" Poor Sansonete was dismayed and disgusted to think that someone had got in first with the news and so

deprived him of a handsome tip. He was correspondingly
relieved to find that no earthly messenger had forestalled
him, and returned to Gandia with a fat purse and all the
latest gossip from Oñate for the nuns. The Abbess had
been writing to Luisa and wondering what to send her
nephew by the messenger. "Does he need anything? I
have been tempted to make him some enjoyable presents...
but all those I thought of caused me scruples except the
one I did send by Sanson . . . for the cell of my son and
father" (March 7, 1552). That present was the delightfully
practical one of a broom !

Meantime Doña Luisa was using all her influence to
obtain a visit from her favourite brother. She wrote to his
old friend, the Cardinal de Cueva, got her husband to
write to the General to ask that Francis might be ordered
to Zaragoza. Ignatius replied direct to her, with his usual
tact, that he "would not formally order him" to visit
Zaragoza but that it might be arranged later. There is a
delicate reproof. "I am sure that your ladyship is not sister
to Father Francis by blood alone, but still more by soul
and by that desire for the divine glory which does not seek
personal pleasures and consolations but only that which
best serves the good of souls and the glory of God"
(August 20, 1553).

Corespondence, as well as visitors, made heavy calls on
Francis's time. There was one letter in particular which
was not easy to answer without bitterness, one written in
July, 1551, by Don Luis, Infante of Portugal, who had so
cruelly insulted and wounded Eleonor. There was an
awkward note of veiled apology at the beginning, then a
sincere and humble petition to be remembered in Francis's
prayers and Masses.

"The holy duke" had only been in Guipúzcoa seven
months when he celebrated his first public Mass, but he
was already known as the Apostle of Euskadi. The local
nobles addressed a charming letter to him. "We owe you
the deepest gratitude for the light you have shed on the

whole of Christendom. These mountains are most deeply in your debt, for to them you have brought a light-bearer and stirrer-up of souls, the former Duke of Gandia. Vergara thanks you." Golden opinions and expressions of gratitude poured in. "God has indeed made this holy man a messenger of salvation." "The townsfolk are so reformed that they preach to their neighbours" (perhaps not an unmixed blessing for the neighbours!). "Those who knew nothing of the Christian life have learned it. Many priests are reformed. The whole town [Vergara] begs Father Francis on its knees to stay within its walls."

That Lent of 1552 Francis organized his fellow Jesuits and sent them out by two and two through the country. He himself was continually on the go, muffled in a shabby black cloak against rain and snow, shod with black *alpargatas*, local sandals of coarse canvas soled with hemp. The Sundays of Advent he had preached at Oñate, Mondragon, Segura, Vergara; "nothing flowery about his sermons but all very much to the point," was the comment of one listener. Christmas Eve he was tramping the streets of Vergara with Father Ochoa, the Navarrese superior, begging for alms towards their Christmas dinner. On St Stephen's day he preached in San Pedro, on the Epiphany, though hardly recovered from an attack of gout, at Ascoitia and from there revisited Loyola. One of his companions wrote Ignatius an amusing account of the Loyola visit. "He wished to stay in the Madalena Hospital as you did . . . to eat at the same little table where you sat and sleep in the same cell as you did. We found the ass your Reverence left at the hospital seventeen years ago, still fat and strong and most useful. He is very privileged and even when he breaks into the enclosed garden he is not punished !"

Juan was no longer with him for this stay at Ignatius's old home. He had been sent to the university at Alcalá de Henares in September, 1551, travelling south with Araoz, who was on his way to Valladolid, but, as his father was to learn later, was getting more enjoyment than knowledge from his first two terms.

Just before Lent, 1552, Francis went further afield, to Vitoria and on to Bilbao. At both these places all Masses were finished in churches and convents before nine o'clock so that everyone could go to hear him preach. He refused no monastery or convent which begged him to preach, often dragged himself into the pulpit half dead with fatigue but never failed to electrify his audience. "Everywhere, at the passing of this man, enmities ceased, fervour was relit, towns begged him to found houses of his Order" (Suau).

Besides all this travelling, preaching, interviewing, visiting the sick, the poor and the countryfolk, he was kept hard at work giving the Spiritual Exercises to visitors at the hermitage, laymen and clerics. In those eight months after his first Mass he won many recruits to the Society of Jesus. One of these was Bartholomew Bustamente, Canon of Toledo, secretary and adviser of the late Cardinal de Tavera. He had built, with the Cardinal, the splendid hospital of St John the Baptist, near the Puerta Visagra at Toledo. So gorgeous was it, with its ornate gateway and the founder's tomb by Berruguete that local wits made cutting remarks about the length of time the Cardinal and the Canon would be kept in Purgatory for the sin of extravagance. The elderly canon (he was fifty-two now) had heard so much of the holy Duke that at last curiosity induced him to mount his mule and ride north in shortening autumn days over the wind-swept Castillean plateau and up into the Cantabrian mountains. He reached Oñate, met the duke with a barrow of wood and stone for the still unfinished building, fell at his feet, says Ribadeneira, told him he wished "to imitate and follow him in this state and mode of life." He did the Exercises and entered the Company. Instead of a comfortable, well-cushioned old age at Toledo he was to spend the next few years as Francis's companion on those ceaseless journeys here, there and everywhere through Spain and Portugal. He was to play Sancho Panza to the saint's Don Quixote and to supply the humorous relief which has been preserved by the earliest biographers in all its frank and delightful naïvety.

There were others too, nobles like Sancho de Castilla and Pedro de Navara, priests like Diego de Guzman and Gaspar Loarte. All did not become Jesuits but all, after doing the Exercises under Francis, were anxious only "to seek and find the divine Will," "asking grace of God that all intentions, actions and works may be directed purely to the service and praise of His divine Majesty."

CHAPTER XVIII

HERE, THERE AND EVERYWHERE

SPRING was here. Snow on the mountains was shrinking. Great patches of gorse on grey rocks were like the gold damascening on Toledo steel. Swallows and storks flew north on their way to countries Francis would never see. Young fronds of bracken were tightly curled like bishops' croziers. They reminded Francis of a vision which had haunted him day and night after Eleonor's death, a jewelled mitre which glittered before his eyes in the daytime and glowed in the darkness. It was not for a bishop's mitre or a cardinal's red hat that he meant to renounce the world, and at last he had spoken to God with a familiarity worthy of St Teresa: "Forgive me, dear Lord, but I can bear this no longer. I vow that unless this vision ceases and you promise me the lifelong poverty of a religious I will not wear a habit nor take vows."

The visionary mitre had vanished. He had escaped the red hat which Julius intended for him, by his hurried flight from Rome to Oñate. He was free now from responsibilities and from what St Benedict calls "the accursed vice of private property." He went gaily about his business, begging, digging, sweeping (the Poor Clare's present had been most appropriate !), tramping through the green pastures and thick woods, often alone but for a brother and his beloved angel guardian. He paused in the fields to talk to the lean, stocky men, with faces as brown and hard as the oak and walnut from which they made the chairs and tables and beds in their farms. Children ran after him, sure of a smile and cheery word. Sometimes as he went he thought out the series of Lenten sermons he was planning for Vergara, to begin on Quinquagesima Sunday. "*Miserere mei, Domine,*" how deeply he felt the conviction of sin without which the spiritual life is a house built on sand, how keenly too he felt the joy of release from sin. "Thou shalt make me hear of joy and gladness and the bones that were humbled shall rejoice . . . Be favourable and gracious unto Sion, build Thou the walls of Jerusalem." There were terrible breaches in those walls, many of them made by enemies within the gates. To cleanse and rebuild was the task for which Ignatius destined the Company of Jesus.

Then came a letter from Ignatius asking him to start at once for Lisbon, if he could and thought right to do so. Humanly every instinct and feeling rebelled against being torn from his dear hermitage to plunge again into court life, to meet the King, Queen and Infante who had so cruelly wounded Eleonor, to undertake a mission which needed almost superhuman tact, courage and diplomacy. There was no hesitation. "If Thou desirest sacrifice I will joyfully give it."

The third Sunday in Lent his sermon in San Pedro was on the duty of obedience. Resolved to take no money for the journey, he and his two companions, Bustamente and Domenech, tramped Vergara with bags on their shoulders for alms (March 19, 1552). They were snatched from the small, dirty inn at which they had dismounted in Casa de la Reina by the Duchess of Frias, wife of the Constable of Castille, who kept them with her for several days to help her to arrange details of the Poor Clare convent to be founded there by Francis's aunt, Sister Francis.

The former Duke of Gandia was vastly deceived if he fancied he could stay incognito in the Jesuit house of San Gil, Burgos, where Father Estrada was superior. He was detained, mobbed in the streets, nearly suffocated by the crowds who pressed to hear him preach, to beg instruction and advice.

It was the same in Valladolid. It was to be the same in every town during the ceaseless journeys through Spain and Portugal for the next nine years. No wonder that he

was sick of it, that sometimes he turned angrily to his companion. "One would think I was some wild beast the way
they rush to stare at me." Then, checking himself, "After
all what am I but a half tamed beast?" It was the irony of
life that he who had fled to Oñate for a solitary and contemplative peace, should spend his remaining years (except for the ten in Rome) in continual travel, in complications requiring the most delicate handling, holding posi-
tions of great responsibility and authority.

Every turn and corner at Valladolid was familiar, the
gorgeous plateresque façade of San Gregorio, the lovely
little oriel window where Prince Philip, as a new-born
baby, had been shown to the delighted people, the noble,
soaring arches of the Benedictine church, with Berruguete's inimitable *retablo*. All was familiar, yet unreal as a
dream, while he walked the dusty streets in his travel-
stained habit, where he had once ridden on his beautiful
Arab, himself magnificent in velvet and gold and jewels.

Familiar too was the long road south-west, hills, houses
and plain all dust-coloured, through Simancas, a heap of
tumbled, red-brown roofs piled up the hill, dominated by
the huge, five-sided castle, to Tordesillas. A vain journey,
except for seeing his daughter Isabel, for Juana la Loca
not only crouched and jibbered as she had done when
Francis first came here thirty years ago, but now her
blasphemy and horror of holy things were such that men
believed her possessed. The Marquis of Denia, who had
known Francis here as a page, was still in charge and had
been a generous benefactor to Oñate.

Holy Week was spent at Toro, forty miles south-east of
Valladolid, on the Ebro, giving the Exercises to the Infanta Juana, Charles V's daughter who was betrothed to
her first cousin, Joaõ, crown prince of Portugal. Francis
was with the young princess twice a day for two hours and
gained an influence over her which lasted all her life. Her
pet amusements were card-playing and novel-reading.
Gambling had always been a vice which Francis had par-

ticularly disliked and forbidden in his household. Now, in obedience to his wishes, the Infanta destroyed all her playing-cards and handed over all her romances. They were beautifully bound in tooled and gilded leather, so it is to be hoped that Francis, more civilised than Savonarola, did not consign them to the flames.

A forced journey of forty miles over the mountains and Salamanca was reached on Easter Eve. During Francis's visit to the great university town, which lasted till April 29, the bishop, the chapter, and the whole personnel of the university, from the Rector to the newest student, crowded to hear his sermons and conferences, some, no doubt, in the dark room on the ground floor, with its whitewashed walls and vaulted ceiling, where, three years later, Luis de Léon was to lecture. Narrow benches and desks and the long side passage for outsiders were packed. Francis, as usual, won all hearts, that of the Rector among them. Don Antonio de Cordova, son of the Count and Countess of Priego, had been appointed Rector at an unprecedentedly early age. Now, to the pride and delight of his family, he was to be made Cardinal by Julius III at the special request of the Prince Regent. He had read and heard of the Society of Jesus, felt drawn towards it, written to the General to ask his advice as to whether the red hat should be accepted or refused. Without waiting for the answer from Ignatius Antonio refused the Cardinalate and followed Francis to Oñate.

For after all, the journey to Lisbon did not materialize. Francis was ready to start from Salamanca, fully conscious of the difficulties which lay before him at Lisbon and Coimbra. Simon Rodriguez, kept from accompanying Xavier to India by command of the King, had been appointed first Provincial of Portugal by Ignatius. The Jesuit college, founded at Coimbra in 1542 as a missionary seminary for the East, had within five years over a hundred students from the noblest families in Portugal. Rodriguez's personal magnetism made students and novices as devoted to him as were the royal family. His eccentric methods were copied by his subjects. Juan Fernandez (who was now doing wonderful work with Xavier in Japan) had been made to ride through Lisbon dressed in his fashionable clothes, mounted on an ass with his face to its tail. That was only one instance of many such. Ignatius, hearing of these oddities and of Simon's too great popularity at court, had summoned him to Rome. The King refused to let him go. Forced to action, Ignatius appointed to succeed Simon as Provincial Father Diego Miron, one of those who had accompanied Francis to Rome.

Francis had now been commissioned to perform the Herculean task of smoothing over difficulties between Miron and his predecessor, persuading the King to let Rodriguez leave, Rodriguez not to make the position impossible by remaining, and Miron to go slowly at first.

However, as he was ready to leave Salamanca for Lisbon, a letter came from Araoz telling him that he was not needed in Lisbon, so, gladly, he turned homewards and was back in Oñate by July 7, when he wrote to console the Countess of Priego for the ruin of her ambition for Antonio.

Ignatius, that shrewd judge of men, had specially exempted Francis from Araoz's jurisdiction. Araoz, ruffled by this and by the choice of Francis instead of himself to go to Lisbon, had persuaded Ruy Gomez, his friend and Philip's chief minister and adviser, that it would be unwise to interfere in the Portuguese affairs at the moment. If Francis's journey had not been cancelled and he had reached Coimbra in the spring of 1552 instead of sixteen months later a scandalous quarrel might have been averted.

Back in Oñate he wrote to put Rodriguez's side of the question to Ignatius. The ex-Provincial, as well as taking his supersession as a personal grievance, as did the king and queen, saw the mistaken methods of Miron, his Prussianism and rigidity, undoing much of the good work which had been done. "So a great insult for our friends,

surprise of everyone, gossip among our enemies and depression among our brethren . . . In human judgment
when the foundations of a building are taken away it will
be destroyed entirely unless the Holy Ghost holds it up
with His hands. And, as we have no right always to expect
miracles, I myself prefer to sin through rashness rather
than through negligence." He then suggests that Simon
Rodriguez should accompany the Papal Legate on his
return to Rome, which would obviate any suggestion of
disgrace. Unluckily Rodriguez himself, unable to endure
exile and the ruin of his work by Miron, rushed back to
Coimbra (February 1553) and by his presence made confusion still worse. One of his Portuguese friends intrigued
in his favour against his superiors, and finally Ignatius was
compelled to order him to Rome in disgrace, "in the
power of obedience." So serious was the disaster that a
hundred and twenty-seven members left the Society in the
province of Portugal.

Francis had not been having too good accounts of Juan
since the boy had gone to Alcalá de Henares to study with
his younger brother Alvaro. It was only natural that Juan,
in reaction from the excessive austerities of Oñate, should
have flung himself whole-heartedly into the amusements
and pleasures of university life. He became popular with
the Prince Regent, just home from a tour in Germany and
the Netherlands which he had hated, and with the power-
ful Ruy Gomez. But to run into debt to the tune of ten
thousand ducats for clothes, servants and horses, was to
overstep the mark.

Francis had been told of some of these doings, but on
his return to Oñate he was met with news that was still
more unexpected. Juan had married Doña Lorenza de
Loyola, without having breathed a word of his plan to his
father.

Ignatius was exceedingly angry. He had refused several
advantageous offers for his great-niece's hand, and now

foresaw the inevitable slander that he had used his influence with the Duke of Gandia to conclude a match so
favourable to his own house. He refused to countenance
the affair. Francis, seeing that what was done could not be
undone, and perhaps with a secret sympathy with the im-
petuosity of his favourite son, went over to Loyola and
gave the young couple his blessing and approval. Juan did
better for himself in the world than any of his brothers.
He became a gentleman-in-waiting to Don Carlos, Spanish ambassador at the court of Lisbon and major-domo to
the Empress Maria.

Juan, however, was not the only member of the Borgia
family to cause trouble. Carlos, whose pious fit did not
last long after he had left Oñate, grumbled in public about
his father's generosity to religious, contributed little and
that grudgingly to the Gandia College and absolutely
refused to pay the sum promised to the Roman College.
He assaulted and beat a certain Dom Gaspard de Centelles
in the streets of Valencia and killed one of his friends. The
whole of the Valencian nobility took the side of de Centelles, except Pedro Galceran de Borgia, Francis's half-
brother. The costly lawsuit which followed cost the duke
a sum far larger than that which he had grumbled about
his father spending in charity. There was worse to come.
He and his uncle were mixed up in a series of assassina-
tions which split the whole kingdom of Valencia into
rival factions, and in the course of the vendetta a natural
son of the Viceroy was murdered (1554) by Francis's
other two half-brothers, Felipe, a knight of Montesa and
Diego, a cleric of one of the principal churches in Valencia.

As if the troubles in his family and the quarrels among
his spiritual brethren were not enough, acute tension had
grown up between Francis and his first Jesuit friend Antonio Araoz. Araoz had been scolded by the General for
having prevented Francis's journey to Lisbon. He believed that Francis, having a vocation to the contempla-
n

tive life, should remain buried at Oñate, leaving the active apostolate to those better fitted for it. Ignatius knew better and Francis was under obedience to his wishes, however gently and tactfully they were expressed. The first half of 1553, in fact, was a continual tug-of-war between the wishes of the General and those of the Provincial.

Francis had gone down in the autumn of 1552 with a worse attack of fever than usual and took so long to recover that he was sent to the seaside in November. This grey, stormy sea, its huge white-capped waves thundering day and night, flinging huge masses of brown rocks about as if they were children's toys, was a very different sea from the Mediterranean as he and Eleonor had seen it on the way to Barcelona, sapphire shot with amethyst and powdered with diamond dust. Over this stormy Atlantic Sebastian El Cano, native of Guetaría, on this very coast, had returned after circling the globe. From across this grey ocean had come those Aztec princes whom Francis had seen with Cortes at Toledo, decked out in gold and emeralds and rubies and feathers. Down south over this sea had sailed from Lisbon, nearly thirteen years ago, Francis Xavier, to be followed by a long line of his fellows— Xavier who now lay dying on San Chian, deserted and alone, murmuring his last prayers in his childhood's Basque.

Those three months in Rome, Francis Borgia had seen through Ignatius's eye the misery, darkness and wickedness he was sending his sons out to fight. Francis himself —as what generous soul has not?—heard the call of 'the people that sit in darkness and in the shadow of death.' His work for missions, his continual prayers for them, the last words of his diary, "Desire to shed my blood for His love," all prove it. But, as he was to write later to one longing to go east, a man's India lay not necessarily in Asia, but where obedience bade him stay and work.

Even the soft Cantabrian air and the languor of convalescence could not keep Francis idle. News came of a

terrible sacrilege in Lisbon. He set out preaching reparation through the country, while a priest from Hernani
translated his sermons into Basque as he preached. He was
back in Oñate for Christmas, the last Christmas he was to
spend there, and for the new year of 1553, a year of troubles, doubts and the imposition of a heavy cross, the appointment to a position of great authority and responsibility.

CHAPTER XIX

DUST OF EGYPT

PROBABLY Francis, with his occasional power of seeing future as present, knew that it was his last farewell to Oñate. "God hath indeed given thee eyes," he had written, "that by beholding the beauty of His creatures thou mightest love Him in all and everything and give Him thanks for all." These last two years and four months, broken as they had been by journeys and missions, yet had been in the hermitage the period of quiet and humble obedience, and absence of responsibility which laid the steady foundation for the next nineteen years of action and authority. It had been the nearest realisation he was to know of the dream of solitude and contemplation which had lured him as it had done Oviedo. In spite of difficulties, like his divided loyalties to Ignatius and Araoz, it had been a happy time, among these gay, simple, devout people, these wooded mountains and soft green pastures, under the pale sky and the white clouds sailing in like laden galleons from the Atlantic. "Everywhere there is beauty," a later Basque poet was to sing, "But my heart cries out for Euskadi."

Francis wrote from Salamanca, where he spent the Feast of the Assumption (1553), to tell Ignatius that, in obedience to his wishes and to three urgent letters from John III, backed by one from Nadal, he was again on his way to Lisbon. The hundred miles from Salamanca, over the foothills of the Sierra de Bejar, through Plasencia to the Portuguese frontier at Villar Formosa, the hundred and thirty-five miles on to Coimbra, were done at record speed, for Coimbra was reached on August 23. Bustamente, as usual Francis's travelling companion, could generally be relied on to supply comic relief. An accident happened on this journey which was nearly the end of *"mi buen viejo"* (my good old man). The travellers had reached a wild pass of the Sierra de Estrella, where a rough narrow track, with no room for two abreast, cut perilously along the steep side of the mountains, a precipice on one hand, overhanging blocks of granite on the other.

Francis was ahead, lost to the world, deep in contemplation. The good Bustamente was jogging along, his rosary in his hands, his attention slightly distracted by the danger of the path, when suddenly his mount slipped on a loose stone and mule and man went rolling down the precipice. The yells of Bustamente and the servants brought Francis abruptly back to earth. "Jesus, Father of mercies, help you !" he cried, and at that moment some jutting rocks and bushes stopped the fall. It was still a ticklish position, but somehow mule and rider were hauled back on to the path, Bustamente breathless and shaken but still grasping his beads. Oblivious of Francis's swift prayer the old man exclaimed that all thanks were due to our Lady and her rosary.

There was no rest for Francis in the Jesuit College at Coimbra, in the Rua da Sophia, on the outskirts of the old town which rose above the winding, white Mondego on the chalky spurs of the Sierra da Lavrão. The little chapel could not hold the crowds which flocked to hear *el Santo Duque*. Nobles, burghers, poor folk, doctors, professors and students from the world-famed university, jostled the Jesuit rector and students and Jerome Nadal. He, after refusing to join Ignatius in Paris, had been swept off his feet by Francis Xavier's first great missionary letter and had entered the Society in Rome, 1545. For the past two years he had been travelling through the four Jesuit provinces in Europe explaining the Constitutions of the Society and the spirit of the Exercises. This was his first meeting with Francis and started a friendship which remained firm in spite of very human differences and disagreements.

Francis was off to Lisbon in five days, but as a listener wrote to Ignatius, "the memory left by his swift passage will never be wiped out."

Four days sufficed to cover the hundred and forty miles over mountainous roads to Lisbon, reached on August 29, 1553. Poor Bustamente, after his life of ease and artistic work at Toledo, must surely have worked off a good deal of the Purgatory predicted for his extravagance. He was rewarded at Lisbon, though, for some of his trials and miseries. This was not the first time he had been at court, for he had accompanied Cardinal de Tavera on an embassy to the Emperor, but the memory of the stiff ceremony of the imperial state probably made the friendly familiarity of the Portuguese royal family all the more surprising.

That first interview at the palace was not an easy one to face. Perhaps it was more embarrassing to those "who had done the wrong." Queen Catherine had not seen her cousin and playfellow since she had left Tordesillas to be married twenty-eight years ago. She would certainly not have recognised the slim, smart young Adonis in this tall, gaunt figure in worn black habit and cloak stained with mud and snow, dark hair turning grey. The brilliant grey almond-shaped eyes were the only thing that had not changed. As the Jesuit came into the audience room King and Queen advanced and the King took off his hat, unprecedented mark of respect. Francis knelt and remained on his knees through the interview, with true courtier's tact giving as his reason for doing so that, being a little deaf, he could hear the Queen better so. As a matter of fact, with her low height and dumpy figure, he was about on a level, when kneeling, with her heavy face and opaque dark eyes. He was then taken through the palace to visit Don Luis, the King's sister and sister-in-law.

There was another royalty more delighted than anyone to welcome an old friend, the heir's wife, Juana, to whom Francis had given the Exercises at Toro a year ago. Miserably home-sick, hating Portugal and Lisbon, not cheered even by the prospect of the baby she was expecting in four months' time, she took on a new zest in life after Francis's arrival which was hardly flattering to her husband. He amused and cheered her by inventing a new pack of cards, twenty-four virtues and twenty-four vices. The winner at this edifying game was the one with most virtues in his hand ! He wrote little rhyming couplets for the cards and the game became so much the rage that Bustamente began to indulge in scruples over such frivolity ! His pen ran away with him as he wrote to Rome about astounding marks of royal favour, palace servants arriving every day at the Jesuit house laden with dainties for Francis, which he took to distribute in the hospitals, the special four-poster with heavy curtains arranged by the Queen for the Holy Duke, her doctor sent with bandages and a linen cap when Francis paid the penalty of his height by bumping his head against the lintel of the door and getting a large lump on his forehead. In fact the old man cackled as loud-ly and proudly as a hen that has just laid an egg, and at such length that poor Polanco, buried under correspond-ence, advised more brevity. "Your style is excellent but if you were to prune it a little when writing of unimportant things it would be better still."

The trivialities of that month at Lisbon, however, were only a camouflage for the real business of Francis's miss-ion. The new provincial, Diego Miron, a Valencian, with the mind of a petty official, showed genius in rubbing everyone up the wrong way. Rodriguez, unable to keep away from his old sphere of action, had rushed back from Spain in the spring and had only been induced to leave Portugal again in June (1553). Poor Nadal had arrived to find everything in confusion and even the good which Rodriguez had done obscured, if not undone. His diffi-culties, if they could not be entirely eliminated, were at least lessened by Borgia, who was exempt (as were Araoz and Estrada) from his authority as Commissary General.

Before Francis left a great function took place, in presence of the King, the inauguration of a new Jesuit house, the first for professed fathers outside Rome. Seven Jesuits pronounced their vows. Three postulants were received and clothed. Nadal wrote that "Dear Father Francis's kindness, humility and holiness, with his competence in spiritual affairs, are a real blessing. He has helped me more than I can express."

Francis himself, almost smothered by royal favour and universal popularity, was weary of 'dust of Egypt', as he called them to Ignatius. He was not free even when he escaped from Lisbon, after visiting the plateresque beauty of Belem, where Xavier and so many Jesuits had said or heard their last Mass before embarking on the voyage to the far East which barely half of them survived. Cardinal Enrique, the King's brother, induced Francis to stay at Evora, with its arcaded streets and Moorish look. Francis preached in the cathedral (October 5), and four days later had the pleasure of a visit to George de Mello, his favourite relation and companion in Provence and at Gandia.

Cordova, nearly two hundred miles away, was reached a week later and there, to Bustamente's relief, a halt was called. Antonio de Cordova's mother, reconciled now to his renunciation of worldly honour, and Don Juan de Cordova, one of the cathedral canons, had given funds to found a Jesuit house there and Francis spent the winter helping in its inauguration. With his usual mixture of zeal and humility he insisted on teaching the youngest class grammar, but was prevented from wasting time and energy by being told that he was no good as a schoolmaster as he had forgotten both declensions and conjugations !

Nadal, who had come on to Cordova, shows Francis in his new aspect. "Father Francis is well. If formerly he was inclined to be retiring and to shut himself up at Oñate, he is now most fervent, diligent, active and determined to help on the Company with all his strength and powers. He is making a crowd of plans for it . . . When I see him again, he will give me more" (To Ignatius, March 25, 1554).

This enthusiasm was to increase and later to cause trouble with Araoz and other superiors who were more cautious in their methods and considered prudence necessary as well as faith.

Francis had planned, after the winter in Andalusia, to visit Luisa in Zaragoza and return to Oñate in the summer, but the murders in Valencia by his son and brothers had raised such a storm that no Borgia was safe there or in Aragon. Carlos himself was forced to disappear for a year. Luckily for Luisa she had had a brief glimpse of her brother on his way to Portugal in the preceding spring (1553).

There was a bizarre incident after Francis had left Cordova and was on his way to Plasencia. Two masked cavaliers rode up to him, but instead of attacking him, warned him that it was dangerous for him, a Borgia, to travel without armed protection. Francis thanked them, said that *he* had wronged no man so feared none but God and (typical touch) "since the enemies of my house are, after all, gentlemen and Christians, they will not disgrace themselves by murdering an unarmed religious."

Francis had fancied himself free from the menace of the red hat after 1552 when the Emperor had urged his claims, but in 1554 it fell again. The Infanta Juana (now mother of a posthumous son, Sebastian, born January 20, 1554) had written to her brother Philip begging him to use his influence with Pope Julius III for the elevation of her dear Father Francis to the Sacred College. Philip, unwillingly preparing for his voyage to marry the English Queen, Mary Tudor, was only too delighted at once to please his sister whom he was leaving as regent and to win honour for his old friend. All this was *secret de Polichinel*. Rome, Sicily and Spain buzzed with the news. Francis's own attitude is something of a mystery. He had been terrified by his vision of the mitre, had fled from Rome to escape being made Cardinal, three years ago. There was no doubt about the feeling of Nadal and other Jesuits. Nadal writes, "I talked freely three time to Francis, then ill in bed at Tordesillas, and told him that, if the hat arrived, I should no longer believe that all were equal in Christ since someone wished to be ennobled." And still more strongly in a long letter from Zaragoza to Francis himself. "I both know and feel that it is not for the service of God, the good of the Company and your own good that you should advance yourself in a way and manner other than that prescribed by the Company . . . When I think about this I feel as angry as Master Jerome Domenech [who had written from Sicily indignant at the idea of Francis being made a Cardinal]. Please God your example may not open a door to the ambition of those of the Company who are of noble birth and have relations able to procure them hats and dignities . . . I see the devil's finger in all this" (June 17, 1554).

Araoz too writes Ignatius from Valladolid a letter which seems to end in a sharp sting of sarcasm. "R. [Francis] has resolved to accept the appointment . . . The judgments of God are wonderful, for that which formerly agitated him now pacifies him."

The editors of the *Monumenta* believe that Francis was unwavering in his refusal. Suau, largely on the evidence of this letter of Nadal's, thinks that he had scruples about refusing to obey the Pope's express wish. He need not have reproached himself for his indecision when he remembered what Ignatius had written to him two years before describing his own doubts as to whether he should advise Francis to accept or decline the hat.

"At first I felt I must oppose it with all my power. Yet, uncertain what was the Will of God, when there were so many reasons for and against, I told all the priests here to say Mass and all the lay brothers to pray for three days that I might be guided for the greater glory of God. During my hours of deliberation on the matter these three days I was filled with fears and did not feel able to speak or act against this nomination . . . At other moments these fears vanished. So the conflict continued. Sometimes I was afraid, sometimes not. At last, on the third day, a firm decision came to me . . . to oppose this matter with all my strength, both with Pope and Cardinals" (June 5, 1552).

Ignatius's description of his own doubts and scruples applied to Francis's now (1554), but these were promptly ended by the General's letter telling him to take his final and simple vows. These forbid a Jesuit to accept any ecclesiastical dignities or titles unless expressly commanded to by the Pope. Francis accordingly took his vows (August 22, 1554) and wrote to Juana, now Regent, begging her to ask her brother never again to threaten him with the cardinal's hat. Unless a Pope actually ordered him, against his own will, to be made cardinal, an unlikely possibility which never materialised, Francis's mind was now at rest. He knew that he could, as he did, wear the plain black Jesuit habit to the end of his life. Once again the snare was broken and he was free.

CHAPTER XX

COMMISSARY GENERAL

"TEN years ago to-day since the Cross was laid on me at Tordesillas," was the entry in Francis Borgia's spiritual diary for June 10, 1564. Nadal before leaving Spain called together at Medina del Campo the first Congregation of Spanish professed Jesuits, Araoz, Torres, Estrada and Borgia; Bustamente and Villanueva were also permitted to attend. The Congregation decided to divide the peninsula into four provinces, which stung the delicate susceptibilities of Araoz. He remained Provincial of Castille, and Miron of Portugal. Estrada was appointed to Aragon and Torres to Andalusia. Francis, who had not yet taken his simple vows, was appointed by Ignatius as Commissary General of Spain and a year later his jurisdiction was extended to Portugal and the East and West Indies. This post, superior to that of provincial, was abolished in 1565, at the second General Congregation of the Society. It opened the door to difficulties and misunderstandings between Commissaries and provincials, and it was natural that Antonio Araoz, Ignatius's own relation and the first Jesuit to land in Spain, should be hurt to see a man who had only been a religious for three years put in a position of authority over him. Indeed the next eleven years were continually disturbed by strained relations between the two former friends.

There was a certain amount of right on both sides, as is nearly always the case in human quarrels. Araoz was touchy and susceptible, saw insults where none were intended, was not above resorting to the stale device of threats of resignation. A close friend of Philip II and of Ruy Gomez, Prince of Eboli, his was not a character strong enough to remain immune from the temptations of court life. In later years his spirituality was dulled by what Francis had called 'the dust of Egypt'. Also he was forced to watch Francis, whose vocation he considered to be for the contemplative life, embarking on undertakings which he himself judged to be rash, starting new foundations without either money or men enough to make them a success, and launching into other adventures which showed more zeal than common-sense. He had been ruffled too by the advent of Nadal to expound the Constitutions "as if we needed to be reformed in Spain !" Ignatius, after weighing the matter, however, had judged that the advantages of Francis's appointment outweighed the disadvantages and Francis, unwilling as he was to undertake authority and responsibility, had no alternative but obediently to shoulder the 'Cross' and to carry it to the best of his ability.

When the news of his appointment arrived he was at Tordesillas. Philip, before he sailed in July for his marriage in England, had summoned his old friend and begged him to see if he could do nothing to break down the mad queen's horror of holy things. Francis was at Tordesillas for two months but could make no impression on that twisted, darkened mind and soul. His daughter Isabel did her best to make him come and stay with her, specially as during his time there he was laid up with a bad attack of gout in his feet. It was useless. He remained in the miserable little local hospital, ministering to the sick as soon as he was up and about again.

It was probably during this visit that his son-in-law, the Count of Lerma, played a singular and ill-bred trick on him, by placing on the altar a portrait of Eleonor, painted as St Catherine. Francis came in, said Mass and went out to the sacristy without a sign of having seen the picture. His server, all agog at such a strange incident, could not restrain his curiosity and asked if the Father had recognised the picture. "Yes, I saw well enough that it was Eleonor but God gave me strength to be unmoved, to remember her only to pray for her soul, as I always do. Be kind enough though to tell the Count of Lerma to keep the picture in his room. The altar is not the proper place for a portrait of Eleonor, even painted as St Catherine."

This self-control was no sign of lack of feeling. That his love for his wife was still strongly alive is shown by a well authenticated incident in one of his visits to Loyola. Juan, going into his father's room, was horrified to see him on his knees by the bed, shaken with sobs. He ran to ask what had happened. His father lifted a face streaming with tears, yet radiant. "Your mother has just visited me, Juan. Before she returned to heaven she asked me to give you her blessing."

After the two months at Tordesillas Francis was summoned to Valladolid by the Infanta Juana, now Regent in her father's and brother's absence. She had hardly waited to recover from the birth of her boy before she had fled from Portugal, leaving him in charge of his grandmother, Queen Catherine, and took no further interest in him, devoting all her energies to governing Spain. Francis continued to have the greatest influence over her during her regency, which lasted till Philip's return to Spain in September 1559, an influence which, unfortunately, caused the most bitter jealousy and scandal.

The next seven years were a maelstrom of activity, travel, dissensions and sorrows. A programme of Francis Borgia's journeys during that time would be merely a list of the chief towns in the Iberian Peninsula, from Burgos to Granada and Cordova, from Lisbon and Oporto to Zaragoza. There were many other adventures besides Bustamente's fall over the precipice. On their way from Castille to Andalusia that autumn they had arrived at a small inn in the Sierra de Morena which only boasted one small guest-room, with bare walls and a mud floor. The Jesuits took possession. Francis went into it, knelt down and was immersed in his evening prayers, never noticing that there was already luggage in the room. This belonged to a traveller who had gone out for a stroll and who, on his return, found in his room a shabby cleric on his knees oblivious of the world and intrusion. The traveller, furious, began to curse the intruder for his impertinence and prepared to reinforce words with blows. Francis's companions and the inn servants, hearing the noise, came crowding to the door. Francis was still on his knees, no longer praying but humbly begging pardon for his unconscious offence. His enemy was soon informed that this was the former Duke of Gandia, the Emperor's cousin, and, covered with confusion, was only too honoured to be allowed to share bed and board with so distinguished a fellow-guest.

There was another occasion when Bustamente, in an extra fit of piety while on a journey, begged Francis to pray for him what he prayed for himself. The result of this was a violent fit of fever and such an agonising headache that the poor old man's head felt "as if pierced by pointed nails." Having got more than he bargained for Bustamente confessed that his courage was not equal to Francis's and begged for the speedy removal of this 'favour'. The fever left him. "The example of the saints is to be admired but not always to be imitated," as Francis remarked later when reproving a novice whose eccentric penances emulated those of Coimbra. Indeed Bustamente, like any ordinary mortal, found a saint neither a pleasant travelling companion nor a comfortable bed-fellow. One day as they were walking through the streets of Valladolid Bustamente remonstrated with Francis over his extraordinary behaviour, striding along, head bent, muttering to himself and beating his breast—hardly the appearance for the director of the Princess Regent in the capital city. "I was suddenly filled with a terror of hell," answered Francis, "my proper place."

That vivid realisation of hell, begun by the friar's sermon at Zaragoza, remained with him all his life. When remonstrated with about his carelessness when travelling, he answered with a laugh. "I have a good steward who goes on ahead and provides better rooms than I deserve. That is my fear of hell." 'Father Francis's steward' was for long a proverb in Castille.

Certainly his appearance on a journey did not dispose innkeepers to give him their best rooms. His cloak and habit were always disreputable, for the good ones sent by relations and friends were given away to the poor or the sick in hospitals. He wore a battered old straw hat to keep off the sun in summer and an old felt which did not always keep out rain or snow in winter. Our Lord's commands to His disciples were literally obeyed. "Take nothing for the way but a staff only, no scrip, no bread, no money."

Begging was not only resorted to on the journey but through the streets of any town where he was staying, where he soon became a familiar sight. He was extremely thin now, not much more than a walking skeleton, and this accentuated his great height. The thick dark curling hair had turned grey and receded from the high forehead, making the aquiline nose jut more strongly and the cheek and jaw bones as prominent as they are in the death mask. The fine hands, with their long sensitive fingers, were roughened and scarred with hard work, brick-laying, gardening, scrubbing and helping in the kitchen. One morning the Regent came to the Jesuit house in Valladolid to call on her director. He was in the kitchen, helping brother cook to prepare dinner for some expected guests. He asked leave to go and see a visitor. "Well, do not be long," was the busy cook's answer. So, after a short interview with the Infanta, Francis hurried back to the kitchen.

In the intervals of cleaning pots and pans, however, he still continued to preach and to draw crowds. One day the mass of people outside the Jesuit church of San Antonio attracted the notice of the military governor of Valladolid, Don Juan de Moschera, who was riding past. Told that the Jesuit who had been Duke of Gandia was preaching, he burst into a torrent of loud and blasphemous abuse against the Company and all its members. His immoral life was public property but this scene of almost insane violence created further scandal. Francis, told of it, said only that he would say Mass for the governor for the next eight days and ask the whole Community to pray for him as well. The fierce soldier of fortune became a lamb, asked pardon of Francis on his knees and offered as a gift his house in Simancas, begging only to be allowed a small room in which to end his days. Francis accepted the offer, thought at first of making the place a house of studies, then decided to open it as a noviciate. It was the first noviciate in Spain, one of the earliest outside Rome after the one begun by Nadal in Palermo five years before.

Francis had thought of superseding his beloved Oñate, too far away now, by a hermitage at Yuste in the Estremadura. That dream was never realised. It was the Emperor who came to die in the cloister of the Hieronomite friary there. But Simancas became for Francis the true successor to Oñate, the refuge where, far from the court and the world, he was at his happiest and most peaceful.

The noviciate opened in 1555 with twelve novices. Francis wrote to Ignatius at the end of July. "We have now thirty-four fathers and novices who live from day to day by alms, but we have never yet wanted for anything." Bustamente was appointed Master of Novices but the Commissary General himself drew up rules and time-table. There were two hours' prayer daily, one in the morning, one in the evening, two conferences by the Master, one on the Beatitudes, the other on the Constitutions. Saturday afternoons were occupied begging up and down the steep, crooked streets of the little town. Once a month two novices, taking turns, trudged the seven miles to Valladolid and spent the day working in the hospitals, a work which was a favourite one of Francis's. They had his example to inspire them, saw him, cloak thrown off, sleeves turned up, washing patients, cutting and cleaning

o

their nails and hair, dressing putrefying sores and doing all the most unsavoury jobs. He was warned to be careful of a patient who was seething with vermin (a nasty indictment of the hospital attendants). He shrugged his shoulders and finished attending to the wretched man. One old woman in the Madrid hospital became quite an old friend, for she had been in for three months with a bad leg. It became gangrenous and one morning Francis found her in tears because the surgeons had decided that it must be amputated. He cheered her, touched the putrid mass, promised to pray. The next day a piece of diseased bone, which had caused all the trouble, came away and the leg was saved.

Francis spent part of the autumn of 1554 in Salamanca and moved on to Plasencia in October. This little town, like Toledo, was perched on a steep hill, circled on three sides by the river and guarded by the towered walls built by Alfonso VIII of Castille, its founder. The bishop, Don Gutiere Vargas de Carvajal, was a worldling and a notorious gambler, a vice for which Francis had never had any sympathy. Judging personal intervention useless, the Commissary General, as usual, had recourse to fervent and continual prayer. The bishop not only entirely changed his mode of life but gave generous help in founding a Jesuit house in the town, which Francis generally managed to visit at least once a year.

The foundation of Jesuit houses and colleges through Spain were his special desire and work. He had already founded one at Cordova in 1553 on his return from Lisbon. Nineteen more were inaugurated before 1561, Avila, Cuenca, Plasencia, Seville, Granada, Simancas, Murcia, Monterey, San Lucar, Zaragoza, Medina del Campo, Toledo, Ocaña, Belmonte, Montilla, Segovia, Logroño, Palencia and Madrid.

Not all were successful. Many offers were accepted with more enthusiasm than prudence. Postulants whom the Provincial of Castille (Araoz) had refused were accepted by the Commissary General. Francis was quite aware of this fault of impatience and had confessed it in a letter to Ignatius. "I am always eager to build, even on wooden piles, and I am keen to found Jesuit colleges and houses in all the important towns, even if money is scarce" (April 27, 1553). Araoz, watching these impetuous and often imprudent adventures with a more worldly eye, must often have felt inclined to anticipate Talleyrand's remark, "*Surtout pas trop de zèle!*"

Francis was again at Plasencia in Lent, 1555, when a messenger galloped in from Valladolid with an urgent summons from the Regent for Father Francis to come at once to the old Queen, who was dying. He left post-haste, reached Tordesillas on Passion Sunday, March 29. Dying had brought no return of sanity. It was waste to linger in that terrible place, haunted by nearly forty years of prison, madness, misery and hatred. He withdrew to Simancas, only twelve miles away, to be within reach if needed, and spent Passion Week in peace with his dear novices. He was sent for again by the Marquis of Denia, found the Queen sinking but comparatively clear in mind and delighted to see him. Asked if she wished to receive the last Sacraments and to declare that she died in the Catholic Faith, she answered "Yes." She began to recite the Apostles' Creed with Francis but wandered off into the Nicene Creed. Francis remained with her and sent to Salamanca to ask the Dominican theologians there if she could receive the last Sacraments, which before, believing her possessed, they had said she might not do. Permission was given. The dying woman was anointed, but owing to violent fits of sickness, could not receive the Viaticum. Francis was with her when she died early on Good Friday morning and was able to write to Charles V that his mother's last words had been, "Crucified Jesus, be with me."

Such a death after all those years of mad hatred of religion was more than a seven days' wonder. Spain counted it a miracle worked by the holiness of Father Francis.

The death of the Pope, Julius III, which had occurred at Rome a few days earlier (March 23, 1555) meant a loss to Francis's dearest project, the Roman College, of a yearly gift of five hundred crowns. Cardinal Caraffa, elected after the twenty-two days' pontificate of Marcellus II, was far from likely to continue his predecessor's generosity. He hated Spain and everything Spanish with a bitterness only to be found in a Neapolitan noble. Not only did he regard the Society of Jesus as a Spanish institution, because of its founder's nationality, but he had an old quarrel with Ignatius who had refused to merge his little company into the Theatines of which Caraffa was head. Ignatius was sitting by the window of his little room when news of the result of the election was brought him. "A visible change came over him and all the bones of his body shook."

The German College, one of his favourite foundations, had to be closed, and all the Roman houses of the Society were reduced to direst poverty by the papal enmity. Paul's insane dislike of Spain touched Francis nearly, for, after allying himself with the French, the terrifying old man actually considered a Bull of Excommunication against Philip II. It would have been the duty of the Commissary General to publish the Bull in Spain, excommunicating his own sovereign and friend, a terrible dilemma which might well have caused a nationalist rising against the authority of Rome. The Regent Juana, however, was equal to the occasion, primed perhaps by Francis. She forbade the entry of any papal emissaries into Spain, so that ports and frontiers would be closed against the bearers of the Bull. Paul reconsidered his rash action and the danger was averted.

Ignatius's life was drawing towards a stormy sunset. There was the Pauline persecution, and though he cared nothing for the Pope's hatred of him he could not be blind to the menace to his Company. There was too the quarrel with the Sorbonne, which had so far made impossible the foundation of a Jesuit house or College in Paris or anywhere in France. Luckily this had at last been ended after a conference in Rome between four French theologians and Lainez and Polanco. Ignatius was worried too about a return to excessive mortification on the part of the Commissary General. Antonio de Cordova had written (October, 1554) begging the General "to tell him to take more care of himself, not to abstain all the time, but sometimes to eat a little chicken, kid or fish." Ignatius's reply was to put the Commissary General under obedience (as regarded health) to a lay-brother. This brother Marcos had formerly been a choirboy in the chapel at Gandia, then had been sent by the Duke to his aunt, the Duchess of Medina Sidonia at San Lucar, where he became choirmaster. He resigned his position there to enter the Society and remained in charge of his former master till Francis's death.

Francis was back at Alcalá de Henares in the autumn of 1555. He had been mobbed there on his last visit by students and professors when he had slipped into a class-room to listen to a lecture. A project was in the air at Rome, of which he knew and approved, that he should be sent on a mission to England (in 1556), where Philip was having a very difficult time as the husband of an amorous, nervy and elderly wife, and as king-consort over a lot of burly, beef-eating, beer-drinking northerners who hated and despised him. Juana, though, took fright at the dreadful thought of losing her precious director and wrote so strongly to the General that the project was shelved.

Francis too wrote to the General from Salamanca, his musical heart rejoiced by a new decision about the singing of the Holy Week and Easter Offices. "As to the tone, it should be full, simple, without affectation so as to be more devout, shorter and so needing fewer voices." He ends: "Begging the divine Majesty to give your Paternity many happy Easters" (May 19, 1556). This was to be the last of his series of fifty letters to Ignatius. (The first was written from Monzon, July 18, 1542, in very beautiful Italian!) In two and a half months Ignatius was in heaven.

CHAPTER XXI

STORMS

FRANCIS was at Valladolid when he received from Ribadeneira the news of Ignatius's death in Rome, July 31, 1556. The General had been failing bodily for some time but the end came suddenly and unexpectedly. "You can well believe the loneliness and unhappiness that I have felt, humanly speaking, when I think of us, his children, left here in the desert while he, our father, is joyfully gathering the harvest which he sowed with such continual tears." So Francis wrote (September 18, 1556) on receipt of the news. The greater the personality the more painful the blank when it is removed. It so often seems that the work which has been the creation of individual genius must collapse when such inspiration and driving force ends. Short-sighted human beings find it difficult to realise that, if the work is good in itself, it will continue and thrive even when its originator no longer guides it. Francis himself did realise this. "I firmly believe that to-day the Company will begin to increase," he ends this same letter to Father Carillo, "that, with fresh strength granted from our father's home in heaven, it will renew its youth like the eagle."

Indeed, looking back over the twenty-two years since the first vows at Montmartre and the sixteen years since the new order was confirmed by Paul IV, its growth and expansion seemed little short of miraculous. At the time of its founder's death the Society of Jesus had fifteen hundred members, sixty-eight houses, nine provinces in Europe (Portugal, Italy, Sicily, Lower and Upper Germany, France, Castille, Aragon and Andalusia), and three provinces outside Europe, the East Indies (including China and Japan), Brazil and Ethiopia (in process of formation).

Ignatius in Rome had been the power-house, the head-quarters of this worldwide organisation. It would be a difficult task to elect a successor, a terrifying responsi-bility for that successor when elected. The man who seem-ed most fitted for the post, Diego Lainez, at the time of Ignatius's death was himself lying dangerously ill under the same roof. His work, though, was not yet finished. He recovered and, elected Vicar-General, summoned the first General Congregation of the Society to meet in Rome that November, a date later postponed till the following spring (1557).

A difficult question now arose for the Spanish fathers. Philip II, since his father's abdication in October, 1555, King of Spain and all the Spanish possessions, was at war with the new Pope, Paul IV. There was a truce at the moment, unlikely to last long, and Nadal, who was again in Spain, considered that the Spanish Jesuits should leave at once before the frontiers were again closed. He urged this strongly when they all met at Simancas in October. With Bustamente as their spokesman the Spanish fathers disagreed with Nadal, announced their intention of re-maining in Spain for the present and begged him to do the same. Nadal with his usual pitiless sincerity wrote in his diary, "I did not disguise my feelings. I entirely disap-proved of their suggestions and did not hide my anger. Finally I announced my intention of leaving the next day and did so."

Francis himself, naturally enough, had no wish to pre-cipitate a crisis by hurrying to Rome against the wishes of the Regent Juana and especially at this moment when the Emperor had just landed in Spain on his way to Yuste, with his two sisters, Eleonor, widow of Emmanuel of Portugal, and Maria, widow of Louis of Hungary. He was prepared, under obedience, to be in Rome with the others, by March, 1557, as he wrote to Lainez (October 28, 1556), but he saw nothing to be gained by starting now. He was still human enough to lose his temper badly with Nadal.

He was not the only one to do so. "Father Francis was angry with me for my outspokenness, so were all the others," reported Nadal. "Far from being subdued I told Father Francis himself, who was emphatic, that I respected not what he had been but what he now is." Nadal, seeing things from the Roman angle, left in dudgeon. The others went back to their respective work, Francis to Alcalá de Henares, whence he was summoned by the Emperor, who was asking why his old friend had not yet visited him.

Francis set out with three companions, Bartholomew Bustamente, who, unexpectedly enough, had been so rigorous with the novices at Simancas that it had been found necessary to replace him, Father Herrera, a favourite of Francis's whom Nadal disliked, and the good Brother Marcos, to see that the Commissary General did not overdo fatigues or penances.

It was a bitter journey in December, more than a hundred and fifty miles across the wind-swept plateau of Castille, then over the Sierra de Gredos, where the steep, rocky defiles reminded Bustamente painfully of his journey to Lisbon. Francis was not looking forward to his interview with Charles, whom he had not seen for ten years. It was an open secret that the ex-Emperor's prejudice against the Society of Jesus was a deep-rooted one. That stormy petrel, Bobadilla, had sown the seeds of it. They had been well nourished by other ecclesiastics, notably by the Emperor's confessor among the Hieronomites of Yuste, who had charitably remarked that if the Jesuits were not agents of Satan himself, they were spies of the Grand Turk. A letter from the Regent was received on the way, telling her director that her father proposed to insist on his leaving the Jesuits and becoming a friar at Yuste and his confessor.

Altogether the Commissary General had plenty to occupy his mind as he let his mule pick its way up through the mountains. Life just now was full enough of difficulties, beside which the ordinary cares of new foundations

were child's play. There was that terrible blank where before he had always felt behind him the breadth of vision
and sound wisdom of his Father in God. There was the
continual strain of the friction between himself and Araoz,
his difference with Nadal, the wonder how the two loyalties of religion and patriotism were to be re-adjusted. As
to the task immediately before him, he could only pray
that the Holy Ghost would inspire him with the words
best calculated to soften the obstinate old man's ingrained
prejudice against the Order of which he knew so little.

Charles was not yet in his quarters in the friary at Yuste.
The additions were not finished enough for him to move
in till February. He was still in the palace of the Oropesas
in Jarandilla, a little village through which Francis had
often passed on his way to Plasencia, twenty miles further
west, to which he went on after his visit of two or three
days (December 19-22, 1556).

Francis wrote an account to Lainez of his interviews
with Charles, who had made to Quijada, his faithful majordomo, the somewhat obvious remark: "Father Francis is
very different from when he was Marquis of Lombay."

"I told him [the Emperor] all about the Company, of
which he had not a good opinion, owing to unfavourable
information," wrote Francis. "He remained satisfied with
everything and neither replied to nor contradicted anything which was explained to him. I won that, thanks to
the great strength which God grants to simple straight-
forwardness and truth . . . The Emperor received me with
more affection than ever and we continued to discuss the
service of God during interviews of three hours" (Alcalá,
Dec. 28, 1556).

Ribadeneira gives a much more racy and detailed account of the first interview, which he had from Francis
himself, and of the one the following day when he told the
story of his 'conversion' and gave the reasons for becoming
a Jesuit. "I saw that the Company combined the active and
contemplative lives, Martha and Mary, so that it was the

best imitation of Christ and His Apostles." Charles, still unconvinced, thinks it would have been more fitting to join an older and better-known order. "The old orders were once new," Francis pertinently remarked. "Age is no guarantee of goodness. Much is said against the Company but surely we who live in it must know it best." "I must believe you as I have always found you truthful," grumbled Charles, "but there are too many young men in your Order." "If the mother is young, how can her sons be old?" flashed Francis. "If that is the only fault you can find, time will cure it by giving those young men grey hairs in twenty years' time. But I can show you some grey hairs now."

Bustamente was summoned and the Emperor greeted an old friend, for the former Canon of Toledo had been sent to him by Cardinal de Tavera over some Neapolitan business and had been on the Tunis expedition in 1535.

Altogether the visit was a great success and Quijada was told to speed the parting guests with two hundred ducats, a mean enough alms, but the Emperor had always been known for his economies.

Francis, after his rush to Jarandilla and Plasencia, was back at Alcalá before the New Year. He was joined there by the Provincial of Portugal, Miguel de Torres, and his companions, on the way to Rome for the Congregation. War however had broken out again between Philip and the Pope, and Spanish subjects were forbidden to go to Rome. Francis, as well as being in a cleft stick between his duty to attend the Congregation and the diplomatic necessity of not offending the Regent, the Emperor or the King, was suffering from the aftermath of a severe hæmorrhage so was in no fit state to travel. He wrote to Lainez a letter which, while expressing his will to obey his superior's wishes, does not disguise his extreme unwillingness to go to Rome unless absolutely necessary. "Prepared to sacrifice myself, I am willing to obey, but however much I try to overcome my weakness it is no secret either to the fathers or to the doctors that my life is at stake" (March 24, 1557).

Never before nor after did he plead health as a reason for avoiding a duty. In this case it was a perfectly legitimate excuse and also a reason for urging that the Congregation should meet in Spain, preferably at Barcelona. So keenly did he desire this that not only did he add to his letter to the Vicar General ten good reasons for it but he also sent to Rome Brother de Ribera to press the matter. He might have guessed that it was hardly likely that the anti-Spanish Pope, with enemies of the Company at his ear, would consent to this.

The combination of the active and the contemplative life, as Francis said to the Emperor, and as St Thomas had remarked three centuries before, was the Christian ideal. His own just now was a prolonged struggle not only with men and difficulties but with himself. He had indeed conquered those bodily passions which had been so strong, but his hot temper still flared suddenly at opposition, as it had done with Nadal. Mercifully, like all generous natures, his temper was over as quickly as it began. He was incapable of bearing malice or sulking. His body, worn by ceaseless mental effort and by those cruel penances which even now he sometimes indulged in, put up less resistance to the periodical attacks of fever and gout which were one of the greatest physical curses of the age. Chronic indigestion, the result of too fierce fasting, and the severe hæmorrhage of spring, 1557, inevitably weakened overstrung nerves and explain those occasional outbursts of temper and a rigour which he rarely showed to any but himself.

Mercifully there was his beloved haven of peace at Simancas, among the novices to whom he showed himself rather as an affectionate father, or even brother, than as a disciplinarian. He amused himself and them by inventing games, such as he had provided for the homesick Spanish princess at Lisbon. He wished to be treated as one of the least of them, not as the 'Holy Duke'. On one of his visits, a novice more noted for zeal than skill in the kitchen, went into the garden to gather herbs for a special dish in honour of the Commissary General. The result was appalling. No one could eat it, except Father Francis, who, to the general amazement, finished his portion, bitter with wormwood as it was. The miserable novice soon heard of the result of his cooking, ran in and flung himself at Francis's feet with deep apologies. "My dear child, God bless you, for you are the only one here to give me what I really need."

One winter day Francis was detained at Valladolid, but late as it was, would not defer his escape to Simancas. He set out on foot, alone, in wind and snow. Night fell. It was so late when at last he arrived that the house was shut for the night, as he was not expected and everyone was in bed and fast asleep. He knocked and knocked, standing in the thickly falling snow, but the dormitories were at the other side of the house and no one heard. At length a wakeful novice heard someone at the door, went down to open it and was horrified to find Father Francis, white with snow and shuddering with cold but cheerful and smiling. "Do not worry, my dearest brother, for the Señor cheered me while I was waiting. I remembered that it was He Who sent snow and icy winds on me and all His works are full of infinite joy and beauty. So I felt glad that He should chasten me and I was glad with the gladness He has in His works, as a lion or some other wild animal is torn to pieces before a great Prince, solely to give him pleasure." There is the echo here of old court days, of bull-fights at Valencia, but still more of his own saying: "God hath indeed given thee eyes that, by beholding the beauty of His creatures, thou mightest love Him in all and every thing and give Him thanks for all."

Indeed gratitude, 'giving thanks', was in him, as in all generous natures, a deep and continual virtue. Every page of his Spiritual Diary, jottings meant for no eye but his own, breathes it. Over and over again comes the phrase,

"I gave thanks, I gave thanks." "During the twenty-four hours of the day I will give thanks." "Thanks be to God for what He has torn up and destroyed." "Hope that He will grant me the Cross. *Ut dictum est, Deo gratias!*"

CHAPTER XXII

PASSING

THERE was a lull in the Spanish alarums and excursions over the meeting of the General Congregation, but there was to be no peace for Francis except for brief, precious days at Simancas. John III of Portugal died on June 11, 1557, and in the following month the Commissary General received an urgent summons from the Emperor, now settled in the new wing which had been added to the friary. Charles unburdened himself of tangled diplomatic difficulties which he felt no one but his cousin could unravel. The new King, Sebastian, son of the Infanta Juana, so Charles's grandson, was only a child. The regency was vested in his grandmother Catherine, Charles's sister, for Juana, who had never returned to Portugal since she had left directly after her baby's birth, was still Regent of Spain, during Philip's prolonged absence in England and the Netherlands. The Emperor was anxious that if the little king died the crown of Portugal should revert to his other grandson, Don Carlos, through his mother, the Infanta Maria of Portugal. He was also anxious about Sebastian's marriage, somewhat prematurely, as the poor child was only three and a half. He wished it to be not to a French princess but to a daughter of his sister, Mary of Bohemia. The old scandal, too, had cropped up again which had ruined the Cardinal of Visieu, Eleonor's friend, fourteen years ago. Was there any truth in the report that John III had married his sister-in-law without a proper dispensation? If so Sebastian was the son of a bastard, and Don Carlos, after the old Cardinal Enrique, the rightful king. Yet more: Charles wished to induce his niece, the Infanta Maria of Portugal, to come to Spain and visit her mother, Queen Eleonor, now frail and failing in health. Altogether a fine bundle of business which Francis, already overloaded with cares and responsibilities, felt little like shouldering. Yet, if he did not, the situation would probably be mishandled and his refusal would damage, if it did not destroy, the favour in which the Society was held by the Infanta Juana and now, more or less, by the Emperor.

One thing during his stay at Yuste gave immense pleasure both to Father Francis and to Brother Marcos, the music at the friary. Charles had found the friars' singing of the Divine Office much below his high standard. He had imported Flemish singers, and when not satisfied with the singing, expressed his feelings in lurid military language. He still had his little organ, like the one Francis had left at Gandia, though his gout-twisted fingers were too crippled to strike the notes.

Francis and his companions set out through the fertile valleys and the woods of the Estremadura, scorched by the blazing August sun. Beyond Plasencia they descended into the valley of the Tagus, which was an inferno of heat. As well as Brother Marcos and Bustamente, Francis had with him on this journey Father Denis Vasquez, afterwards his confessor and the author of a life of him. Just over the border into Portugal Francis and Vasquez went to the village church to say Mass. It was one of Francis's rules when travelling to spend the night somewhere near a church, though this often meant pushing on till late, staying in an inn even more filthy than usual, or sleeping in the open. Sometimes there would be a difficulty about his saying Mass, the local priest or sacristan being unwilling to put himself out. Then Francis would turn with a smile to his companion. "The time has come to invoke the secular arm." And when it was revealed that the shabby, unknown traveller was the former Duke of Gandia, difficulties vanished as if by magic. This particular morning when he and Vasquez returned to the inn where they had left Bustamente they found the old man on the point of being lynched by the inn-keeper and a furious crowd. With incredible stupidity he had remarked to his host that it would be a good thing if the little King were to die and the crown of Portugal be united to that of Spain. The man, a keen patriot, began to curse his guest so loudly that neighbours came to join in the fray, and but for the opportune arrival of Francis and Vasquez, Bustamente would have been in a very unpleasant position. After this escapade he was sent back over the frontier.

The last stage to Evora lay through cork woods, which shaded the plateau, but the heat had done its work on an exhausted body and Francis only just managed to reach the town before collapsing altogether. Nothing would bring down the fever. Frantic messages were sent to Lisbon for the court doctor, but when he arrived he could hold out no hopes. The end seemed inevitable. Delirium was over. Francis lay to all appearance dead, eyes closed, the high Borgia nose, sunken cheeks and temples those of a corpse. Yet, behind those closed lids, the keen mind still worked. He was aware of the irony of life, the broken wreck who had left the world to prepare for death in the cloister at Yuste, yet was still immersed in international complications. Himself, who had also renounced all and fled to Oñate, which was to be, he had said, "his oratory and his tomb, where he could live in lonely contemplation." And here he was, dying because his body was worn out by ceaseless activity and travel, and he too had been caught in the net of royal intrigue.

They thought him dead, but as the priest carrying the Viaticum entered the room, he sat up in bed and cried aloud, "*Ave verum Corpus!*" The doctor had given up hope but he himself knew better, with that obscure instinct of the body which is deeper and surer than any medical verdict.

He opened his eyes again to find not only Vasquez and Marcos, but all the Jesuits in Evora round his bed in floods of tears. There was a quick flash of impatience. "What use

are all these tears? Would they prevent my death if God
wished to recall me from exile?" Then a glimpse ahead.
"Alas, my day is not yet over. There is still a long road
for me to travel, many labours for me to endure. This fruit
is not yet ripe for heaven. In four days' time we will start
for Lisbon."

They did, but the adventures of this journey were not
over. The Queen sent a litter for the invalid and a royal
barge to ferry the party over the Tagus to Lisbon. A sudden storm rose, swept the unwieldy craft down the river
and looked like driving it out to founder in the Atlantic.
Francis, alone calm, cheered his terrified companions and
the still more frightened crew, and Lisbon was reached
late that night.

The Queen could not do enough for her cousin. He
was installed in the charming country palace on an island
in the mouth of the Tagus. The September weather was
glorious. The convalescent got up and about. Then one
day he visited the Franciscans in their friary facing the sea,
warned them to evacuate it, collected his own little company, and to their amazement, took them back to Lisbon.
That very night a furious cyclone ruined the friary and
destroyed part of the palace, the ceiling of the room Francis had occupied crashing down. This tempest, Ribadeneira tell us, "blew from the uttermost parts of the East
Indies and brought a pestilence which spread through
Europe and caused many deaths" (September, 1557).

The public object of his mission was a visitation by the
Commissary General of the Jesuit houses in Portugal. No
one but the Queen-Regent and the Cardinal knew his
secret mission. He wrote a couple of letters to Yuste saying that the Queen was sending a verbal answer by him as
she was unwilling to put anything on paper. Naturally, as
verbal promises can always be denied or evaded, the end
of this arduous mission was words, words, words. One
thing, though, Francis, still racked with fever, did learn in
Lisbon and reported to the Emperor on his way back, the
P

deep-rooted and bitter antagonism of the Portuguese royalties and people to the idea of a Spanish sovereign, whether that sovereign was Don Carlos (Portuguese on his mother's side) or any other claimant. The marriage project was not rejected and the Infanta Maria consented, much against the grain, to pay her mother a short visit at Talavera. Altogether a great deal of trouble and suffering for very little result.

After his first visit to Yuste Francis had gone on to the Jesuit house he was founding at Avila. Now, in the autumn of 1557, he came again to the towered, walled city, with the apse of its Gothic cathedral jutting from the wall like the stern of a huge galleon. On both these occasions he went to the Convent of the Incarnation, a fort-like building a little way outside the Puerta del Sol, up a slope of dun sand, patched with scorched, purple moss. St Teresa has told of these visits and of the help she gained from the 'great contemplative', in her *Way of Perfection*, her *Autobiography* and the *Relations of her Spiritual State* which she wrote for her Jesuit director, Rodrigo Alvarez. Francis settled all her doubts and left her "exceedingly comforted." It is most regrettable that the correspondence which followed between the two saints should have entirely disappeared.

Once more Charles called his old friend to him, and, a most unusual mark of favour, put him up in the friary itself instead of in the village. He fussed round in the guest-room, rather to Quijada's annoyance, and had the newly hung Flemish tapestry replaced by depressing black draperies from his own room! Francis found a scene of desolation on his arrival, for there had been another terrible hurricane on December 15. Two of the imperial chimneys and several houses in the village had been blown down, as well as many of the splendid trees in the garden which was one of Charles's hobbies.

The Emperor seems to have had an instinct that this would be his last meeting with his most intimate friend.

He returned all the reports which Francis had sent him
from Valladolid with the assurance, "None but myself has
seen them." What a mine of treasure these personal and
political reports would prove if extant! He discussed a dis-
pute in progress between Duke Carlos and Alonso de
Cardona, Admiral of Aragon. (The Borgias seem to have
had a passion for expensive law-suits.) He was surprised
when Francis begged him to show all possible favour to
the admiral. It must be confessed that Francis's reply to
his astonishment bears the stamp of the grandee rather
than that of the saint. "Probably the Admiral needs the
land most and it is a good thing to help the needy." He
does not mention this in his account of the visit to
Lainez, but remarks that his and Vasquez' being in the
friary "is a mark of favour and distinction which he does
not show even to his nearest and dearest. He gave me
many proofs of gratitude for my friendship and my past
and present desire to serve him. In order to overwhelm me
by his kindness he sent me alms which, in spite of his
poverty, he forced me to accept. He added that, if he had
more, he would have given more but that, poor himself,
he could give little to the poor. This is a great sign of
friendship which he wishes to show me" (December 23,
1557).

Once again in the New Year of 1558 the question of the
General Congregation loomed on the horizon. War-clouds
too everywhere darkened the sky. Philip had defeated the
French at St Quentin (August, 1557) and, if he had had
his father's energy, would have entered Paris within a few
weeks. The corsairs of Dragut Reis were sweeping the
eastern Mediterranean and in June a hundred and thirty
Turkish galleons appeared in the Bay of Naples. Reggio
and Sorrento were sacked, convents raided and young
nuns sent to the harems of Constantinople. Travel was
dangerous equally by land or sea and, as might have been
foreseen, the anti-Spanish Pope had forbidden the Congregation to be held anywhere but in Rome.

The Spanish Jesuits had two alternative routes, both without attraction. They could go by land and, if not stopped or arrested at the frontier, attempt to make their way across the enemy territory of southern France. Or they could sail from Barcelona, with a good chance of capture by the sea-wolves and the prospect of ending their days as galley-slaves on the rowing benches of Moslem pirate ships. One thing at least was certain. The Commissary General would not attend the Congregation. He had been ill on and off all the time at Lisbon, where the west wind blowing in from the Atlantic, warm and wet, had never suited him. Then, after an attack of gout which left him so weak that he could hardly stand, he had an acute and painful attack of bladder trouble, which became chronic and, while still violent, made it impossible to sit a mule or even endure the jolting of a litter. The Provincial of Aragon, Estrada, was also prevented by illness from going and Bustamente, now Provincial of Andalusia, was detained in Spain as well.

Francis arranged for the Portuguese fathers to go by land, the Spanish by sea. The Provincial of Castille, Araoz, started overland from Valladolid without waiting for orders. He was stopped at the Perpignan frontier and sent back so that Francis's formally signed acceptation of the Constitution with which he had been entrusted, as well as a long memoir of suggestions for the conduct of Jesuit houses, did not reach Rome till the autumn. By then the three months' sitting of the General Congregation was over (June 2-September 10, 1558). Diego Lainez had been elected General by thirteen votes out of twenty and the Pope had approved the choice.

In September too Charles V had died at Yuste. He kept calling for "Father Francis" in his last illness. Even in his agony his sensitive ear was offended by the harsh voice of Bartolomé Carranza, Archbishop of Toledo. Francis set out from Valladolid to attend the Emperor's deathbed as he had done that of his mother, but was met by a messen-

ger with news of Charles's death. He found himself left
with a last sign of trust and affection which he did his
best to escape.

"His Majesty has appointed me executor of his will," he
wrote from Valladolid to Lainez. "I wished to be excused
but her Highness [Juana] ordered me with great decision
to accept . . . So I shall be forced to spend the winter here
in spite of my wishes and my health, for this place never
agrees with me in winter. My former misery has begun
again, as well as gout, which punishes me as I deserve"
(October 25, 1558).

The death of Charles meant more to him than the passing of a friendship of over thirty years. "We have seen the
end of the greatest man in the world," he wrote. It was
indeed the end of an era, the exit from the stage of Europe
of the greatest layman of the sixteenth century, the going
of the Middle Ages when men had lived hard and died
hard under the banner of Christ.

Francis preached the funeral sermon before the court
at Valladolid. The high stone gallery in the great Benedictine church, the three huge pillars on each side of the choir,
the gorgeous movement and glitter of Berruguete's vision
of the Communion of Saints, were hidden with black
hangings, which struck eye and mind with the same start-
led horror as the violet-veiled statues of Passion Week.
Francis looked down on the crowded church, black-veiled
women, black-clad men, pale upturned faces a dim blur in
the gloom. His beautiful, resonant voice gave out the text.
"Lo, I have made haste to flee far off and to abide in the
wilderness. I waited for Him Who hath saved me from
cowardice, from the stormy winds and tempest."

Past and present were strangely blended. It was nearly
twenty years since he had listened to Juan of Avila's words
on the beauty whose swift corruption had stricken him to
the soul, the sharp snapping of threads planned to weave
patterns lovely in form and colour, the vanishing of 'castles of wind'.

"Behold Thou hast made my days a span long, and verily every man living is but vanity, for he walketh in a vain shadow and disquieteth himself in vain. We bring our days to an end as it were a tale that is told."

CHAPTER XXIII

DARK NIGHT

THAT year of 1558 had brought several deaths which touched Francis Borgia more or less closely. A companion related that one day that autumn he was going with the Commissary General to the palace at Valladolid when the superior stopped suddenly in the street with the words *"Requiem eternam dona ei, Domine!"* Asked the reason for his exclamation, he said that his daughter Isabel, Countess of Lerma, had just died at Tordesillas, only twenty-six years old. When he had finished his conference with the Infanta Juana he asked her prayers for the Countess's soul. She, and another friend to whom he made the same request, could hardly believe such self-control possible. To the expostulations of the latter Francis answered that, having given God all his heart and all his affections, he could hardly cry out if they were crucified.

He had too another royal funeral sermon to preach before the New Year. News of the death of Queen Mary of England reached Valladolid on December 28. A solemn Requiem was celebrated the next day in the Jesuit church of San Antonio before the assembled court and council. This death too was the end of an epoch, of a thousand years of Catholicism in England, for the succession of Elizabeth was to mean the final break-away of the country from the traditional unity of European culture.

Philip II, now a consolable widower, was to return this next year to his beloved Spain which he had no intention of ever leaving again. The enemies of the Society and of the Commissary General looked forward eagerly to the King's advent. Not content with whispered complaints of her director's extraordinary influence over the Regent, jealous courtiers spread stories of their immoral relations. She who never showed her face, was never seen except veiled and swathed from head to foot in deepest mourning, and he a wreck from gout and fever, little more than a skeleton kept going by sheer force of will!

One of the most admirable of human qualities is the power of mind and will to dominate the pain and weakness of worn-out body and overstrung nerves. There is a deeper courage, hidden from human eyes, that of the soul which, though deprived of all light and consolation, still clings steadfastly to God and in its utter desolation only echoes the words of its Master, "Why hast Thou forsaken me?" St Teresa, St John of the Cross have striven in vain, like all the great mystical writers, to express the inexpressible, to paint that terrible blackness which they have called the Dark Night of the soul. It is permissible to think that Francis Borgia, long past what St Teresa calls the Prayer of Quiet, had now reached this stage of the mystic way. There are in his letters notes of "Sadnesses and melancholies," weariness, weakness, "agonies," which seem to point to something deeper than mere bodily ills or mental worries. Perhaps too he who so often saw future as present was aware of the oncoming storm whose mutterings were already to be heard in the distance.

The prayer of St Ignatius for his sons was that, like the Apostles, they should be insulted, slandered and persecuted. That prayer was answered even in his own lifetime and is still taking effect to-day.

The Emperor had not been the only man in Spain to be prejudiced against the Society of Jesus. The Archbishop of Toledo, where Francis had founded a Jesuit house in 1557, though a personal friend of the former Duke of Gandia, was consistently hostile to the Jesuits who, as he acidly said, "paraded their saint as countrymen do the heads of the wolves they have killed!"

There had been worse trouble in Zaragoza, where religious and secular clergy chased the Jesuits out of their new house on the accusation that they had diverted alms from other and older foundations. Francis's sister Luisa, Duchess of Villahermosa, paid for her courage in housing the refugees at Pedrola by being excommunicated by her uncle the Archbishop of Zaragoza. It needed a strong protest from the Regent to bring the deadlock to an end. There was a more dangerous enemy still, the Dominican Melchior Cano, said to be the best preacher in Spain. He denounced the Company of Jesus from the pulpit, giving the somewhat strange reason that its members urged people to frequent the sacraments. He also wrote to the Emperor's confessor at Yuste, Fray Juan de Regla, that his chief objection to these meddlesome 'friars' was that they "change the gentlemen who fall into their hands from lions into hens," "soldiers into women and gentlemen into merchants!" There was a reason for his dislike, for he believed that the influence of Araoz had prevented him from getting a better-paid post than the bishopric of the Canaries. The campaign against the Society had been going on for the past three years (1556-1559) in Seville and Granada, and even before that one of the fathers had written gaily from Cordova: "The talk is that we are all to be burned, Father Francis the first of the lot." Jesting words, but they were echoed seriously enough by Francis himself in a letter to Ribadeneira (1558). "Lutherans have been unmasked here and plenty of people are saying at court and in Castille . . . that we are the cause of these errors, that I have been arrested, others strangled and one hung. Or we are to be burnt. Such is common talk."

It was true that a nest of Lutheranism had been unearthed in Valladolid in May, 1558. Charles had written urgently to Philip at Brussels and Juana at Valladolid, threatening to return himself to public life if they did not ruthlessly suppress what Francis had called "this abominable leprosy." The Holy Office moved. Its dungeons were soon full. Francis was forbidden by Diego de Alava, President of the Council of the Inquisition, to leave Valladolid. "They want my opinion and consider it necessary for me to stay here till after the *auto-da-fé*" (October 25, 1558).

This did not take place till May 21, 1559. It was a solemn and full-dress affair, with the Regent and Don Carlos present in state on the grand stand in the Plaza Mayor. Near them was seated Doña Magdalena de Ulloa, Luis de Quijada's wife, and a fair, slim boy of twelve, with yellow curls and bright blue eyes who, as Francis Borgia probably knew, was an illegitimate son of the late Emperor. It was Don John of Austria, the future victor of Lepanto.

There were thirty condemned prisoners, fourteen of them sentenced to death, five of whom were members of a distinguished family of Jewish converts, the Cazallas. One of those found guilty was Doña Maria Enriquez, sister of Francis's son-in-law, the Marquis of Alcañices. She was to be led to the scaffold, dressed in the dreadful San-Benito, with a lighted candle in her hand, before being taken back to prison, a shattering ordeal for a sensitive, highbred woman. Francis was commanded to break the sentence to her. "I had to comfort and strengthen her to enable her to submit bravely," he wrote to Lainez. "I succeeded, thanks to God, Whose help was very necessary. I managed to cheer her so that she, who would have preferred death to such infamy and who left the prison more dead than alive, was so Christian that she felt the knowledge gained of truth and the pardon of her sins more than repaid her for the loss of honour, position and personal dignity" (June 16, 1559).

The summer passed. Philip was on his way home. Francis, for all his bad health, was still visiting and inspecting his foundations and enjoying those brief days of happiness at Simancas, among his novices and his flowers. He loved his garden. One day he picked a bunch of the sweet scented Indian pinks that the Emperor had grown at Yuste and tied them up as a present for a prince who was visiting Valladolid. He loved the music and the sound of the fresh young voices in the little chapel where he sometimes spent six or seven hours in prayer and, like Xavier, would remain wrapt in ecstasy while saying Mass till his impatient server, coming back after an hour or more, would have to bring him to earth by pulling his chasuble. His three special devotions were to the Passion, to the Blessed Sacrament and to our Lady, and these he was never tired of impressing on the novices. He gave them plenty of sound practical advice about preaching too, afterwards published in his *Advice to Preachers*. Humility was to be the Alpha and Omega, "lest, having preached to others, I myself become a castaway." There must be no eccentricity in matter or delivery, sound stuff suited to the mentality of listeners and, above all, sincerity. "Let the preacher consider himself only as a piece of artillery, with which God will batter and overthrow the proud walls of Babylon, and his own share in the business no more than a cold and heavy lump of iron or brass, with dirty powder, black, ugly and useless till touched by the fire of the Holy Ghost."

That humility he practised himself, sometimes with embarassing results. He would kneel at the novices' feet and answer remonstrances by saying that Christ had knelt to wash the Apostles' feet but that he himself was another Judas. One day he came into the kitchen and offered to help. The brother who was acting as cook and was very flustered over some unexpected guests for dinner did not know the Commissary General by sight and asked him curtly if he was capable of cooking. "No," was the answer, "I am not much good at anything except washing up." "Well, hurry up then and clean all those dirty pots and pans stacked in the scullery." The poor brother's apologies, when he discovered whom he had been ordering about, were met with a laugh.

All was peaceful these long, hot summer days in the former house of Juan de Mosquera, where he himself lived quietly in one corner. The additions that had been made when it was taken over as a noviciate were reminiscent of Oñate, poor, adobe walls, bare cells, nothing on the floors even of parlour and refectory except some coarse rush mats. The great yellow bulk of the castle dominated the little village, with its wide moat, its mighty walls of huge, rough stones, grey below, warm fawn where they rose to the battlements. The south gateway with its iron-hinged and studded door had a grille for the sentry who guarded what was no longer a palace but a store for royal archives. Down below, the half ruined brick tower of the church soared like a minaret above the tumbled brown roofs, and the tangle of crooked streets, half paved with lumps of stone, were generally crowded by women and girls carrying slim earthenware jars of water balanced on their hips, by donkeys in gay scarlet harness, mules with jangling bells and patient, wide-horned oxen being led to drink after their day's work in the fields. Often two black figures would be pushing their way through the jostling mob, novices begging from house to house and laden with alms in kind, as Father Francis had been at Oñate. He had a wide view from the garden, over the roofs to the poplar-fringed river, the only landmark in a flat expanse of ripening corn, green vineyards and rusty ploughed earth. Far to the east rose one square mountain looking like a giant's castle. The river, placid as a bronze mirror, reflected the tall, slim trees. The far distance melted into a blue only just deeper and more violet than the cloudless sky. Earth seemed transfused by heaven. All was peace.

The Inquisition was not idle. Carranza had incurred the enmity of Valdes, Archbishop of Seville and Grand Inquisitor, by having been appointed by Charles V as Archbishop of Toledo, an honour which Valdes wanted for himself, as Melchior Cano had done. Carranza was arrested (August 20, 1559) and his *Catechism* condemned as heretical. He called Francis as a witness in his favour. The Inquisitors, Cano among them, seized eagerly on this, and struck. The very day that Philip landed at Santander (September 8), Francis Borgia wrote to the General, Lainez. "While at Segovia I received the list of books condemned by the Inquisition, among them one attributed to me, *Christian Works*, a title which I never gave to any work nor even thought of. . . As it could be proved that the works attributed to me are not mine, the Archbishop of Seville and the members of the Inquisition Council were begged to wipe out the insult I have received and to declare that the works condemned were not mine. They did nothing. They answered that what had been decided had been well decided."

The truth of the matter was that *The Practice of Christian Works* which the Viceroy had composed at Barcelona and, when Duke of Gandia, had had published at Valencia, proved such a best-seller that there were various pirated editions, among them one in which a Medina del Campo bookseller had cunningly inserted other matter, some of it Lutheran heresy. Araoz, forgetting all differences and strained relations, worked hard in the service of his old friend. He made public the fraud and the names of the heretical authors. Nothing was gained. The Inquisitor, with his personal jealousy of Carranza and Francis, only replied Pilate-wise, "What I have written, I have written."

Poor foolish Carranza, already in the clutches of the Inquisition, was to spend seven more years in prison, till he was exculpated and released by Gregory XIII, an event noted by Francis in his diary for December 16, 1567, "Joy over the good news about my afflicted friend." Worn out with litigation and prison, the old man died soon after.

Francis Borgia was still at liberty. How long would it be before the dreaded familiars stood by his bed in the Jesuit house at Valladolid or in the noviciate at Simancas? The pack was unleashed. All those who hated the Jesuits, all those who hated the Commissary General for his influence with the Infanta Juana, were in full cry. Philip had written in the spring asking his old friend's advice, as Charles had often done, as to the best men for important posts in the kingdom, and immediately on his return to Spain, had taken that advice. He saw the Commissary

General in Madrid in October and, according to Araoz, "showed him much affection, was more demonstrative than ever before and discussed all kinds of things with him."

Such favour was brief and insecure. Philip, cautious and secretive, listened to talk. He was not likely to believe the gossip about the liaison of the Jesuit and the Princess, but he allowed the five worst scandalmongers to go unrebuked. Ruy Gomez did not lift a finger to help his cousin and benefactor. There was also another matter on which, from the material point of view, Philip had some show of reason. This was the large amount of money collected in alms which left Spain for Rome. The king had no intention of watching this stream, so badly needed to replenish his own empty treasury, flowing steadily into enemy coffers. Prudent as always, he listened, watched and waited.

A letter Francis had written to Lainez a little before the storm broke sounds a note of warning and approaching trouble. "I have only one desire these last months, to shed my blood for the catholic truth of the Roman Church. Yet, even while I desire this," he adds with trenchant humour against himself, "I quite see that I have not courage even to endure a mosquito bite! Yet it will truly be a death for me to have to die without shedding my blood for Him. Here I am, ready, if God will grant me the opportunity as He has given me the will" (Valladolid, June 29, 1559).

Martyrdom, unsought and unavoidable, might be easy to bear. It is always easier to face great tragedies than small pin-pricks or "mosquito bites." But Francis, ready as he was—too ready, some thought—to suffer humiliation, had not only himself to think of. He had to realise the fact that it was only one step from the condemnation of his work to the Inquisition prisons, only one step further from prison to the stake. It is one thing for a missionary to be done to death by heathen savages. No martyr's palm or crown awaited those who, clad in the grotesque San-Benito, made an *auto-da-fé* as popular a show as a bull-fight. If the best known Jesuit outside Rome, the Commissary General of Spain, Portugal and the Indies, were to be arrested, it was likely that all the work of the last eighteen years in Spain would be destroyed, all the favour Francis had won with Charles V undone.

Antonio de Cordova saw this and wrote to Lainez as frankly as he had spoken to Francis. "Father Francis avoids esteem and fame to such a degree that I have told him several times that such contempt for his honour and reputation lessens the charity he owes to those nearest to him and to the Company. I think that, in his great love for God, as he cannot give his life for God he prays hard to win martyrdom by the sacrifice of his good name, even to our prejudice. . . It seems as if, to try him, God has allowed Satan to strike all that belongs to him, his children, his house, his person. I only hope that, to increase His servant's sanctity, God will not allow the devil to get hold of the Company as well!"

If Francis was in a difficult position, Diego Lainez was in a worse one. Rome was buzzing with rumours about the troubles in Spain. The Society had had none too easy a time with the anti-Spanish Pope, and this complication was meat and drink to all its opponents. No news came for weeks either from Borgia or Araoz, and when at last the General did get a letter from Araoz it was two pages of complaints (someone else in Rome got eighteen!) about the Commissary General's rashness, the 'scandal' of sending such large alms to Rome, the lack of confidence shown to himself by telling him nothing. Lainez's reply did not beat about the bush. The alms were 'apostolic' rather than 'scandalous'. Nothing had been kept from the Provincial of Castille. "I call bread bread and wine wine." Then, to his amazement, Lainez learnt at the beginning of February, 1560, that Borgia had left Spain.

"I hear you are at Evora," he wrote to him, "I hope not because you wanted to hide yourself in a corner and entirely forget about your post. . . Now that you are peaceful and can write to me by a safe route I wish you to tell me (1) about your office, if you are carrying on and why you are in such obscurity; (2) if this is your reason for going to Portugal; (3) about the persecution raging against the Company" (February 9, 1560).

The explanation was that Francis had seized the opportunity afforded by an invitation from Cardinal Enrique, great-uncle and heir of little Sebastian, to attend the opening of the new university at Evora. He noted in his diary for October 25, 1566, "Act of thanksgiving for leaving Egypt seven years ago," to commemorate the anniversary of his crossing the frontier with Bustamente, another father and Brother Marcos.

His departure left the stage clear for Antonio Araoz who, apparently paralysed by his presence, now woke to speech, activity and volumes of complaints. It was all very unedifying. Lainez was right to make fun of the dismal prophecy of one brother that "The ruin of the whole Company is at hand," but none the less its work in Spain was being jeopardised by quarrels which opened a breach for its numerous enemies. Araoz had had legitimate reason to differ from Borgia, who was naturally autocratic, impatient, capable of organisation on the grand scale but inclined to push on to conquer new worlds, leaving to others the tiresome and difficult job of consolidating the old conquests. It is the nature of saints to trust absolutely to the divine Providence. This, to the eye of commonsense, is mad rashness. It was not so rare for some of the Jesuit houses Francis had founded on insufficient foundation and left entirely dependent on alms to find themselves penniless and foodless. Araoz, then, had had cause to complain in the past of Borgia's arbitrary arrangements and occasional outbursts of impatience or hot temper. Yet Francis's faults had not been committed for his personal advantage but for the greater glory of God. His temper flashed and was gone. He was always generously ready to apologize and make amends. Araoz's many good qualities were already tarnished by the fatal blight of court favour, too often deadly poison to religious life. A confidant of Ruy Gomez's and favourite of the King's, he was to revert more and more to the worldliness from which Ignatius had rescued him.

Meantime the love and enthusiasm with which Francis was welcomed in Portugal were some balm for his wounded spirit. If he were too ill to preach in the cathedral the Cardinal said, "It is enough if he only comes and lets the people see him." Ill as he was, he preached a series of Lenten sermons at Evora in 1560, lifted on to a mule or carried when unable to walk to the cathedral. There was the same affectionate reception at Lisbon from the Queen Regent. He moved on from there to Coimbra, Braga and Oporto, preaching, visiting the Jesuit houses and, at the bishop's request, founding a new one in Oporto. This, one of the most beautifully situated towns in the peninsula, lies at the mouth of the Douro, its noble houses and churches rising terrace above terrace from the river banks. "Healthy and temperate air and renowned for contemplation," says Cepari, and there in spite of work Francis found peace for a while. He preached, he gave Communion to thousands, he went through the streets ringing a little bell to call the children to catechism (an echo of the bell which his namesake had rung in Goa and Malacca and through the untrodden islands of Malay). But his best hours, five or six a day, were spent before the Blessed Sacrament in the little chapel of the new Jesuit house, lost "in highest prayer" (Cepari).

The lull was badly needed, for neither the storm in Spain nor Francis's bodily ills showed any signs of abating. In September came a letter from the General summoning him to Rome, in order to relieve him of his onerous duties and to give the fathers in Rome the benefit of his experience. Lainez saw that this was the only way to cut the Gordian knot.

q

Francis started from Oporto, was seized with gout, had to return by easy stages, then back in Oporto narrowly missed being killed by the fall of a heavy church grating.

Paul IV had died at the end of 1559, and the new Pope, Pius IV, at Lainez's request, ordered Francis to Rome. Cardinal Ippolito d'Este (the Duke's brother and Francis's cousin) added his persuasions. Nadal, who had left Rome in November to try and patch up things in Spain, found Araoz very difficult. "I had to handle him very carefully. In fact, to speak frankly, I was displeased with him." Of Francis he wrote, "I most earnestly desire his good and consolation. It seems to me that the best thing for him to do is to return to Spain" (January, 1561). That would indeed have been to put his head into the lion's mouth. Then someone suggested he should be sent to the Council of Trent, a course which Lainez vetoed. Theology was not Francis's strong point, nor was tact. Saints can be extremely inconvenient and it was no secret that Francis, for all his desire of martyrdom and his self-sacrificing work, had become a difficult problem. His work in Spain was done. He had outgrown it. A heavier cross, a more bitter cup were waiting for him in Rome.

PART III
IN AUTHORITY
(1565-1572)

CHAPTER XXIV

BEAST OF BURDEN

"I HAVE only one desire," Francis had written, "to shed my blood for Christ." He was not to shed his blood, but short of that, he had already endured a veritable martyrdom of mind and body. He was prostrate at Oporto when Nadal arrived in Spain (January, 1561). As if a combination of fever, gout, bladder trouble and rupture were not enough, he was now disabled with the recurrence of a nervous paralysis which had temporarily crippled him at Evora a year ago. "As it has attacked the fingers of my right hand I tell myself it is the finger of God striking me. If it gets worse it will save me a lot of work, such as writing. If the whole old man could stay paralysed, so much the better" (January 31, 1561).

Heart trouble and paralysis were both the result of nervous exhaustion, struggles with terrible difficulties and worse still, the necessity for a decision as to whether it would be for the best to go or stay. He had confided to Lainez how evenly balanced he found the arguments on each side. If he went to Rome he would be accused of showing by flight that he had a guilty conscience, accused too of seeking worldly advancement, and so undoing all he had done in Spain these last ten years. A winter journey, too, was impossible for reasons of health, a summer one dangerous from corsairs. Could he perhaps be relieved of his office? Allowed to retire and die in peace in the Jesuit house in Lisbon? "If however your Paternity decides that the Brief is to be obeyed, give the order. All difficulties will then be swept away by virtue of obedience" (November 25, 1560).

Nadal did not get to Coimbra till June, 1561. There he was met by Francis, who made to him a general confes-

sion of his whole life, as he had done to Ignatius in Rome
eleven years ago. "I told him to make his own decision
and he answered that he had decided to go," wrote Nadal,
and the decision once made, Francis acted with his usual
promptitude. He embarked for Bayonne, so as to avoid
passing through Spain, was driven back by contrary winds
and started overland (July 12). Nadal and the others were
alarmed. There was the risk of being arrested in Castille,
the certainty of Philip's anger being roused by this abrupt
departure. Rashness, however, was justified and the frontier crossed in safety. From Bayonne the fugitive wrote a
long letter of explanation and justification to the King.
Unluckily the original is lost, and as Suau points out, the
draft given by Vasquez shows signs of touching up. Early
biographers had, many of them, a passion for Ciceronian
periods, whose stately pomposity too often eradicates
all the trenchant sincerity and human nature of the origi-
nals.

The fire flamed up more violently than even in Castille.
Araoz's tongue and pen were equally fluent. The King
was furious. The Grand Inquisitor was angrier. Even
Francis's friends blamed him. Nadal, very prudently, drew
up a memoir disclaiming all responsibility. It would be
fatal for him to incur Philip's wrath. He wrote to Lainez,
"The storm raised by Father Francis's departure is so
violent and the sea grows so rough that it will not be easy
for us to defend ourselves" (November 5, 1561).

As the ex-Duke of Gandia had slipped through his fingers, Philip struck at his relations. Diego Borgia was
dragged from sanctuary in the Poor Clares' convent in
Madrid and beheaded for the murder of the Duke of Segorbe's son seven years before. Felipe only escaped the
same fate by a hurried flight to Africa.

Amid all this turmoil no one seems to have realised the
obvious reason for the Commissary General's journey to
Rome, obedience to the orders of the General and the
urgent summons of the Pope. It was for the best in the

end. The storm would never have abated as long as he remained in Spain or Portugal. It was impossible for him to
carry on the duties of his office, under the displeasure of
King and Inquisition as well as the now open hostility of
Araoz. His work there was done and it was good, in spite
of occasional rashness and impatience, such imperfections
as mar all human achievements.

Thus far his work and his outlook had been confined to
the Iberian Peninsula. Rome, head and centre of the universal Church, opened to him a horizon beyond the rising
sun in China and Japan, beyond the setting sun in Mexico,
Peru and Brazil. "To recount in detail the fruitful years
which Francis Borgia lived in Rome would be to write the
whole history of his Order," says Suau, and indeed the
next eleven years are as crowded as Titian's canvas of the
'Gloria' which rejoiced Charles V's eyes at Yuste.

Francis Borgia reached Rome on September 7, 1561,
two months after he had left Spain. He visited the Holy
House of Loreto on the way, the first of several pilgrimages there by which he showed his devotion to the Mother
of God. Lainez was not in Rome. He had been sent to
France by the Pope with the Cardinal Legate, Ippolito
d'Este. Alfonso Salmeron, whom Francis did not know so
well, was left in charge as Vicar General, but the following year both he and Lainez were sent as Papal theologians to the fourth and final session of the Council of
Trent and Francis was made Vicar General of the Order.
His health had much improved in the dry, clear air of
Italy, and the universal affection and admiration with
which he had been welcomed had proved the best of
tonics. The Pope, in particular, went out of his way to
show favour, so did the Pope's nephew, Charles Borromeo, Cardinal Archbishop of Milan, Grand Penitentiary
(1563) and administrator, living in great state in his princely palace but himself austere and mortified.

Even in the ten years since Francis Borgia's last visit an
immense change was visible in Rome. The splendour, lux-

ury and license of the Renaissance had faded and the new spirit of the Counter-Reformation, which would be more accurately named the Reformation within the Church, had introduced a strictness of life and morals which was to be still more accentuated under the next Pope, Pius V. Francis, who had nothing in common with the artistic and intellectual glories of the Renaissance, was entirely at home in the new atmosphere. John Addington Symonds, in his great work on the Italian Renaissance, has emphasised, perhaps over-emphasised, the fact that this new spirit was that of Spanish piety, austere, in spite of its splendour, martial, unfaltering in its defence of the Church and Faith, and fearless in its attacks on heresy. The Council of Trent had defined the dogmas of the Catholic Faith. With the need, as always, had arisen the man. Ignatius of Loyola, less even than Francis Borgia, had not been a great intellectualist, humanist or theologian. Yet, on lines of daring innovation, he created the Order which was the one best fitted both to attack heresy and to defend the integrity of dogma. And after him Francis Borgia was not only to carry on but to consolidate and widen his work.

Meanwhile Francis, as Vicar General, went quietly on his way. He preached in the Lent of 1562 in the Spanish church of Sant' Iago to a mixed congregation of cardinals, nobles, professors and poor people. The last, like the Basques, understood not a word of his Castillean, but they recognised sanctity when they saw it. In spite of the beautiful Italian in which he had written his first letter to Ignatius, Francis never felt too sure of himself in that language. When he went to interview the Pope at the Vatican he always took Polanco with him to interpret if necessary or to clear up difficulties. When an important letter had to be written to any of the Italian superiors too he would explain that Polanco was writing for him.

His two special friends outside his own Order were Pope St Pius V (elected 1566), and Charles Borromeo.

Michele Ghislieri, the stern and austere Dominican who
was head of the Inquisition in Rome before he was made
Pope, had determined to make a Holy War against Islam
the outstanding event of his Pontificate, and it was natural
that he should realise the value of Francis Borgia as an ally.
Borromeo, when ordained priest (1563), came to sleep in
the Jesuit house of Santa Maria della Strada the night after
saying his first public Mass, and celebrated his first private
one in the little chapel on the altar which Ignatius of Loyola had used and at which Francis now celebrated his
Mass every morning. The next year the young Cardinal
did the Spiritual Exercises under Father de Ribera and
was so deeply impressed by them that he began to lead a
life of sanctity which his Papal uncle considered extreme.

The Council of Trent ended at last, but Lainez did not
get back to Rome till February, 1564, and soon after he
notified the provincials that Francis Borgia had been appointed Assistant of Spain and Portugal, "for which he is
well fitted, thanks to his spiritual gifts, his prudence, experience and many other qualities which God has endowed him with."

It was good for Francis to know that he was appreciated,
that his work during the absence of Lainez and Salmeron
had been successful, but once more there was trouble, this
time, luckily, nothing to do with him personally. Borromeo had suggested to Pius IV that the Jesuits should be
put in charge of the new seminary to be founded in Rome.
Cardinal Sabelli wished them to give the examinations of
candidates for Holy Orders. Cardinal Farnese intended to
send them round to visit and report on parishes. All this
was favourable to the Society but of course it raised a
storm of angry and jealous protests. Suddenly the Pope,
alarmed at his nephew's change of life, his extreme austerity and determination to be a saint, also turned against
the Jesuits who had caused this. He refused even to see
Lainez or listen to explanations. Father de Ribera, who

had given the Exercises to the young Cardinal Archbishop with all too successful results, thought it diplomatic to ask leave to be sent on the Indian mission.

The storm blew over. On July 31, 1564, the anniversary of Ignatius's death, the Pope visited the professed houses of the Society in Rome, as well as the Roman and German Colleges. He repeated his orders for the Jesuits to direct the new seminary, though Lainez saw that this was a sign of favour to be avoided if possible. The house was bought for the seminary but never used, for the project was abandoned after Pius IV's death in the following year.

These complications, on top of all his work at the Council, were too much for Lainez, who had been ailing for the last year. Determined to say Mass on the Epiphany, a feast for which he had a special devotion, he just managed to do so, then sank into Francis's arms, with the murmur, "Take me to my room, Father Francis, for I shall never again stand at the altar of God." He died a fortnight later, without having named a successor, but the fathers round his bed saw him, when past speech, fix a long and imploring look on Francis Borgia. The next day the professed fathers in Rome elected Francis Vicar General, so it fell to him to summon the second General Congregation of the Company of Jesus for June, 1565.

He made a typically generous and impulsive gesture towards Araoz by wishing to prolong his appointment as Commissary General of Spain, until it was pointed out to him that this was exceeding his powers, as such appointments ended with the death of the general who had made them.

The Vicar General had a strenuous time during the next few months. Not only had he to arrange for billeting and feeding the professed fathers from all the European provinces, but money had to be conjured from somewhere to reinforce the slender pittance of alms which barely sufficed for the needs of the Jesuits in Rome. His former position in the world and his many friends were useful. He wrote himself to many of them, to Antonio de Cordova asking him to beg, to Miguel de Torres, telling him to obtain from the young King Sebastian and from friends in Portugal all possible help. The Duchess of Frias (who had put up Francis on his way from Oñate) had in her will left the Society a thousand ducats. Somehow they must be got to Rome. The *buen viejo* Bustamente was also appealed to. At last enough money was obtained to cover expenses, lodgings for everyone were arranged and the second General Congregation opened its sessions in Ignatius's old room. In that small cell thirty-nine electors were crowded, among them St Peter Canisius and Blessed Ignatius Azevedo, afterwards Apostle of Brazil. A week after the opening on June 21, 1565, began the four days of prayer which were the preparation for voting. It was fairly obvious on whom the choice would fall. Francis begged all to be swayed by no worldly consideration but to judge by merit alone. He wished privately to impress his own unworthiness on each elector, but Salmeron and Ribadeneira wisely dissuaded him.

St Ignatius had clearly defined in the Constitutions the qualities he considered necessary for the head of the Society, close union with God through prayer, charity, humility, mortification, wisdom, judgment, vigilance, perseverance, capacity for successful organisation, honour, authority and the requisite amount of bodily health. Such a combination of virtues seemed impossible except in a great saint. Ignatius of Loyola united them all. So, the electors believed, did Francis Borgia.

The first scrutiny of votes showed that, by thirty-one votes out of the thirty-nine, Francis Borgia was appointed General of the Society of Jesus (July 2, 1565). His diary for that day had the words, *"Dies meae crucis"* (day of my crucifixion).

Tragedy or suffering had marked each stage of Francis's progress in sanctity. His severe illness in 1536, the death of the Empress and that of Eleonor each in its turn perfected his detachment from the world and from self. Persecution, calumny and enmity had broken the last remains of his natural autocracy, arrogance, impatience and hot temper. Man is not perfect, but Francis shows few traces of his old faults in the eleven years between his departure from Spain and his death. The *Spiritual Diary*, printed by Suau at the end of his Life of St Francis Borgia, and also published in the original Spanish in the *Borgiana*, was found among the Jesuit archives in Rome and was meant for no eye but its writer's. It begins February 1, 1564 and continues, with gaps due to illness or loss of the books, till February 1, 1570. Love of God, humility and desire for suffering are its chief notes. "I have prayed to the Holy Ghost for love, to lose the love of created things, to give all to Him and to love with the love with which He loves us" is entered on the first day, and on the last, "Desire to shed my blood for His love."

These copy-books, whose cheap, common paper is so thin that the ink blots through the page, are a marvellous revelation of the inner life of a great saint. The writing is irregular, broken, sometimes quite illegible, with an upward sweep of optimism, that of a man living at high nervous pressure controlled by an iron will. There are two autograph letters of Francis's among the archives in Simancas Castle. One was written by him when Marquis of Lombay in 1530, in a firm, even, dominant hand. The other is addressed from Barcelona during the last year of his life to Philip II, in the weak and broken scrawl of a hand hardly able to grasp a pen, signed "*su obedientissimo servidor Franco.*"

A week after his election as General, Francis writes in his diary, "I offer myself, my blood and my life, for the Company." He began the Exercises on July 11 "for my reform and that of others," and from now on the refrain is repeated again and again, "To do His Will or die." "To die or be made wholly His." "To be taken or given grace to govern or to be relieved of office." All human wishes or desires were shed or submerged entirely in the desire to do the Will and work of God.

"September 3," he notes, "the Congregation finished, with grace and thanksgiving." Polanco, less brief, has described how Francis ended the sessions "by an explanation of the virtues necessary for us. Finally, amid general emotion, he kissed the feet of each one. All embraced with many signs of mutual affection and left Rome very satisfied."

The end of Francis's farewell speech is very individual. "I will add only one word about myself. I beg you to behave to me as you would to a beast of burden. It is not enough to load them. One must see that they keep going. If they stumble one helps them. If they are slow one whips them. If they fall help them up. If they are worn out take off their load. I am your beast of burden. Treat me as such . . . Have only one heart, one soul. Bear one another's burdens so that I can bear yours. Fill me with joy that your joy may be perfect and no man can take it from you. . . I kiss your feet, begging God that they may be swift as harts' feet to tell of peace and happiness and that, at last, having reached the heights, they may enter into rest eternal."

CHAPTER XXV

SEVEN HILLS

THE Viceroy of Catalonia had written that he was
more in his element on horseback scouring the
country for brigands or game than sitting cooped
up at Council Meetings. The Commissary General had
covered thousands of miles on foot or on a mule during
his continual travels through Spain and Portugal. The
General of the Society of Jesus was not to leave the seven
hills of Rome for the next six years, except for one journey
in northern Italy, a rare pilgrimage to Loreto, and visits to
Frascati or Tivoli to convalesce after attacks of gout or
fever.

The house at whose door he had first met Ignatius, the
garden on which the windows of his room had looked
down those four winter months fifteen years ago, were
now to be his home. The little church of Santa Maria della
Strada, where he had first received Communion from
Ignatius's hand, was now the centre of his spiritual life.

The church, old and dilapidated when it had first been
handed over to the Jesuits, in spite of periodical patching,
was now totally inadequate for the congregation who
crowded it. Not only was it not weatherproof, it was dangerous and might collapse at any time. The necessity for
rebuilding it was urgent. The Chancellor, Cardinal Alessandro Farnese, promised to be responsible for the expenses of the work (1566). A year later the General wrote,
"If the Cardinal does not soon make up his mind, as he
promised us he would, we shall begin work, trusting to
the purse of God, Who is even more rich" (October 10,
1567).

Though the Cardinal had consented to back the bill
for the building of the new church of the Gesù, four

thousand five hundred crowns had to be raised for the purchase of the site. Not trusting to 'God's purse' alone the General wrote a host of begging letters, to the Empress Maria, wife of Maximilian II, to the Duke of Bavaria, the Viceroy of Catalonia, his cousin the Duke of Medina Sidonia, the Spanish provincials and others. One of his best recruits at Oñate and one of the dearest to him of the younger generation, was no longer there to help. Antonio de Cordova had died in the spring of 1567 and Francis's letter of condolence to Antonio's mother, the Marquesa de Pliego, shows that his detachment from earthly things had in it nothing cold or inhuman. "I am the one who needs to receive comfort rather than to give it. . . I confess to having said, when I heard of his death, 'What a loss for us' . . . I let myself be overcome with sorrow. . . How easily the flesh is blinded and how easily it gives way. . . It continues obstinately to consider gain as loss. Señora, why did God give him to you? Why did I receive him at Oñate? So that he should belong entirely to Jesus Christ on earth and in heaven" (March 11, 1567).

Francis hoped to have the foundation of the new church laid on March 25, 1568. "I should be happy if the church which is to bear His Name could be begun on the day on which He began to take on human flesh." But the ceremony could not take place till the Cardinal Chancellor got back from Sicily, and it was only on June 26, 1568, that he solemnly laid the foundation stone which the Cardinal of Augsburg had blessed.

The old church was poor and miserable. The house adjoining it was also far too small to hold the increasing number of professed fathers. But it was filled with the spirit of Ignatius. The little bare cell upstairs, with its white walls, its heavily beamed ceiling, its window looking on to the Blessed Sacrament in the church, was still a power station from which radiated light and heat, comfort and wisdom. The life, so strenuously filled with prayer and work, which he had lived, was repeated in his successor.

It was no longer possible for Francis to spend six or seven
hours in contemplation, caught out of time and space, like
St Paul, seeing and hearing things "which it is not lawful
to utter." There was little time left for relaxation or for
sleep, in the tiny room next the high altar, in the narrow
camp-bed, without head or curtains. When business over-
flowed its limits it was sleep, not prayer, that was curtailed.
He writes to one of the Poor Clares at Gandia: "If you
could only see my work by day and night! I do nothing
but read and write letters, busy myself with rules, Constitutions, professors, classes. You will understand that
the little free time left to my poor head it spends in rest
or in asking help from our Lord, like a sword carried here
and there but not knowing where it is. Time slips away.
Enough. Let us work and keep silence" (January 13,
1568).

That enormous correspondence, flung like an invisible
net across and round the world, grew daily, weekly,
monthly. Nearly seven hundred letters of Francis Borgia,
written between 1565 and 1572, are published in the *Borgiana*. The notes for twenty letters, written in one day alone
(May 8, 1568) fill twenty pages of close writing. How
many hours a day were spent at his desk, with constant
interruptions, writing or dictating to Polanco letters to
Jesuit superiors, fathers in Europe, Asia, Africa and the
New World, to Cardinals, bishops, nuns, to his children
and relations in Spain. He kept in touch not only with
Carlos at Gandia, often in the throes of a fresh lawsuit,
with Juan and his wife, with his widowed brother-in-law,
the Duke of Villahermosa, with his sons-in-law, the Marquis of Alcañices and the Duke of Lerma, with the Poor
Clare nuns at Gandia and Madrid.

Messengers came and went between Rome and Gandia,
taking presents from the General to his son, his grandson
and namesake whom he had never seen, and the other
three grandsons. Carlos acknowledges a terrestrial globe,
with the naïve remark "I never knew how small the world

was till I saw this," also a book on hunting, a watch, which gives rise to pious remarks on the flight of time, statues of saints, a *retablo*, etc. Francis, in his turn, received several cases of sugar from the famous Valencian factories, seven boxes of jam and sweets from the Poor Clares of Gandia, among whom (1567) he numbered three sisters and three granddaughters. Two years later more cases of preserves arrive in Rome. "They are not necessary," he dictates before setting out on a pilgrimage to Loreto, "do not send any more."

Juan perhaps received more letters than his brothers. He was gentleman in waiting to the unfortunate Don Carlos, as was his brother-in-law the Marquis, and later Spanish ambassador at Lisbon. Francis's younger sons were not forgotten. Ferdinand was a knight of Calatrava, and a marriage was arranged for Alfonso by his father through Carlos (1567). A touching letter came from an old servant who begged the General not for an answer but for prayers, "I was born to serve you all the days of my life." Long and pious effusions from the Gandia convent, where his half-sister was now Abbess, continued in spate. "Not wishing to weary you," writes his sister Elizabeth; but they did! Francis wrote resignedly but despairingly to the Provincial of Toledo: "I write to my sisters so that your Reverence may not think me inhuman. Please believe me, my dear Father, that I love them as sisters and because their goodness compels me still more to love them. But I have always felt that unnecessary letters are not exactly a pleasure. Still, I will write" (June 15, 1569).

There were other letters, less intimate and perhaps more important. Among the "princes, lords and kings of Christendom" who, Ribadeneira tells us, corresponded with the General, were the Cardinal of Augsburg, the Duke of Savoy, the Empress Maria, her four daughters, the Duchess of Milan, the Duchess of Ferrara (wife of Francis's cousin Alfonso), the Princesses Magdalena and Helena of Austria, Don Francisco de Toledo, Viceroy of

r

Peru, Catherine de Medici, Queen-Mother of France, Philip II of Spain, the Queen Regent of Portugal.

Such a herculean task would have been impossible but for the help of Father Juan de Polanco, who had been Ignatius's secretary and right hand and had probably known more of the inner working of the founder's mind and spirit than any of the younger generation of Jesuits. His entrance into the Society had been adventurous, for he had escaped by a rope from the window of the room in Tuscany where he had been imprisoned by his family to prevent his wasting his talents with the new eccentrics.

The Toledan, Alfonso Salmeron, whom Francis had just met in 1551, was in Rome during the General Congregation of 1565 and after the election of the new General. He was the outstanding figure of the three original companions of Ignatius still alive. The erratic and fiery Bobadilla, after incurring the founder's anger by his rash behaviour in Germany, had been the only one to vote against Lainez's election as General and was now wandering to and fro, mounted on a white horse and, as Salmeron caustically said, "making elephants out of flies." Simon Rodriguez, under a cloud too since the turmoil in Portugal, had been forbidden to return there from Spain. Salmeron had known Ignatius from the beginning and always his life had been closely linked with that of Lainez. The two had been Papal theologians at the various sessions of the Council of Trent, and that neat head and parrot profile contained not only the deepest theological knowledge but wisdom and shrewd common-sense. Such a man was invaluable to the new General, and Francis showed his appreciation by inducing Salmeron to bring into some order the chaos of notes which were the only deposits of his enormous learning. The last twenty years of his life (1565-1585) were spent mainly in this task, in which he was helped at Naples by the young Robert Bellarmine.

Another famous Jesuit had been in Rome for the General Congregation, St Peter Canisius, the Dutchman who,

as a young student, had been converted by Peter Faber at
Cologne and was to become the second Apostle of Germany and a Doctor of the Church. He and the General did
not always see eye to eye, one keen on local needs, the
other with a wider outlook on the work of the Society.
Francis had already written with more than a touch of impatience to tell Canisius he wanted too much for the College at Innsbruck, and expected "a new man for every
hour." The two were agreed that Salmeron had been the
greatest theologian at Trent, but it was Canisius who was
set the gigantic task of drawing up the Catechism of the
Council of Trent and was sent by the General the orders
of the Pope to answer the Protestant calumnies in the
Centuries of Magdeburg.

There was one Jesuit in the house who saw even more of
Francis, Brother Marcos, still the stern nurse with the wil-
ful child when prudence was being drowned by mortification. How often he had to knock at the General's door,
as he had done in old days in Spain, to tell him it was time
to stop praying and go to bed, and what a deaf ear he
turned to the pathetic plea, "A little longer, Brother Marcos, just a little longer."

One personality stood out vividly in the crowd of students, novices and priests packed uncomfortably into the
small house. Pedro de Ribadeneira, like Salmeron, was
Toledan. A page in the splendid house of Cardinal Farnese, he had run away at the age of sixteen to fling himself
at the feet of Ignatius, and though one of the wildest and
most undisciplined of his novices, had been one of the
dearest to his heart. It was in a letter from him in Flanders
that Francis Borgia had learnt of the death of Ignatius,
and it was under obedience to Francis that Ribadeneira began to write the life of the founder (1566). His was to be
the first published biography of Francis Borgia, the best
of all the earlier ones because of its first-hand knowledge,
its sincerity and honesty, and the source from which the
hagiographers of the next three centuries mainly derived

their information. Vital incidents stand out in the liquid flow of Ribadeneira's beautiful Castillean like rocks breaking the ripples of a sunlit stream. He was often out with the General in his walks through Rome and tells how one day they met a rider on a thoroughbred horse whose points were set off by resplendent harness. Ribadeneira, with a true Spanish eye for a good horse, was surprised to see that his companion, once the best rider at the Spanish court and owner of famous stables, had not even noticed the beast. Roused from his abstraction Francis's answer seems slightly irritated. "Thanks be to God, Who has delivered me from horsemen and horses." That he had not really lost his judgment for horses is shown by another incident, this time on his way from Valencia to Madrid in 1571. He met a cavalier on so beautiful an Arab mount that he could not help expressing his admiration. The man dismounted at the next inn and sent back his horse, begging Francis to accept it as a gift. It was returned with a message of thanks and a remark that so fine a beast was not fitting for a poor religious.

There were many of these walks through Rome, from the Piazza Navona, often deep in water when the Tiber was in flood, to the malarial quarter by the Trinità dei Monti, where pestilences usually were worst, through the maze of narrow old streets round the Maria della Strada into the straight wide avenue newly finished by Pius IV (now the Via Quirinale) up to Monte Cavallo, over the yellow Tiber by the Ponte Sant' Angelo, under the grim round tower of the castle, to St Peter's, where the scaffolding still hid the façade and the great dome left unfinished by Michael Angelo at his death in 1564.

Again and again the General was summoned to the Vatican by Pius IV, and still more often by Pius V. The latter, Francis Borgia and Charles Borromeo, the late Pope's nephew, were three outstanding figures of the Counter-Reformation. There was another, a simple priest living with a few others by the poor church of Santo Girolamo della Carità but known as the Apostle of Rome, St Philip Neri. The Jesuit General and the humble Florentine had apparently little in common but sanctity, but one saying of St Philip's might have served as the motto for St Francis Borgia. "Throw yourself into God's hands and be sure that, if He wants anything from you, He will give you all you need for the work."

Francis always took Polanco with him to the Vatican and often Cristobal Rodriguez as well, whose life had been an adventurous one: an embassy to Cairo, a mission among Calabrian brigands, infirmarian at Malaga in charge of seven hundred plague-stricken patients, chaplain to the Spanish fleet. He was to be chaplain on Don John's flagship, at the battle of Lepanto.

The Pope and the General made a striking picture as they paced to and fro in the Raphael rooms upstairs or in Bramante's great court. The Pope was sixty-eight, but the fire and resolution of youth still burned in the frail body emaciated by mortification, and in his fierce face, with its keen eyes, long nose and thin lips. The General too was no more than skin and bone, but his great height made him tower above the bowed figure of the old Dominican. The dream of Pius V's pontificate was to unite the princes of Christendom in a great crusade against the Turk. While the Jesuit fathers had been in Rome for the Congregation the Turkish fleet under Piali and the famous corsair Dragut had invested Malta (May 18, 1565). It was only saved by an heroic defence by the Knights of St John under La Valette and the somewhat tardy arrival of the Spanish fleet in September. Since the end of the truce in 1552 the Sultan Suleyman had never ceased hostilities against the Emperor, and Transylvania and Hungary were under Turkish dominion. At his death in 1566 Suleyman left his son an empire of forty thousand square miles and a fleet which had never been defeated. Little wonder that Pius V had resolved to strain every nerve to drive back the power of Islam and to prevent the Mediterranean from being a

Turkish lake. In Francis Borgia, head of the Church's
newest Order, founded and organised to meet the needs
of the day, in him, a Spaniard whose ancestors for the last
three hundred years had been engaged in the fight to make
and keep Spain Christian, Pius V found the ally whose
power and experience he considered would be invaluable.

Fond as he was of the Society and friendly with the
General, yet the Dominican Pope made two enactments
entirely contrary to the spirit of Ignatius. He wished it to
be compulsory for all Jesuit fathers to sing Office publicly
in choir, while none were to be ordained priests till after
they had been professed, that is, taken their final vows.
Francis argued and entreated. Pius was adamant. The
Society obeyed his wishes during his lifetime but was released from them by his successor, Gregory XIII.

There were many ghosts for the former Duke of Gandia
as he passed through the Borgia apartments on his visits
to the Vatican. There was the well-known Pinturicchio
profile of Alexander VI, egg-shaped head, massive, sensual face with piercing dark eyes, high-bridged nose like
Francis's own, bull-like solidity of neck and shoulders; the
Pinturicchio of Lucrezia, like some pretty, foolish dairy-
maid, long, butter-yellow hair, milky skin, blue eyes and
rosebud mouth; that red devil Cesare, with his fine-cut
aquiline nose, delicately sensual, cruel mouth and sleepy,
heavy-lidded eyes.

Sometimes the way would lead past the square corner
house or the other, also an inn, which had both belonged
to the low-born Vanozza, mistress of Alexander VI, and
mother by him of Francis's grandfather, Juan, second
Duke of Gandia. There was a darker memory still, that
corner by the Jewish quarter where the city's filth was
tipped into the Tiber, where the searchers' nets had fished
up Juan's body, fouled by slime and ordure, gashed with
wounds, still in his satin doublet, with his purse full of
gold, and long golden spurs on his high riding-boots.

The ghosts that haunted the Vatican, the Castle of Sant'

Angelo, the dark streets of the Giudecca and the turgid river were those of men and women whose names, whether rightly or wrongly, stand for all the wickedness and violence of the Italian Renaissance, for adultery, incest, murder, cruelty, treachery. Their blood ran in Francis Borgia's veins. He had been conscious in himself of passions which, if not controlled, would lead him also to disaster. "The dragon which wears me out," "these two beasts of hot temper and lust," "I am in the power of my passions," "that I may be delivered from my passions," these notes continually recur in his diary and show that, saint as he was in the eyes of the world, he was more and more acutely aware of his own imperfections.

There were no more of the old excessive penances. His own body, the digestion which Ignatius had foreseen would be ruined by extreme abstinence, the frequent gout and fits of fever were all better mortifications than any he could have imposed himself. The penances given by God are so much more stimulating to the soul's growth than those imagined by man. Francis had always known that love is inseparable from sacrifice, the greater the love the greater the sacrifice. He knew too that the best sacrifice of all is the sacrifice of self, the nailing of the human will to the Divine as Christ was nailed to the Cross.

He had written that little time was now available for contemplative prayer. Araoz had been right, so had St Teresa, when they saw in the former Duke of Gandia the makings of a great contemplative. But St Ignatius knew, as St Thomas Aquinas had known, that the most perfect, as it is the most difficult life, is the one which unites the contemplative and the active.

Every available moment was snatched from business to pray. "Continual prayer made a habit of finding God in outward things, so all places became an oratory, all things material for recollection and prayer." His tiny room near the high altar became "his corner of refuge and retreat, a nest where he escaped the bustle and tumult of business"

(Ribadeneira). His life was the expression of the spirit of the Exercises, "the love which shows itself more clearly in works than words," of that wonderful prayer of St Ignatius, "Take, O Lord, and receive my entire liberty, my memory, my understanding, my whole will."

CHAPTER XXVI

FOUNDATIONS

" I KNOW you will be sorry for me because of your great love for me and because you know how much against the grain this is with me," wrote Francis on his election as General to his dear Antonio de Cordova. "However, as it has so pleased our Lord, that is reason enough for me to rejoice to serve Him. If the slave dies on the cross, then he dies on it with his Master. One of the trials of this cross is that it entails such a rush of business, especially at first, that one has scarcely time to breathe . . . But I can fancy, with pleasure, how you will cheer me, bid me be of good courage, bow my head and lift the cross" (Rome July 31, 1565).

The General Congregation indeed bequeathed the General a huge legacy of work. It had elected four Assistants for him, Antonio Araoz for Spain, an Italian, Benito Palmio for Italy and Sicily, Diego Miron (Simon Rodriguez's successor at Coimbra) for Portugal, Brazil and the Indies, and Everard Mercurian (the Belgian who would succeed Francis as fourth General) for France and Germany. They also decreed the foundation of a professed house and a noviciate in every province, the revision and publication of the Constitutions.

The appointment of Assistants entailed residence in Rome. Borgia wrote an affectionate and charming letter to Araoz the very day after his appointment, claiming his help "since the pilot who steers the ship is so wretchedly weak," welcoming him to Rome and suggesting he should arrive in October "before the rainy season begins" (July 29, 1565). The answer to this was a curt letter from Philip at Segovia (September 8) forbidding Araoz to leave Spain. Francis replied with a diplomatic hope that the delay in

Araoz's departure would only be a short one (October 26).
He also wrote a personal appeal to Ruy Gomez, as well as
one to Araoz, telling him of the Pope's death and his own
need of help. "Fly to help me carry this cross which my
bad health makes so heavy. The Pope was in good health.
I never expected to outlive him. Come quickly" (December 15). Polanco also wrote that Araoz's presence and help
would certainly prolong the General's life.

No one in Spain doubted that it was Araoz's own desire
to stay at court which inspired the difficulties made to his
departure. An imperious communication from the King
(Madrid, March 2, 1566) brought a final refusal to let
Araoz go. There was nothing left for the General but to
submit.

Araoz never came to Rome. He was chosen by Philip
as his confessor, and Nadal, who had been named Assistant
in his place, wrote caustically from Mayence: "God help
the Basque if he is the King's confessor. If he is not, God
help him to be what he should be, a good religious"
(February 20, 1567). "The Basque," whose conscience
apparently troubled him not at all, continued to scribble
to his superior and old friend what Francis described as
"most friendly and affectionate letters eighteen sheets
long." He died in the year after Francis. "More and more
friendly with Ruy Gomez, more and more overwhelmed
with business, he paid hardly any attention to apostolic
work for several years" (Suau).

The Congregation had strongly recommended that
existing foundations should be strengthened rather than
new ones made without enough men or money. Francis,
realising his own old faults of rashness and impatience,
saw the wisdom of this advice. He wrote to an old friend,
Francisco de Toledo, Viceroy of Peru, who had offered to
endow a new college, and regretfully refused. "The Congregations considered that colleges should be closed down
rather than new ones opened. This year it has been necessary to shut three." A rule was made that twenty was the

smallest number of Jesuits to justify a new foundation,
and the General was forced to refuse another offer from
Juan de Avila, whose funeral sermon on the Empress had
so deeply impressed him. "The scarcity of workers in
many parts is such that it is only with great difficulty that
I dare open new colleges in Spain."

In spite of this new prudence the decision of the General
Congregation to have a professed house and noviciate in
every province was carried out, and during Francis's
generalship houses were founded at Toledo (1566), in the
house of the Count of Orgaz who has been immortalised
by the famous El Greco painting of his funeral, at Valencia, at Seville and a new one at Valladolid (1567). This last
was in the parish of San Esteban, adjoining the church of
St Ambrose, now the Scots' College.

Francis must surely have had a pang of regret when the
noviciate at Simancas was closed, to be superseded by one
at Villarejo, for Toledo, and another at Villagarcia, a few
miles out of Valladolid. This, the childhood home of Don
John of Austria, was given on her husband's death by
Doña Magdalena de Ulloa, widow of Don John's tutor
and the majordomo of Charles V. In all, eleven colleges
were opened in Spain between 1565 and 1572.

France had, so far, been a fallow field. The Society,
though favoured by the King, Henry II, the Cardinal of
Lorraine and most of the bishops, had been prevented
from founding a house for students at the Paris University by the enmity of the Archbishop of Paris and the
Faculty of Theology. The ban had only been finally lifted
and full participation in the privileges of the university
accorded to Jesuit students after the visit of Lainez in
1563. Borgia now wrote to Catherine de Medici and to the
young king, Charles IX, obtained from Parliament the
revocation of the last unfavourable edicts and founded
colleges at Lyons, Avignon, Never, Pont à Mousson,
Roanne, Bellom, Verdun and Bordeaux. Colleges were
opened in Belgium at St Omer, Tournai, Liège and Lou-

vain, in Bohemia at Olmutz, in the Tirol at Halle and Innsbruck (for which Canisius so eagerly demanded masters),
in Germany at Würzburg, Fulda and Spires. A Polish
province was inaugurated with five colleges and the General even dreamed of founding one in Russia.

Besides foundations, the first two years of Borgia's
generalship were occupied by the revision and publication
of the Constitutions. These rules for the government of
the Society had been composed by St Ignatius (1547-1550)
and confirmed in every essential by the first General Congregation after his death. The edition printed under Francis's supervision in 1567 is, but for a few slight alterations,
the same as that published by Mercurian in 1580, which is
still the official constitution of the Society of Jesus.

There was however one important change in the day's
routine which Francis had urged, though unsuccessfully,
on the first General Congregation. St Ignatius had laid
down one hour of private prayer a day, to include the two
particular examinations of conscience at midday and night
of a quarter of an hour each. Francis, empowered to
lengthen this time, wrote, "The morning there will be
three quarters of an hour's prayer, not counting the two
quarters before dinner and bedtime. This last is to be increased to half an hour, so that there will be half an hour
divided between vocal and mental prayer" (October 6,
1565).

This rule was not a hard and fast one. Spain was allowed
to continue the unbroken hour's meditation which was
customary there. Nadal wrote that in Austria and Germany
"The fathers find it difficult to meditate for half an hour
after dinner as they go to sleep and waste their time!"
(February 20, 1567). So the meditation was changed to the
morning, on an empty stomach instead of on a full one!

Another important work undertaken under Francis's
supervision was the rule of studies for Jesuit Colleges.
This occupied the learned Father de Ledesma from his
return to Rome after the Diet of Augsburg (1566) till his

death nine years later. His work is the basis of the famous *Ratio Studiorum* published in 1583.

Francis, not a great scholar himself, was a shrewd judge of intelligence as well as of character. Aware of young Robert Bellarmine's great promise, he arranged for him to leave Padua for Louvain in 1568. He was fully conscious too of the organising gift and able personality of Alessandro Valignani, a young Neapolitan noble who had entered the Society in Rome (1565) and who was to leave two years after Francis's death to be one of the greatest Visitor Generals of the Jesuit missions in the East. In the Roman College, housed in a big bleak monastery given in 1560, there were names of professors and students to become famous beyond their own circle of a hundred and fifty Jesuits and the six hundred students, soon to be over a thousand. Francisco de Toledo, Ledesma and Emmanuel de Sa were some of the professors; Christopher Clavius, afterwards teacher of Matteo Ricci, and the best known mathematician in Europe, was a student. Another student, Jean Leunis, was to found the Sodality of the Blessed Virgin in the College, a devotion specially dear to Francis's heart.

The General Congregation had decreed the foundation of a noviciate as well as a house for professed fathers in every province, and this too was a work to which Francis eagerly put his hand. He had never let the grass grow under his feet. He had written when at Barcelona that the idea of a good work should be followed at once by action. Within three weeks of the dispersal of the Congregation in September, 1565, he had inaugurated noviciates for Rome and the other Italian provinces. That in Rome was specially needed, not only because Rome was the head and centre of the Society as of the Church, but because the house near the Piazza Minerva was crowded to suffocation with professed fathers, students and novices. The General's former position in the world was useful, for it had brought him into touch with many who proved generous benefactors. Luigi Crici, Bishop of Tivoli, had given the Society a site on Monte Cavallo (the Quirinal). This was only a mile away from Santa Maria della Strada, but was high, cool and healthy, well above the malarial swamps which bred fever and pestilence, and it contained a small, half-ruined chapel of St Andrew. It had been intended for a convalescent home for sick fathers, but Francis saw in it the ideal spot for his noviciate. Funds for the foundation were promised by the Duchess Juana of Aragon, mother of Marc Antonio, Duke of Pagliano and Hereditary Grand Constable of Naples.

Francis threw himself heart and soul into the work. The house was to resemble as far as possible his dear Simancas. All was to be plain, bare, severe, redolent of holy poverty, so as thoroughly to try the vocation and perseverance of novices, as had been laid down by Ignatius in the Constitutions. Building was actually begun on August 12, 1566; and the tall, thin figure in the shabby habit, an old straw hat in summer, an equally battered felt in winter, became familiar, striding up the long slope to Monte Cavallo or hobbling with a stick or the help of a companion's arm after an attack of gout or fever. Francis notes in his diary prayers and Masses said "in joy and hope," a triduum of Masses ending on St Andrew's day, 1566, and visits to the building to oversee and hasten the work.

It was delayed by a terrible pestilence which broke out that year (1566) in the marshy quarter by the Trinità dei Monti and swept through the city. Four thousand homes were stricken. In some religious houses ninety out of a hundred were ill. A fervent philanthropist, who had turned his house into a hospital but found himself unable to cope with the numbers of sick and dying, was put in touch with the Jesuit General. Francis obtained alms from the Pope and the well-to-do, divided the infected area into fifteen parts, put each in charge of a Jesuit father and lay-brother, organised ambulances and the distribution of food and medicines. Finding this inadequate he hired another

house and made it into a central hospital, served by forty
Jesuits. Largely thanks to his organisation, the epidemic
was at last checked and when another began two years
later the Pope at once put him in control of the administration of public relief funds and their distribution.

At last, in spite of checks and delays, the additions and
alterations at Sant' Andrea were finished. There was a great
function when the first Mass was said there on St Andrew's
day, 1567, Cardinals, bishops, religious, the Duke of Pagliano and as many princes and nobles as could squeeze in.
But it was later, when the thirty novices were settled in,
that Francis was happiest there, for it was his oasis in a
wilderness of worry and affairs, just as Simancas had been.
"If my heart were opened," he said, "it would be found
full of noviciates."

Up there, in the cool air, there was a wide view over the
roofs of Rome to the unfinished dome of St Peter's on one
side and the gaunt, towering ruins of the Baths of Diocle-
tian on the other, across the Roman Forum, with its
crumbling arches and shattered temples, to the Colosseum,
south-east towards Frascati and the Alban Hills, north-
east to Tivoli and the Sabine Hills, south-west across the
Campagna and the twisting Tiber to Ostia and the sea.

The garden was sweet in spring with the heavy scent of
freesias, the perfume of hidden violets, starred with tiny
red wild cyclamens and pink-tipped daisies frail on their
long, swaying stems. Roses and nightingales under the
marble-white moon brought memories of those halcyon
days at Toledo, when Charles and Isabel, Francis and
Eleonor had dreamed happily in silence. Tall cypresses,
black-speared against the sky, unchanging through the
year, were entirely Italian in their bronze beauty. The
copper gleam of oranges, their wax-white bloom among
the shining leaves were like the 'Earthly Paradise' of Francis's early days. There were other flowers too, Indian pinks
such as the old Emperor had tended at Yuste and Francis
at Simancas, herbs for the kitchen, but not that bitter

wormwood of the Simancas novice whose dish no one but
Francis could swallow.

The air was murmurous with young voices and low
laughter for, said the General, in recreation time "let them
be free to do as they will . . . nothing organised and formal
but with joy and liberty in our Lord." They might sing
too, "not in public places but in the garden during recreation . . . or even in the house if it is to help or cheer an
invalid."

Music still held first place among the arts, as it had always done, with Francis. No one could rejoice more than
he at the reformation and re-birth of church music. The
present Pope, Pius V, had been one of the eight Cardinals
appointed by Pius IV in 1564 to put into effect the decision
of the Council of Trent to "exclude from churches all such
music as . . . introduces anything impure or lascivious, in
order that the house of God may truly . . . be called the
house of prayer."

The singers from the Pontifical choirs had declared such
reform to be impossible. It looked as if music would be
banished from the Liturgy when Palestrina was told to
compose a Mass which would satisfy both reformers and
choirs. His Mass of Pope Marcellus was judged by the
eight Cardinals to fulfil all requirements. The Pope, a
keen musician, declared it to be "the music of the heavenly Jerusalem" and appointed Palestrina composer to the
Papal chapel.

Francis, who had always been austere in his religious
compositions, could not have been other than eager to put
the new reforms into effect in the Roman Jesuit houses,
though it was for St Philip Neri, not for Francis, that
Palestrina composed his *Arie Divote* and songs to our
Lady.

The first novice master at Sant' Andrea was succeeded
by one of his novices, Father Fabio de Fabi, a young Roman noble of great holiness. During the seven years that
Francis was General there passed through the hands of

these two men novices who were afterwards to be famous. Claudio Aquaviva, a Neapolitan noble and favourite chamberlain of Pius V, became fifth General of the Society. His nephew, Blessed Rodolfo Aquaviva, son of the Duke of Atri, went to the East, was sent on a mission to the Great Mogul and was martyred with four companions in Salsette (1583). From Poland came Stanislaus Varsiwieski, the poet, Peter Skarga, the famous orator and St Stanislaus Kostka, model and patron of novices. He, after tramping across Europe to be received into the Society by Francis Borgia, died less than a year later at Sant' Andrea, aged eighteen, on the feast of the Assumption, 1568. Matteo Ricci, who entered in 1571, was the first Jesuit to reach Pekin in 1611.

Francis loved, above all human things, to be with his novices, to enjoy their eager enthusiasms, to control their eccentricities, to encourage their devotion. He wrote for them instructions which were afterwards widely applied. Humility, simplicity, sincerity, these were still the *leit-motif*, as they had been in his *Advice to Preachers*. "Preach from heart to heart" was said for superiors and novice-masters as well as to novices. "Be pitiful rather than angry." All must be moulded, gently but firmly, to the spirit of the Cross, be taught to remember that religious life was a continuous cross, a ceaseless exercise of renunciation and mortification. New and extravagant penances were to be discouraged, tasks to be allotted with common-sense and sympathy, not overtaxing the will or bodily strength. "The simplicity of doves and the wisdom of serpents" were to be combined.

So Ribadeneira tells us after watching Francis in his dealings with those under his authority. There was little, if anything, left of the autocratic and impatient commander of men. It was not "Do this or that," but, "Will you, for the love of God?" or a gentle suggestion, "Do you not think so and so?" Confession of a trivial fault brought the reply, "God did to you as He did, brother, or why should

s

you confess it to me?" The community of religious life was emphasised, sympathy with the sorrowful and weak and, hardest of all, with the stupid. "No servant of God should say 'I have one head, two eyes and hands'. Those of his fellows are his also for he must share their labours and needs as if they were his own. As St Paul says, we are all members of one body and must be weak with the weak, sad with the sad." Complaints about well-meant but unsuccessful efforts were silenced by the words, "The intention counts, not the execution. Where there is zeal there should be no blame." Grumbles about bad weather or discomforts met with no sympathy. Those nine years of continuous journeys in Spain and Portugal had left room neither for ease nor rest. "It is a marvellous thing to see a man reared in such splendour and luxury tramping the roads in sun and rain, winter and summer, night and day, in such wretchedness, often sleeping on the ground, often with nothing to eat, in order to visit a few poor religious. And think of the gladness and joy with which he did it, having always before his eyes the journeys and weariness of Christ our Redeemer" (Ribadeneira).

'Gladness and joy', Francis himself dwells on this side of the religious life, the love which turns all suffering and sacrifice into pure gold.

"If religious life could be tasted like wine, no great noble alive but would enter religion to enjoy the sweetness of this holy drink. But, because it is impossible to know the happiness of such life till one has entered it, many flee from it, terrified of the poverty and harsh outside of this holy state. They do not see the riches and interior favours with which our Lord rejoices the hearts of those who faithfully serve Him in religion" (Ribadeneira).

CHAPTER XXVII

HIGH MOUNTAIN

FRANCIS Borgia's horizon as a child had been the walls of Gandia, the *huerta* and the low grey foothills; as a Viceroy it had included the menace of the French frontier on the north, that of the African corsairs on the west. As Commissary General he had gone further afield, but only between the Bay of Biscay and the Straits of Gibraltar, the Atlantic and the Mediterranean. Now that his bodily activities were confined within the gates and on the seven hills of Rome, his vision widened till, as from "a high mountain" he was "shown all the kingdoms of the world." In St Ignatius's mind he had watched the shadows shifting across the magic mirror of the world. Now those shadows materialised as visible and tangible as those Aztec princes, in gold and jewels and feathered cloaks, whom he had seen climbing the steep streets of Toledo in the train of Cortes. There had been in their sullen, dark faces the tragedy of a proud, conquered race, without hope here or hereafter. It was nearly fifty years now since Mexico city and the Aztec empire had fallen. The great Cortes had died, as Columbus had done, poor and neglected, abandoned by the emperor for whom he had won a new empire. The country still needed missionaries. No Jesuits had yet followed the Franciscans and Dominicans who were fighting against overwhelming odds. Francis continually remembered Mexico in his prayers and Masses for the missions. At the moment he could do no more. His hands were full enough carrying out the directions of the Congregation in Europe.

There were foundations to make, education to be widened, talent encouraged to supply new colleges with masters and professors, but his outlook extended far beyond

Europe, east and west round the world. His finger was on the pulse of every Jesuit mission. Like Ignatius, no scheme was too vast, no detail too small for his attention. The directions he drew up for Visitors in Spain were to be applied everywhere. "Your business," he wrote to Busta- mente, "is to comfort and cheer all you visit . . . Let them find a very loving father in you, pleasant and gentle" (February 2, 1567). The general instructions of a month later were in the same key. "The Visitor must be cheerful and rejoice over the good he finds and the work under- taken. Let him approve or, if something needs to be changed, it must not be done sharply or discontentedly . . . Let him be simple and straightforward, loved, not feared, both by those in authority and those under them."

Before this he had written to the Visitor for the Indies, telling him that eastern customs were not to be changed unnecessarily, that Japanese Jesuits and converts must be properly fed and looked after, since fear of starvation and misery retarded the conversion of bonzes, that missionar- ies arriving in the East "should be warmly welcomed and treated lovingly . . . specially if they are foreigners, for there is neither Greek nor barbarian nor Scythian in the Company but all are one in Christ Jesus" (Jan. 10, 1567).

And a little later that same year to Peru: "Do not run after useless dangers. Martyrdom may benefit you, but what is more important is the work of those sent out" (August 13, 1567). He discussed the thorny question of slavery with Ignatius de Azevedo, who returned to Eur- ope (1569) after promulgating the Constitutions in Brazil. He encouraged Manuel Texeira to try and enter China, though Matteo Ricci, who was to be the first to found a mission in China, did not join the noviciate of Sant' Andrea till a few months before Francis's death. He warned Japanese converts that they could not too be careful not even to appear to countenance pagan rites.

The refrain of his instructions to missionaries is "zeal combined with prudence, a firm foundation rather than a showy edifice." This is insisted on in his directions to Father Ruiz de Portillo, former novice master at Simancas, now (1567) Provincial of Peru. "Wherever our brethren may be, let their first care be for those already converted, their first aim to strengthen these in the Faith and to help them save their souls. After this they may convert others not yet baptised, but let them proceed prudently and not undertake more than they can carry through. It is not desirable for them to hurry here and there, to convert heathen with whom they cannot afterwards keep in touch. It is better to advance step by step and consolidate conquests already made . . . They are not to risk their lives unnecessarily in excursions among unconquered people. The swift loss of life in God's service may be advantageous for them, it is not for the greater good of the many, for there are only a few labourers for the vineyard and it is difficult to replace them." The same advice is sent to Goa. "The Pope thinks that it is useless to make Christians of those who cannot be kept in the Faith. He says strengthen what you have already won before you push on further" (Pastor).

Not only does Francis keep in touch by letter with all these Visitors and missionaries, he still cherishes a dream of laying down his 'cross' and following in the footsteps of Francis Xavier. "Though I am well on in the fifties I have not yet lost all hope of seeing that country [India] and ending my life there in the service of God and souls" (January, 1567). And again to Father de Ribera: "I still hope to die there and I wish that all those who go out to India, under holy obedience, would realise the great grace which God our Lord grants them in such a sacred vocation. Be of good cheer, my dear Father. We must not let our blood grow cold with age."

"To live under the sky of Portugal, of Rome, of Brazil, it is all the same," he writes to Brazil. "This is no winding by-way but the straight road to heaven, for any who is exposed to all these journeys and wearinesses and gives his life for Him Who died for us and Who promises us, in exchange, life everlasting" (December 24, 1568).

"Let those who go out not imagine they are going in order to baptise millions of Indians, but rather to suffer for Christ Jesus and, like children, to learn to speak savage tongues." Always practical, he asks the different missions to send home grammars and dictionaries so that the study of languages may be begun in Europe and continued on the long voyage round the Cape of Good Hope to Goa or across the Atlantic to South America. Indeed one Jesuit amazed the natives by being able to speak their language when he landed in Brazil.

For all his longing to leave Europe Francis Borgia knew in his heart that his real work was in Rome, for, as he wrote to another would-be missionary, "You will find your India wherever the Company needs you." Not only by the written and spoken word was he the power-house which supplied the Jesuit missions through the world with strength and courage. As near as is humanly possible he fulfilled Christ's command to pray without ceasing. It is seen in almost every page of his Spiritual Diary.

"Let my soul live as if separated from my body." "To nail the old man to the feet, hands and side of the Saviour." "Every hour I offer my life, uniting it with the martyrdom of Christ or the apostles." "I offered myself, such as I am, humbly to go to India or Constantinople and die for Him Who is my God." "To pray for seven things, the reform of the Church, the progress of the Company in Spain, Asia and Greece, the conversion of the heathen, Indians, Jews and Moors." "Prayers for Portillo and Brazil." "Twenty-four hours' prayer for the seventeen provinces of the Company." "Fifteen hours' prayer for fifteen provinces." Continual Masses and prayers "For the missions," "For Florida," "Daily for Brazil, Goa, the whole Company." Such are some of the hurried, all but illegible notes in his diary, ending with "Desire to shed my blood for His love."

That desire, unfulfilled in his case, was abundantly granted in the persons of his spiritual sons. In the Spanish empire of the West he founded missions in Florida, Peru and Mexico. Brazil, which had been under Portugal, was made into an independent province. All these were to grow a rich crop of martyrdoms, untold perils and miseries. Father de Segura, former rector at Valladolid, and seven other Jesuits were martyred within five days in Florida (February, 1571). St Louis Bertrand, O. P., a Valencian like Borgia, laid the foundations on which the Jesuits were to build in Peru. Before his work (1562-1569) the terror inspired in the Indians by the ruthless methods of the conquistadores was such that they often committed suicide, saying they preferred hell to the Spaniards. Philip asked for twenty missionaries for Peru. Such a number could ill be spared, but Francis sent them, under de Portillo. 'New Spain' (Central America) he made into a province (1572). The mission he sent to Mexico arrived there only a few days before his death.

The new province of Brazil gave more martyrs than any other during his generalship. Ignatius de Azevedo, who had gone out as visitor and returned to report in 1569, was supplied by the general with forty chosen young Jesuits. He sailed with them on the Santiago, bound from Lisbon for Brazil. The ship was separated by storms from her convoys and attacked off Palma by Jacques Soury, a Huguenot pirate from Rochelle. During the bloody fight Father Azevedo stood at the foot of the mast with an image of our Lady in his hand and, when the ship was taken, was the first to fall, with his head cleft open. "No quarter for Jesuit dogs" was Soury's order. Those who were tonsured had their heads split. The rest were insulted and ill-treated before being killed. The wounded were stabbed, others tied back to back and flung into the sea. One was blown from a gun. Father Diaz and twenty others on another ship went on to Brazil.

Francis wrote the news to Denis Vasquez in Sicily.

"Our Company in heaven has increased by forty more martyrs, the chief of them our Father Ignatius de Azevedo . . . All forty, because they were going to preach the false doctrines of Papistry and were priests, were hacked to pieces, robbed and thrown into the sea. So blessed Father Ignatius hastened to martyrdom in good company . . . This is enough news and in itself worth much more" (July 24, 1570).

There was one mission in which Francis had a specially personal interest, that of Ethiopia, where his old friend, Andrea Oviedo, alone of the three who had been consecrated bishops, had arrived. He had longed for solitude in the old days at Gandia. For twenty-three years he was to know it in its hardest form in Abyssinia. Persecution, lack of converts, poverty so extreme that he was forced to dig and plant to supply himself with food and had to tear a blank page from his Breviary to write to the Pope, such was his life in the little Catholic community he founded north of Adowa.

"My pity is deep," wrote Francis to him, "to know you stripped, poor, a prisoner, persecuted, reduced to such need . . . but I envy you still more since your soul remains more fervent, enriched and consoled by all these misfortunes . . . Help me, by your efficacious prayers, to obtain from the divine Will that I may be relieved of the weight of government or helped to bear it" (October 28, 1566). Oviedo died in Abyssinia in 1580.

The East added its quota of martyrs. Four Jesuits were attacked on the way from Cochin to Goa, three killed and the fourth sold for a slave. In all during the seven years that Francis Borgia was General of the Society sixty-six Jesuits were added to 'the glorious company of martyrs', while thirty-six more lost their lives nursing those stricken by plague in epidemics in Rome, Spain and Lithuania.

Missions throughout the world owed and still owe Francis Borgia yet another debt of gratitude, for it was he who first suggested to Pope Pius V the foundation of a

Congregation of Cardinals to further the work of mission-
aries and to free them from the interference of sovereigns,
such as those of Spain and Portugal. The Congregation of
Propaganda was not actually inaugurated till 1622, by
Gregory XV, but it was Francis, when General of the
Society, who first conceived the idea.

Francis's desire to shed his blood for the Faith was
granted, as prayer is often granted, in another form. The
worn, exhausted body, which he had so ill used, caused
him a veritable martyrdom of pain and illness. There were
recurrent bouts of the twin inescapable evils, gout and
fever, each attack leaving him weaker than the last. As
Ignatius had prophesied, he had ruined his digestion by
inordinate fasting. It retaliated by chronic pain which at
times became almost unbearable, so that those who saw
him in one of these crises could not believe he could live
through it. Yet he still insisted on abstaining during the
whole of Lent and Advent, writing cheerfully to Nadal,
"My health is better than I dared to hope, only my gastritis
continues to bother and exhaust me" (August 12, 1567).
A visit to Frascati or Tivoli would complete the cure after
fever or gout. "I am leaving for Frascati to rest a little so as
to be able to work harder," he wrote in March, 1566.
September that same year he notes a fortnight's illness in
his diary, followed again by a stay in the Jesuit house at
Frascati where he kept the feast of his namesake of Assisi
on October 4. "I asked God's blessing and a share of St
Francis's spirit of poverty, humility and love of the Cross."
Mid-February and March 25, 1567 the only entries are the
one word "ill," which occurs again June 31, in spite of
another rest at Frascati in late April. A slight illness in the
spring of 1568 was followed by another pilgrimage to
Loreto and then, in the summer, he went down with such
a complication of illnesses that he was bedridden for
months. "I have been ill with continuous fever, twenty
attacks of my old trouble, grown worse with age. One of
my knees is so badly swollen that the doctors and surgeons

in consultation decided to open it. So far it has been treated with massage and plasters." "Thanks be to God, I am much better, but so weak and with so many relapses that I can hardly manage to scrawl my name on the few letters I do sign."

This illness lasted for six months and prevented him from presiding at the triennial congregation of procurators from the various provinces, a task in which Everard Mercurian deputised for him. He begged both this congregation and the next three years later (1571) to accept his resignation on score of health. The request was refused on both occasions.

"Let Him take me or help me to govern well" is a prayer which is repeated again and again in the diary. He felt that a younger and stronger man would be better able to carry on his herculean work, but, as in the case of Ignatius, it was decided otherwise.

During this long illness, when the doctors had given up hope, Polanco kept Carlos at Gandia informed of the invalid's state. His spiritual intuition was stronger than medical science. "The fevers frightened the doctors more than they did me, for I am sure and confident that, though God our Lord had used so much of our Father's work, He will not yet let him rest . . . Our urgent need for his health and life is a guarantee of their lasting" (December 27, 1568).

A worse cross than bodily weakness and suffering had been laid on Francis. He was unable to celebrate Mass for four whole months, and only managed to do so with a great effort on the Epiphany, 1569, as he wrote to Araoz.

Once more the Roman spring came sweeping over the Campagna, flowers making a rainbow carpet for her feet as in Botticelli's picture. The sunshine was warm enough for the convalescent to sit out, in soft air laden with the sweetness of freesias and violets, full of the shrill cries of circling, north-bound swallows. Slowly, very slowly, strength returned, but not fast enough for Francis who had been idle too long. "Why is my force not equal to my will?" he cried impatiently in a letter to Cardinal Hozius in Poland (May 2, 1569). It was not till the end of May that he was able to write to the Empress.

Before then he had managed a pilgrimage to Loreto, in fulfilment of a vow made during his illness. He was still so weak that the doctors were against such a risk, but he insisted. Cardinal Pacheco sent a litter. It was returned with thanks as being too luxurious! The journey took six days, about twenty miles a day, along the Tiber valley, up through beech and chestnut woods, over the Apennines, their peaks still white with winter snow, then down across the flat, green *Marche*, with the Adriatic sparkling in the sunshine. It was six days of physical misery as the feeble, emaciated body was jolted and bumped while bearers slipped and stumbled in mud from melting snow or on stones that strewed the rough track. Bodily misery, but worth while for the peace and blessing of the little Holy House whose rough brick walls, according to tradition, had sheltered the Divine Child, His Mother and foster-father. Francis's devotion to her had grown stronger with age. He had had the famous portrait of her in Santa Maria Maggiore copied and then had it engraved on copper so as to be able to send prints of it to friends and fellow Jesuits, from Japan to Peru and Brazil. Often he had told great ladies that gold, pearls and jewels were better employed to decorate statues of the Mother of God than to display curled hair and white flesh. What a pleasure too it had been when the Sodality of the Blessed Virgin Mary had been inaugurated in the Roman College.

The thirty years of the hidden life of Christ with His Mother were so vivid and present in the dark narrow space of this poor little house enclosed like a jewel in its golden domes and flowery baroque walls. In all those years only one incident had been recorded, the only words of Christ written for us as child, boy and young man. "Knew ye not I must be about my Father's business?" That was the motto of Francis's life now, everything done through, in and for God, all action as well as contemplation his "Father's business." "Drowned in a sea of endless care," he said when pleading to be allowed to resign, but now, strengthened in body and soul, he was resolved on "amendment of life," "determined to animate my fathers and brothers in the Lord to follow their calling more fervently, diligently and strongly," as he wrote to Estrada on his return to Rome from Loreto. "Remember the word of God is a sword which must not be left to rust in the scabbard" (June 30, 1569).

Convalescence was completed at Frascati, where he had already been three times (March, 1565, October, 1566 and April 1567). "He is very brisk and very much the man of business," Polanco had said of Francis, but, in Francis's own words, he found the worries and responsibilities of his position "dusts blurring the spiritual vision." But up here, in the cool, clear air of Frascati there was peace and healing, quiet but for the splash of falling water reminiscent of Moorish palaces. South along the slopes of the hills ran the old Via Latina, further south the more famous Appian Way, past the Lake of Albano and the sinisterly beautiful Lake of Nemi whose jade-green waters hide the wreck of Caligula's galley.

But Francis was interested in none of these things. As he sat in the deep shade of pines and ilexes he did not imagine the swinging tramp of the legionaries along the two-thousand-year-old road, nor the strange ritual of human sacrifice by Nemi, nor Horace with his odes to the wine and women of Albano. The blue lake, the green of beeches bright against the sombre shapes of pine and cypress, sharp as the clear notes of a flute above the muted bourdon of a cello, he loved them, as he had loved them all his life, but as a means, not an end, the many beauties leading to the one, absolute and perfect Beauty. He had prayed "To live as if deprived of my senses, as if already dead"; only the capacity "To love the Creator in all His creatures" could reconcile the seeming paradox. The creations of man, the glories of Bramante, Michael Angelo and Raphael, the splendour of the Vatican, the Farnese, the Cancellaria, all the magnificence of the golden age of the Renaissance in Rome meant nothing to him. His was the Spanish mixture of austerity and realism, which pierces like a sword-blade straight to the heart of things. He had none of the Italian finesse, the Machiavellian subtlety, the license which had corrupted so much of the personnel of the Church and had rotted the fruit of the Renaissance at the core.

The aim of Pius V, even before the crusade against Islam, was the more urgent crusade against the corruption which had infected so many, from the highest to the lowest. The work of Francis Borgia was supplementary to this, to organise and strengthen the Society which had been founded by Ignatius of Loyola as the storm troops of the Church, and this could only be accomplished by spiritual weapons, by intense personal holiness.

CHAPTER XXVIII

LEGEND

THE General was back in Rome from Frascati on the thirteenth anniversary of the founder's death to superintend the transference of his body from the old church to the new Gesù (July 31, 1569). Peter Faber's body was to have been moved too but, oddly enough after so short a time, the exact spot of his burial had been forgotten and the body could not be found. There were new worries and difficulties waiting, as there generally are after a holiday. The Pope, among his reforms, was changing the organisation of the Penitentiaries (special confessors). He appointed Franciscans at St John Lateran, Dominicans at Santa Maria Maggiore and told the General that the Jesuits were to take charge at St Peter's, the most important centre, at the head of which was the Grand Penitentiary. Francis considered (and the third General Congregation after his death confirmed his opinion) that such an appointment was entirely contrary to the spirit of his Order because it entailed ecclesiastical dignity. The old Dominican Pope, once he had decided on a course, was not to be persuaded to change his mind. He insisted on this, against Francis's wishes, as he had done about having a Jesuit living in the Vatican. The only concession he made was, as Francis explains in a letter to the Provincials, "that he reduced the Penitentiary so as to make it in no way repugnant to our Institutions and manner of life" (April 28, 1570). The Penitentiary at St Peter's was to be composed of twelve Jesuits, Spanish, French, Italian, Portuguese, German, English and Polish.

The idea of putting the Jesuits in charge had originally been St Charles Borromeo's. He had been Grand Penitentiary himself before he had left Rome for Milan in 1565, and now made himself responsible for the heavy charges of the new foundation.

Money, as usual, was short. It was needed for the professed houses in Rome, for the noviciate, for the new church and for the Roman College, the last "a preparatory school, public school, university and seminary all in one" (Brodrick). Francis had the spirit of Franciscan poverty in its most absolute form. He had prayed on the feast of St Clare for "the perfect poverty of this saint and more also." Such perfection of poverty, however admirable from the spiritual point of view, must have proved rather trying for his subjects when it took the shape of such resolutions as that which he notes on July 20, 1566. "To distribute the income of the [Roman] College so that the house remains in more perfect poverty."

Yet somehow faith was always justified, as it had been in old days in Spain. There had been that occasion in the Valladolid college when the Rector had come in despair to Francis, to tell him that there was not a farthing in the house and no food but two small stale loaves. "Ring the bell as usual for dinner." The Commissary General was obeyed. Novices, students and fathers said grace before an empty table. The brother porter answered a knock at the front door. An old man and a young one handed him baskets heavily laden with meat, fish, bread, cheese, wine, fruit and money and left in silence. All sat down to a lavish meal and it was hardly surprising that the messengers were supposed to be angels in disguise. The same thing had happened more than once and now, in Rome, when there was no money nor any apparent likelihood of alms to supply urgent needs, some had always been given in time to avert starvation or debt.

An atmosphere of wonder began to surround such things. Stories were told about them and supplemented by Spanish fathers and nobles visiting Rome.

The Archbishop of Seville had bitterly said that the Jesuits flaunted their saint like a wolf's head. It was true that, still alive, Francis Borgia was already a saint in popular estimation. 'The holy Duke' was a legend, not only in his own country, but beyond Europe.

According to witnesses at the various processes before his beatification and canonisation, miracles had strewn his steps from Lisbon to Zaragoza, from Guipúzcoa to Cordova. It was perhaps not to be wondered at that to him, who lived in eternity while still prisoned in time, present and future should be one. He caught many glimpses of men's fate as known to divine omniscience. As he lay dying he turned with a smile to the faithful Brother Marcos. "After I am dead, Brother, you will go to India and die there." At the time nothing seemed less likely, but so it happened. When on his last journey in Spain, he visited his sister Margareta, wife of Don Frederick of Portugal. Her children were brought in for his blessing. "There is another little girl." She was called and came in, grimy and shabbily dressed, good enough, it was thought, for one who was only to be a Poor Clare. "On the contrary," said Francis, "she will make a good marriage and be the only one left to carry on the family." The others all died and the ugly duckling married the Duke of Pastrana.

There were miracles of healing, both of body and mind: the poor old woman with the gangrenous leg, Bustamente with a splitting head and high fever, others who begged the saint to tell their fever to leave them and it did. Vasquez's faith was put to a severe test when, yelling with the pain of violent rheumatism, Francis told him to bathe in an icy stream near Plasencia. He obeyed and that cure was certainly unusual as well as instantaneous. Devils were cast out, and to avoid too great publicity, Francis would turn his power into a joke. "Surprised?" he asked laughing at those amazed at the rout of the enemy, "Why, do you not know that two of a trade never agree?"

One story, for all its terror, has a strange haunting beauty. After his visit to St Teresa at Avila in 1557 Francis arrived at the Jesuit house in one of the larger towns of

Spain. He was told that a wealthy noble of notoriously bad
life lay at the point of death and refused to listen to any
suggestions of penance and confession. Would Father
Francis go to him? He surely would be successful where
everyone else had failed. Francis hesitated. To go and fail
would be to draw another torrent of blasphemy from the
dying lips, add yet another sin to the already long list. He
knelt before the Crucifix in his cell and prayed for light.
"Go," was the answer, "Go, and I Myself will come with
you as infirmarian and doctor." Francis went. As he entered the sick room he saw beside the bed a tall majestic Figure dressed in a doctor's gown. The Presence touched
Francis to such superhuman eloquence and persuasion
that it seemed impossible for any to resist it. That 'heart of
bronze' remained unmelted and Francis left sorrowing to
pray and pray for the hard heart and blackened soul. Again
the Voice spoke. Again he returned, Crucifix in hand, to
plead with the sinner. The only reply was a flood of blasphemy from the blue lips, ears stopped against the plea of
grace. Then Christ spoke from the Cross. "See how much
thy soul has cost me, to what depths My love has descended to receive thee into My arms, into My glory if, even
now, thou wilt repent." But those ears were deaf to the
divine appeal. The Figure, loosening its right hand from
the Cross, took blood from its wounded side and sprinkled it on the dying man as a priest sprinkles holy water on
a coffin. "Since thou refusest the gift of this blood shed
for thy salvation, depart into eternal damnation."

Goya has painted this scene in the St Francis Borgia
chapel in the cathedral at Valencia. The lower part of the
figure, which he originally depicted naked, still shows
through the draperies which were added later. The four
devils who crowd behind the pillow as they wait for their
prey have none of the satanic power and horror of 'Goya's
Dreams' in the Prado. The saint, in his neatly belted habit
and a nimbus, poses coyly, the Crucifix in his right hand,
his left lifted to display to advantage his elegant fingers,
t

looking as if about to begin a *pas seul*. If he can see this from heaven it must cause him considerable amusement, for his sense of humour, a quality seldom emphasised in edifying biographies, remained with him to the end. After all, humour, like wisdom, is only a right sense of proportion and without it life would often be, humanly speaking, "salt that has lost its savour."

Bustamente, Sancho Panza grown difficult and crotchety in old age, still provided amusement. Now, at the age of seventy, he proposed to go to Florida as a missionary! Francis, aware both of the humour of the suggestion and of its good intention, wrote diplomatically, "Your Florida must consist in resting after seventy years spent in hard work for our Lord." He got amusement too from the interminable complaints of the Rector of Alcalá de Henares, which he compares to the Lamentations of Jeremiah. A Spanish Jesuit wishes to go on a pilgrimage to Sant' Iago. "I am afraid the real reason is to see Portugal, for 'he has seen nothing beautiful who has not seen Lisbon'!" A French Jesuit fancies he would show devotion by walking from Avignon to Rome. "Most edifying, but better to ride than walk, and, at present, better still to stay where you are."

Other incidents were a cause for laughter later, though not always at the time. On one gala occasion the students of the Roman and German Colleges were to join in an entertainment for a large and distinguished audience. The producer was certainly to be pitied, for he had not only to struggle with the usual pitfalls of amateur theatricals, but with accents worthy of the Tower of Babel as well. The German College was guttural with young men from Cologne to Prague. The Roman College, as Father Brodrick says, held "in one little house a miniature of the world." The great day arrived. The General, Cardinals and celebrities were seated in the hall waiting for the performance to begin, when an agitated messenger whispered something in Francis's ear. An argument had arisen as to

which college was to open the programme. Words led to
blows, and (too frequent occurrence with amateurs) the
entire cast resigned and a free fight was in progress behind
the scenes! Francis, seeing that drastic measures were called for, rose to announce that the play had to be postponed
as the hall had been found to be unsafe. It was, but not in
the structural sense as the audience thought when they
filed hurriedly out. The inefficient producer was replaced,
and at the delayed presentation the German students won
so much applause for their acting in St Catherine's Martyrdom that the Palermo College decided to emulate, and
if possible surpass them. A strictly private rehearsal was
being held for the Viceroy's benefit (October, 1569) when
a knocking was heard at the street door. The porter, obey-
ing his orders to admit no one, did not answer. Unluckily
the visitor was the Inquisitor Bezerra, who went away furious at the discourtesy, swearing he would repay this insult with interest. The play was about to begin on the
afternoon fixed when a message arrived from the irate
Dominican saying that anyone taking part in the play
would be excommunicated, as it had not been censored by
the Holy Office! The Viceroy wrote and complained to
Philip about Bezerra. Bezerra wrote to the Grand Inquisitor of Spain about the Viceroy. "The end of all this was a
scandal and loss of credit for all," says Father Martin
Rouelle, who tells the story.

Warned by all this Francis determined to restrain the
passion for the drama which, though it taught rhetoric
and ease of gesture, too often shocked and scandalised.
He wrote to Messina: "These productions cause too much
distraction, so it has been decided to restrict them to one
a year here" (October 1, 1569).

The year 1568, when Francis had been at death's door
for so long, had been a tragic one in Spain and for King
Philip, whose troubles Francis still shared. Early in the
New Year the homicidal insanity of Don Carlos, heir to
the throne and Philip's only son, had rendered restraint

necessary. Mercifully the young man had died in June, like his great-grandmother, recovering enough sanity at the end to be able to receive the last Sacraments. The lovely young Queen, Isabel de Valois, had also died in October, after giving birth to a dead child. The Moors of Granada broke into open rebellion at Christmas. The Duke of Gandia wrote gloomily that he daily expected the Valencian Moors to follow suit. The quarrels of clerics and jealous old men played into the rebels' hands, and it was not till Don John of Austria swooped down on the Moors that the Cross began to drive the Crescent from the valleys of the Alpujarras (December, 1569-November, 1570).

This renewed the Pope's determination to organise the fresh crusade. Suleyman the Magnificent had failed to take Vienna and his fleet had failed to take Malta, but Turkish power had been increasing during his reign and the Turkish fleet had never yet been defeated in a naval battle. The greatest of all the Sultans had died in 1566, leaving his son an empire of enormous extent and wealth and an overwhelming ambition to exceed his father's conquests. Arabia was conquered in 1570. Cyprus, a Venetian stronghold, was next attacked and taken.

Francis Borgia, whose youth and manhood had been shadowed by the menace of African corsairs and Spanish Moors, whose position in the world and power of organisation had been famed, was the obvious choice for Pius V's helper and confidant. The two figures, the white-habited Dominican Pope, thin and bowed, with piercing, deep-set eyes, the Jesuit General, tall and emaciated in his old black gown, the grey eyes as far-sighted as ever, were two of the most familiar figures in Rome, the protagonists of the new holy war. The Pope's first appeal to Christian princes had been met with silence or evasion. Now, with the map of Europe unrolled before them, the outlook was black to any but a saint. France, ruled by Catherine de Medici till her son Charles IX came of age, had been for years in the throes of a civil and religious war between

Catholics and Huguenots. The Spanish Netherlands had broken into open revolt against Philip after the execution of Egmont and Horne in 1568. Maximilian II, who had succeeded his father Ferdinand, brother of Charles V, in 1564, was suspected of Lutheran tendercies. England, under Elizabeth, had definitely broken away from the tradition of Catholic Christendom, and in February, 1570, Pius was to issue his Bull of Excommunication against the Queen. There remained only Spain, the most Catholic country of Europe but the most tenacious of national pride and independence. Philip II could be relied on to do what he could for the Faith, but his fatal procrastination forbad swift and decisive action. Yet he and the Venetian Republic were the only two to respond to the Holy Father's call to arms.

The year 1570 saw nothing but quarrels and dissensions between the Spanish, Venetian and Papal fleets and their various commanders. A united command, a new force was necessary. The eyes of the old Pope turned to the brilliant young prince who had just returned to Madrid, leaving the Moorish revolt crushed. The Pontiff called a council of the powers to sign the Holy League on St Dominic's day, March 7, 1571, in the Dominican church of Santa Maria sopra Minerva, near the Jesuit house of la Strada. Philip's agent, Cardinal Granvelle, raised objections. The Pope ordered him from the room. The meeting broke up, nothing done, and the old man drove back to the Vatican with tears of rage in his sunken eyes.

The Jesuit General was at Tivoli (May, 1571) resting after the work of preparing for the triennial Congregation, before all its meetings and discussions began. Spring was at its most perfect moment. The hillsides were carpeted with flowers, the air full of their sweetness. The fountain spray glittered in rainbow iridescence. All was peace and affection. Francis was loved by those under him, who knew that he spent himself to the uttermost in body, mind and soul for them. Araoz wrote long and affection-

t*

ate letters. All the old difficulties and differences were forgotten. Those two stormy petrels, Bobadilla and Simon Rodriguez, were no longer in the limelight. The *buen viejo*, Bustamente, had died last year. There was a warm comfort, gentle and pleasant as the spring sunshine, in Salmeron's words of loving praise. "The confidence I have always had, and still have, in the wisdom and exquisite charity of your Paternity has never deceived me. I have learnt and as it were touched with my fingers the great care and swiftness with which, like a good leader, you help the Provinces . . . So that in you I seem to see the same heart as in St Paul, with whom you can truly say 'My daily burden, the care of all the churches'."

Francis was only sixty-one, but hardships, work, travel, responsibility and many bodily ills had worn out his body. It was good to sit, as old men sit, and dream in the sun. He had planned what he would say to the fathers when begging for the second time to be allowed to resign. "I am worn out with drifting here and there like smoke, drowned in a bottomless sea of business. You see me old, weak, immeasurably weary, so that I feel it impossible to continue with this burden, which has been beyond my strength all the years that I have borne it." Surely now he would be allowed to say that his work was done, that he might prepare in quiet for the end which could not be long delayed. Thoughts floated through his mind, vague and dim as reflections in water ruffled by the wind. Rumours reached Tivoli from Rome. The Pope's resolve had only been stiffened by the failure in March. Venice was sending secret emissaries to treat with the Turk. Then suddenly the Holy League was signed, sworn and proclaimed between the Holy Father, Philip of Spain and the Serene Republic. Don John of Austria was appointed Supreme Commander both by land and sea of the forces of the Holy League (May 25, 1571).

Don John of Austria, with all the ardour of brilliant and gifted youth, was preparing to take power and respon-

sibility with both hands. Francis Borgia was equally ready
to lay it down. Young Apollo dreamed of conquest, fame
and empire. He who had so long ago been called Apollo
and Narcissus dreamed of renunciation, solitude and
obedience. He felt it was better to look back than to look
forward, now that passion and earthly ties had fallen, as
dead leaves, falling, show the bare tree in all its lace-like
beauty against the pale winter sky. He still caught the echo
of Juan of Avila's voice under the arches of the Granada
cathedral: "All flesh is grass and the glory of it as the
flower of the field. The grass is withered and the flower
fallen."

The procurators from the Jesuit provinces had begun
to assemble in Rome, and the General returned from
Tivoli. There was a summons to the Vatican (June 1). He
went, accompanied as usual by Polanco. The Pope explained that he was going to make yet another and more
urgent appeal for help in the Holy War. Cardinal Commen-
done was to go as Legate to the Emperor Maximilian and
to Sigismond, King of Poland. Cardinal Michele Bonelli,
the Holy Father's nephew, was to go to Spain, to make
Philip promise his continued support to the League, and
then on to Portugal where the young King Sebastian, full
of dreams of adventure and military glory, would easily be
persuaded to join in this last crusade.

The short summer night was ending. Francis could see
the window of his little room outlined by the pearly grey
of dawn, as he had watched dawn change to sunrise that
August morning at Gandia twenty-one years ago. The
Pope wished him to go with Cardinal Bonelli, to give him
the benefit of his experience and knowledge of men and
of Spain. There had not been a moment's hesitation on his
part. At his age and with his health it meant a death sentence, as well as the shattering of his dream of peace and
quiet. His prayer to shed his blood for Christ had not been
accepted in his way, but in God's. But the sacrifice of his

life had been offered and accepted. Juan Polanco had been horrified, had put to the Pope the difficulties and inconveniences which would arise from the General's absence during the Congregation. He had emphasised the General's age and bodily weaknesses. The old Dominican had been inexorable. The business must be carried through and at once.

There was much to do, to be settled and arranged before the hurried departure. Friends and relatives in Spain must be warned of his coming. The Congregation had to change the superiors of six Provinces, to appoint a Provincial and select twelve priests for the new mission of Mexico. Nadal was the obvious choice for Vicar General during the General's absence. How lucky that Polanco was to accompany the embassy to Spain and Portugal. Francis felt that without him he would have been as helpless as he had felt with his right hand paralysed at Evora. He had been an unprofitable servant, yet he had done his best to "imitate the shepherd who gives his life for the sheep, his eyes to weep for them, his tongue to teach them, his hands to defend them." The words of *The Imitation of Christ* which he had pored over during his illness in 1535 came back to him. "Both joys certainly thou canst not have, to delight thyself here in this world and after to reign with Christ. All therefore is vanity, except to love God and serve Him only." That truly was all that mattered. It mattered nothing, less than nothing, when or where the end came, nor where the worn-out body returned to dust. "Into Thy hands, into Thy hands."

CHAPTER XXIX

LAST JOURNEY

UP IN the Mont Cenis Pass the mists drifting down from the snow were penetratingly cold. Down in the Provençal plain the August sun beat with the same fierce intensity on grey rocks, yellow cornfields and green vineyards as it had done when Francis had been drenched with sweat in his armour. This time there was the Jesuit College at Avignon to welcome the General, Polanco and Miron, the three Spanish Procurators and the faithful Brother Marcos. Rome had been left on the thirtieth of June, 1571, Susa, at the foot of the pass, reached on the third of August and Roussillon three weeks later, in wonderfully good health for Francis.

He had left Spain ten years before, a persecuted refugee. Now the wheel had turned full circle. Philip had sent Ferdinand Borgia, Knight of Calatrava, to the frontier to welcome his father home. He carried letters of good wishes from the King, Ruy Gomez and Cardinal Espinosa, the President of the Council of Castille. The progress through Spain was to be a triumphal procession in which Francis's chief difficulty was to remind the eager crowds of rich and poor that the Legate, not himself, a humble Jesuit, was the person who should be fêted. He kept as much as possible to the rule of the religious life while travelling, arranging that the little group of Jesuits should ride separate from the Legate and his splendid suite and each occupy one hour in meditation, taking it in turns so that this mental prayer was continuous.

The entry into Barcelona (August 28) which apparently he had never revisited since he left in 1543, was a veritable triumph. Carlos sent an envoy from Gandia with a large sum of money, a pair of riding boots, a new cloak, habit,

&c. They were refused as being too smart and fashionable. Luckily Brother Marcos put down his foot and ordered their acceptance. They were needed, too, for a witness, present at Francis's Mass in the Jesuit Church of Santa Maria de Belem (in the Rambla) noticed that when the saint unvested after Mass he was very shabbily dressed "with a belt from which hung a rosary of seeds strung on a violin cord,"—intimate and delightful detail. The rosary which was never out of his hands as he walked through the streets of Rome was probably this humble, home-made thing, threaded on an old piece of catgut which had once made music.

It was quite like old times to find the Catalans at logger-heads, the chapter of the Barcelona cathedral engaged in a fierce lawsuit with the royal officials. The Bishop of Mallorca, deputed by the Pope to settle the quarrel, had been unable to do anything. Francis was called in. Peace was made before evening.

If Barcelona had welcomed its old Viceroy with such enthusiasm it was certain that the entry of the former Duke of Gandia into Valencia would be an apotheosis. There were ceremonies, receptions and excitement at every town on the way south: Tortosa, where Francis had taken his oath to observe the Catalan Fueros in 1539; the succession of small brown towns that he and Eleonor had passed on their way north, clustering round high-perched yellow churches or grim Moorish castles; Castellon and Villa Real, their domes glittering in the September sun. The country changed from a silver-point drawing of grey rock and grey trees to a glow of colour, oranges copper among their polished bronze leaves, tall spears of sugar-canes swaying in the light breeze, vines heavy with ripe bunches of green and purple grapes.

There rose the high stronghold of Peñiscola. It was over fifty years since he had landed there from the ship crowded with royalist refugees. The tide of memory rose till it submerged the bodily misery of the swinging, jolting litter. The brilliant train of the Cardinal Legate, the scarlet and purple, the glitter of helmet and cuirass, the tossing of plumes and the curvetting of Arab horses and sleek, well-fed mules, the group of Jesuits, their black habits dusty and travel-stained, rosaries in hand, all the sight and sound and heat vanished. He was a child again, among all those fighting men and frightened nuns, a child on his first journey to Zaragoza, a boy on the road to Tordesillas, to his first contact with darkness and madness and evil, a youth on his way to the court of the world's greatest Emperor. But the most vivid memory of all those journeys was that brief moment in the dusty, wind-swept street of Alcalá de Henares when the eyes of Ignatius Loyola had met his and, unknowing, had decided his future.

Journeys also to Barcelona and back with Eleonor, their two lives so intertwined that it seemed impossible that "one should be taken and the other left." Sagunto, throned on its two hills, threw long shadows across the flat *huerta* that stretched to the still, shining Mediterranean. The red-ochre of its rocks and walls was dark against the orange of the sunset sky. A troop of horsemen was waiting at the gate, Don Carlos, Duke of Gandia, his brother Don Alfonso, his twenty-year-old son, Don Francisco, Marquis of Lombay, all the local nobility. Francis was surrounded and almost overwhelmed, though he told them that their first duty was to welcome the Legate, not a simple Jesuit priest.

The Hieronomite monastery of San Miguel, just outside the gates of Valencia, was reached on September 14 and the next morning the Archbishop, Juan de Ribera, the Duke of Gandia and a crowd of mounted nobles arrived to escort the Legate to the grand reception by the city authorities.

The road to the Puerta de Serranos, with its magnificent battlemented towers and rampart, was thick with yellow dust, thicker still with townsfolk who had hurried out to see *El Santo Duque*. The older ones remembered him well, tall, fine-looking and the fattest man in Valencia. The younger knew him only as a legend, but to see a legend in the flesh is even more exciting than to renew twenty-year-old memories. Half a dozen Jesuits came on in front of the Cardinal's suite. There was no such person to be seen as that fine figure of a man. Where was he? Which was he? No one could recognise the Duke in the skeleton that looked as if it had nothing to cover its bones but the black gown. Young Francisco dismounted to kiss the hand his grandfather held out to him, was quickly given his *congé* and sent on to the Legate, and then Francis, knowing his Valencia by heart, told the men who carried his litter to turn aside, take a short cut to the left and so enter the city by the Gate of St Vincent Ferrar, near the Puente de Real and the citadel of Charles V. So he managed to slip into the Jesuit house close by, having, with the cunning of the old huntsman, successfully evaded notice.

The Legate and his suite were sumptuously entertained in the archbishop's palace, which adjoins the cathedral. Francis, with Polanco, Marcos and the five other Jesuits, remained in the house near the Plaza de Tetuan. Carlos, who had been so mean about the promised contributions to the Roman College, now assumed filial generosity, daily sent his father provisions enough to feed all the members of the Jesuit College and set up the travelling companions with new outfits. Francis, though under obedience to Brother Marcos he had accepted a new habit and cloak, refused a silken girdle, which had to be replaced by a cotton one.

On Saturday, the day after their arrival, Francis drove round with the Legate to show him some of the gardens for which Valencia was and is famous, which make it in truth a bit of Paradise fallen from heaven. Palms, oranges, roses, lilies, carnations, cacti with strange shapes and brilliant colours, the dark, narrow streets, the houses grim and withdrawn, heavily barred windows where black-eyed, black-haired, red-mouthed women dropped roses and carnations to the gallants whose music filled the night with passion, low archways where often the stones were red with blood and moonlight glittered on a drawn blade as a body slumped into the shadows, the fairy beauty of the Lonja with its ranks of slim, serried pillars, the glory of the Audiencia, with its blaze of *azulejo* walls, its intricate rainbow *artesonado* ceiling; how familiar they all were to Francis, how new and strange to the Cardinal's Italian eyes. There was the *Señora de los Desamparados* (our Lady of the Forsaken), dark in her dark little chapel, but a glimmer of gold and jewels; the slim, golden tower of the Miguelete from whose summit the Cid had shown to his wife and daughters the garden of God which he had recovered from the infidels.

Francis was to preach at Low Mass on Sunday morning in the great Gothic cathedral, one of whose chapels is now dedicated to him and filled with paintings by Goya. There was a battle at the Apostles' door of the cathedral. Everyone *must* hear the Holy Duke preach. There was a battle inside too, while a way was forced for Francis to the pulpit through the packed mass of excited humanity. The text was simple. "Jesus came to the city of Naim." Brother Marcos made some notes of the sermon, one of the last the saint was to preach. "There were many reasons why I should escape this ordeal, my bad health, the fatigues of my journey, the want of time for preparation, but I remembered the Patriarch Abraham when God commanded him to sacrifice his son ... I got up this morning, took the ass of the old man, the sword of the word of God and climbed into this pulpit to sacrifice the weakness and hesitation which kept me back."

"The ass and the sword," it was typical of Francis Borgia, this one and only sermon the Valencian saint ever preached in Valencia.

The stay there was short and some of it Francis spent in bed with gout. The Archbishop and chapter came to visit him there and, to his horror, Don Juan de Ribera knelt as he came into the room. Francis cried out that if his Grace did not rise at once he himself, crippled as he was, would have to get out of bed and kneel, gout and all! There were other amusing incidents, told by eye-witnesses. Francis's sister, the Countess of Almenara and Doña Eleonor de Noronha, wife of his youngest son Alfonso, caught him after Mass and tried to kiss his hand. He moved away till he was literally back to the wall and could retreat no further, and the two women, having him at their mercy, fell on their knees and succeeded in capturing and kissing his hands. When he went into church or the cathedral he had to push his way through crowds of kneeling women waiting to kiss his hand. The Jesuit house was always full of men waiting to do the same, or failing his hand, to kiss his habit. These guests were surprised to see the Duke of Gandia standing, bare-headed, while the Jesuit fathers, by the General's orders, sat, with their birettas on. Francis answered expression of surprise with a smile. "God tells sons to obey their fathers . . . The Duke is my son. The fathers are my brothers."

Of course there was a quarrel in progress which neither the King nor B. Juan de Ribera had been able to settle. The Valencia University objected to the Jesuits giving courses of theology at their own college. The Jesuits naturally refused to stop the work for which the college had been founded. Once more Francis was a successful peacemaker.

Meanwhile Gandia was clamouring for its saint. Nothing would induce Francis to go there. He had bidden it his last farewell that August day twenty-one years ago when he had turned in his saddle to look back with the joyful words, "*In exitu de Egypto.*" Since he refused to go to Gandia, Gandia must come to him. Men, women and children came, on horses, asses and on foot, the thirty odd miles north along the dusty, stony track, through vineyards, olive and orange orchards, palms, mulberries, stubble fields and sugar-canes. Seventy miles there and back just to see their Holy Duke pass in the streets of Valencia, or if they were lucky enough to be able to force a way through the crowds, to kiss the frayed hem of his habit or the bony knuckles of his gout-twisted hands.

The Cardinal continued his state progress to Madrid. The General turned aside to visit the new noviciate of the Toledo Province at Villarejo de Fuentes. As he went on to Madrid occurred the meeting with the cavalier whose horse he admired and returned with thanks and the words, "Remind him that I am no longer Duke of Gandia but a poor religious." He caught up the Legate at the gorgeous palace of the Duke of Infantado at Guadalajara, where Cardinal Espinosa received them. The King himself met them at the Dominican house of the Atocha, on the out-skirts of Madrid (September 30, 1571), embraced the Leg-ate and the General and made the state entrance into the city with the Legate on his right, mounted on a mule splendidly caparisoned which was the gift of the city. Francis stayed at the Jesuit house. The new college was not to be opened till next year. At the official reception to the Legate, in the old Moorish palace of the Alcazar, courtiers, ministers and grandees crowded round the 'poor religious' who, ten years before, had been condemn-ed as heretical and forced to flee the country. There was a flagrant omission at one ceremony. No train-bearers had been supplied for his Eminence. Francis slipped from his appointed place and bareheaded bore the train.

The King and court could not make enough of Francis. The Inquisitor celebrated his return by authorising the publication of all his works, formerly censured, now de-clared to be above reproach and most edifying. Araoz waxed eloquent to Nadal in Rome over the success of the General's mission. He was no less than "the right hand of the Highest." The chorus of Hosannas was ceaseless and deafening. The Spanish provincials and superiors assem-bled in Madrid to meet the General. Quarrels were made up, tepidity warmed to zeal, final arrangements made about the organisation of the mission to Mexico. Relations came to claim their share and more than their share of over-full days. There was only one haven of refuge and quiet, the convent of the Poor Clares, where Francis's sister, Juana of the Cross, was Abbess, and his former penitent, the Infanta Juana, a nun. A letter came there one day from the Viceroy of Sardinia addressed to "The most Illustrious Lord, Don Francisco de Borja, Duke of Gandia." Francis handed it back unopened to the messenger. "I do not know where in the world you will find this most illustrious Duke."

One day after Mass he withdrew to the house of his son Ferdinand, shut himself into the chapel and remained there lost in prayer for ten or twelve hours. Was it on Sunday, October 7, 1571?

In spite of Araoz's rose-coloured picture the results of the mission were small. On October 8 the King renewed to the Legate his promise that the campaign against the Turks should be continued next year by Don John of Austria and the Spanish forces, but his only reply to the exposition of quarrels and differences between the civil and ecclesiastical authorities in Naples and Sicily was his usual non-committal one that he would have enquiries made.

Philip was kneeling in the chapel of the palace during First Vespers of All Saints when 'news of a great victory' was whispered into his ear. He remained unmoved, sent orders when Vespers were over that a *Te Deum* was to be sung and only then heard from one of the gentlemen at the Venetian embassy of the smashing victory won over the Turks at Lepanto on October 7 by his half-brother, Don John.

Francis had a personal, as well as a patriotic interest in the news, for six Jesuits had been appointed by Nadal as chaplains to the Spanish fleet, and of the two on board

Don John's flag-ship one was Cristobal Rodriguez, who had so often accompanied Francis and Polanco on their visits to the Vatican.

The time in Madrid drew to an end. Francis was to go on to Lisbon with the Legate, who had instructions from the Pope, "Discuss everything with the Father General and be guided by his advice, talking to those whom he judges likely to be useful." As a parting gift Francis gave a relic of the True Cross to the King for his new church at the Escorial, with the documents of authentication. "These are unnecessary," said Philip, "your word is enough." No doubt Philip specially asked his old friend's prayers that the Queen's imminent confinement might result in the birth of a son. Ana of Austria was his fourth wife, but since the death of Don Carlos, he had been without an heir.

Again Francis travelled west with a difficult mission to fulfil in Lisbon. It was late November. Wind and rain swept down from the Sierras and here and there the passes were under snow. At long last the Tagus widened. The white houses of Lisbon shone in the sunshine and the frenzied welcome to the city was rather for an old friend than for the unknown Legate. "Father Francis is too good for a Spaniard," had always been the popular verdict, "he must be Portuguese." Francis, staying in the Jesuit house of Sant' Antonio, had the pleasure of seeing again, after so many years, his dear son Juan, Spanish ambassador to the Portuguese court, with his wife and daughters at the embassy. There were many former intimates, also many quarrels. Queen Catherine and her brother-in-law, Cardinal Enrique, were eager to pour out to Francis their indignation over the young King's behaviour. Sebastian, now seventeen, as soon as he had come of age had reversed his grandmother's policy and dismissed the officers she had appointed to posts of authority. Old age had not endowed Catherine with self-control. It had only been with the utmost difficulty that Father Torres and the Duke of Feria (Philip's envoy) had dissuaded her from an indignant return to Spain.

Father Luis de Camara, to whom St Ignatius had dictated his autobiography, had come to Lisbon to direct the young King's studies ten years ago, at the Queen-Regent's urgent request. He had succeeded in making his difficult and unruly pupil honest, chaste and popular with his people, but it was beyond human power to eradicate a mad thirst for danger and adventure, an unbalanced desire for campaigns and conquests in North Africa.

Francis and the General Congregation had seen the perils of religious living in palaces and acting as directors or confessors to royalty. The danger of being blamed for every crime and mistake of their penitents was a very real one. It has given the Jesuits a bad name for meddling in politics, a reproach which has stuck to them as firmly as a burr to a dog's coat.

The Queen, furious at her grandson's revolt, attributed to his tutor the fierce independence, the chivalrous visions, the horror of marriage which were results of inbreeding and an insane streak. Lisbon, in fact, was divided into two camps, the King's on one side, the Queen's and Cardinal's on the other, all three of them, said the enemies of the Society, tools in the hands of intriguing Jesuit confessors. Here was a pretty tangle for Francis to straighten out. The Legate's task of persuading Sebastian to join the Holy League was no more difficult than setting dry tow aflame.

Miguel de Torres, Catherine's confessor, came to the General and begged, as he had done three years ago, to be sent East to try and enter the forbidden territory of China. Impossible; his mission was here. The Queen was calmed, induced finally to give up her idea of flight, but not even Francis could make her consent to any of the three father confessors leaving the court. Remained the young King. By infinite patience and charm Francis at last persuaded him to consent to negotiations being opened for his marriage with Marguerite de Valois, sister of Charles IX of France. Luckily for Sebastian it was too late, for she was already secretly betrothed to Henry of Navarre. He himself perished seven years later in the disaster of Alcazar Khebir. His youth, his romance, his charm and the uncertainty of his fate became a legend in the hearts of his people, who refused to believe him dead and were convinced that, like King Arthur, he would return at the hour of his country's greatest need.

The short visit to Lisbon was even less peaceful than the one at Madrid. Apart from the dissensions at court there were differences among the Jesuits themselves and what with the King, the Queen-Mother and Cardinal Enrique continually in and out of the Jesuit houses in Lisbon, Evora and Coimbra religious peace was disturbed, as one father wrote irritably, by "great turmoils in the house which has become no better than a palace."

Hopes of being back in Rome for Easter had been dashed by orders from the Holy Father, received before leaving Madrid, that the Legation was to go on to France. Success had been achieved in Lisbon in that the King had consented to join the League and to negotiate a marriage. Francis, the peacemaker, had healed the open breach between Sebastian, his grandmother and great-uncle, and had privately decided that the next Congregation should recall all three confessors to royalty. The only dissatisfaction left behind him was that of the fathers in Lisbon, Evora and Coimbra over the shortness of the time which could be spared them. "The comfort of his visit has been lessened by its swiftness," wrote one sadly.

Madrid was reached by the New Year. Prayers had been answered and the King insisted that Francis, who had so often carried him in his arms, should be the one to hold the new Infante, Don Ferdinand, at his baptism.

Francis still hoped that the Legation would go on without him so that he could return to Italy by sea. He had stood these six months of continuous travel and crowds better than Polanco and Marcos had dared to hope, but there are limits to physical endurance. Not the strongest will and spirit can drive the weak body beyond a certain point. It was cold in Madrid, with the icy wind sweeping across the bare Castillean plateau. Reports from France told of a winter of bitter cruelty and Francis, child of warm Valencia, had never been able to stand cold.

Letters came from Rome bidding him go on with the Legation. It was his death warrant. He knew it. His loving companions miserably feared it. He had accepted the cup at Rome. There was no faltering now. "We on our part, should not wish for health rather than sickness, for riches rather than poverty, for honour rather than ignominy, for a long life rather than a short one." His life had been a long one, with faults and imperfections of which he was fully aware, seeing them, says Ribadeneira, as one sees specks of dust in the sunlight. But he was not conscious of having deliberately sinned against light. With blood and tears he had gained that iron self-control with which alone he could bridle what he called the wild beast of strong passions. Cruel to himself alone, he had in these last six years shown to those under his authority only charity, sympathy and tenderness, even to those at fault or in revolt. He had won that "detachment from all earthly things" which is not heartless indifference but the perfect sense of proportion which loves God before and above all, and created things only in Him. Being a Spaniard, he was a realist, and the genuine realist knows that there is only one true and eternal reality, God and eternity.

There was perhaps one thing in life which he had regretted, the solitude which he fancied would have given him greater scope for contemplation, for, as Ignatius himself had said, "The more the soul finds herself alone and apart from men the more fit she makes herself to draw near and attain her Lord and Creator." Ignatius, in his greater wisdom, had called him from Oñate back to a life of activity. He knew now that the saint had been right.

He was to say a little later to a fellow Jesuit, during his last illness, "It was when I was Viceroy of Catalonia that God prepared me to be first Commissary General and then General of the Company . . . I learned to decide important questions, to settle rival claims, to adjust differences, to see both sides of a question as I could not otherwise have done. Everything has turned out for the greater glory of God" (Clarke).

CHAPTER XXX

HOMEWARD BOUND

THE journey north was not free from business. The foundations of the professed house at Burgos, where a halt was made, of the college at León and the noviciate at Villagarcia were confirmed. After the brown austerity and bitter winds of Castille it was good to reach the gracious wooded green valleys of the Basque country, to hear the thunder of the Atlantic with its wind-driven, sun-painted spray. The last night was spent in Fuenterrabia, that strange old town with the huge castle of Charles V, looking down across the Bidassoa and across all those centuries since Charlemagne had listened here to the echo of dying Roland's horn at Roncesvalles.

The last view of the Spanish mountains, transparent, opalescent, ridge behind ridge, lovely as a dream; Bayonne and the farewell to Ferdinand who had come so far with the Legation; then came those fifty miles or more across the sandy heather wastes of the Landes, with the tang of salt on dry lips and stinging cheeks as the wind roared in from the Bay of Biscay.

It was the road Francis Xavier had ridden singing gaily on his way to Paris University forty-seven years ago, the road that was to lead him on to Rome, Lisbon, Goa, Kagoshima and the quicklime grave on Sanchian. For him life had been beginning. For his namesake it was ending. Outward things were dim and remote as they were through the white fog that drifted in from the sea. It was often only with an effort that Francis withdrew himself from contemplation, then too often to know a heart-broken longing for reparation for the desecration and profanation he saw all about him.

France had been racked by civil war for eleven years. Everywhere was danger and desolation, ruins and murders. "Justice and security reigned in all parts of Spain, in roads, cities and country, as a result of the observance of the true religion. In France were armed brigands, civil war and revolt against authority, caused by the rebellion of heretics against God" (Ribadeneira).

The arrival at Bordeaux (Saturday, January 26, 1572) was marked by none of the enthusiasm that had been universal in Spain. The Catholics there were comparatively few and afraid of Huguenot force. Indeed soon after the departure of the Legation (January 28) the town was taken and looted by the Huguenots. Jean de Lauze, Francis's host during these two days, was so impressed by the sanctity of his guest that he promised to found a Jesuit college in the city and guaranteed two thousand pounds annually for the expenses.

The two hundred miles from Bordeaux to Blois were covered by the Legate at top speed so that he arrived two days before Francis. For the latter it was a Way of the Cross in body and spirit. The cold was terrible, icy winds, hail and snow. It was difficult for mules or bearers to keep their feet on the frozen tracks. Every jolt and lurch was agony to the poor, wasted, pain-wracked body. The spiritual suffering was worse. Everywhere churches had been defiled and desecrated, sacred images defaced. Only ruins remained in some places. But for the privileged altar it would sometimes have been impossible for the General to say Mass. Two days from Bordeaux (the average covered was twenty-five miles a day) Francis insisted on saying Mass on the stone altar which was all that remained of a church recently destroyed by the Huguenots. All the while tears were pouring down his face. All that day he kept murmuring to himself, "Oh God, the heathen have come into Thine inheritance. They have defiled Thy holy temple. They have destroyed Thine altars and slain

Thy prophets with the sword." The sword had pierced his heart as well. He was mortally wounded by something crueller than piercing winds and driving snow.

Carnival was in full swing when he reached Blois (February 8) and suddenly his litter was surrounded by a wild noisy crowd who pranced round it. The young King was there. The welcome was as strange as a dance of death. Men whispered questions, under cover of fools' jingling bells, whirring rattles and drunken shrieks. Was this a welcome or a mockery? To Francis himself, half dead with cold and weariness, the macabre scene must have been like the sport of devils dragging souls to hell.

The lowering sky, dark as the slate roof, drenched all the warmth of red brick and gold-grey stone of the castle façade. Patches of snow had lodged in the lace-like tracery and on the mounted figure of Louis XI above the main gateway. There was a little shelter in the arcade, with its elegant lozenged pillars and its frivolous ceiling of blue and pink and gold, but the wind whistled across the court and up the open spiral staircase. Logs were burning in the wide open hearth of the *Salle d'Honneur* so that the swan and crown of the iron fireback were hidden, but the heavy overmantel with the salamander of Francis I loomed in the feeble light of flickering candles. A group stood at the far end of the hall. The Queen-Mother sat in a high-backed gold chair, her immense farthingale billowing round her, her boned stomacher sewn with pearls, her wired ruff of lace framing the face of an impassive, stout, dark *bourgeoise*, an odd mask for the astute and treacherous mind. The young King shivered, though he had a furred velvet cloak over his tightly belted tunic and huge trunk-hose. Jewels glittered in his ears, at his ruff, on his thin, restless fingers. The rouge on his cheeks accentuated the consumptive flush under the sunken temples. There was a gleam and rustle of jewels and swords and silken skirts as the Jesuits advanced. Francis's height topped the rest. The habit which Carlos had given him at Valencia was

stained with the dust of Madrid and Lisbon, the mud and
snow of Portugal, Spain and France.

Catherine de Medici and her son treated this shabby
figure as a Grandee of Spain, a cousin of Philip II. He was
begged to sit down and put on his biretta. They had already
received the Legate politely, without saying that the
Queen-Mother of Navarre had forestalled him in bargain-
ing for Margot's hand, or that they cared not a ha'porth
for the Turkish peril. In fact they had received news of the
Lepanto victory coldly, since it meant more glory to their
hereditary enemy Spain and to Don John of Austria.

Francis, so Ribadeneira tells, talked to that female
Machiavelli and her decadent son of their Christian duties,
of their obligation to deal firmly with heresy, which, he
said, would inevitably lead in the end to civil as well as religious anarchy. "If the Faith is lost, so also is your Kingdom." "The sovereigns listened with deep attention and
showed agreement" (Ribadeneira). Those keen grey eyes
pierced the pretence. Catherine shed tears at parting. How
right Lainez had been nine years ago when he saw such
crocodile's tears as 'a comedy'. She even begged as a gift
the rosary hanging at the saint's girdle, probably that well-
worn, home-made one of the seeds strung on catgut.

How exciting and romantic it would have been had
there been a word of truth in the Protestant legend that the
idea of the massacre of St Bartholomew six months later
had been hatched in this interview between the wily
Jesuit, the treacherous Medici and the frightened young
pervert.

Couriers from Rome brought news of the dangerous
illness of the Holy Father and the Legation left Blois hurriedly on February 25, 1572. There was bitter disappointment among the Paris Jesuits, who had hoped for a visit
from the General, even greater joy among those in Rome
who fancied there might be a chance of having him home
for Easter.

The two hundred miles between Blois and Lyons were

u

scarred by the ruins of churches and farms, like a caravan track marked by the bones of those who have fallen by the way. They were endless miles, along straight Roman roads, which seemed to stretch into infinity, flat country without landmarks to tell of the leagues already travelled, long lines of tall poplars, tufted with mistletoe and swaying in the north wind, miserable sheep huddled in the scant shelter of tumble-down walls, here and there a stretch of dead brown heather or a patch of bare brown vineyard, and over all a grey sky that hung like a shroud.

Bourges, with the towering glory of its Gothic cathedral, whose flying buttresses, like angels' wings, seem to lift it nearer heaven than earth; Nevers, with its fine ducal palace and Romanesque cathedral; Paray-le-Monial, with its splendid basilica; Francis was aware of them not as places where his shattered body could rest for a night, but for their churches where he could celebrate Mass in unaccustomed peace. There were so many halts without a church or marked only by a desecrated ruin. Still he insisted on saying Mass, in spite of all that Polanco and Marcos could do, even in roofless shells, open to wind and rain and snow. It was little short of a miracle that the martyred body had lasted so long but, before Lyons, the limit of endurance was reached. His spirit, "sustained only by the Bread of Life" (Ribadeneira), could no longer whip on 'brother ass', the body. One bitter morning, at the end of his Mass in a ruined chapel, Francis collapsed on the frozen ground and was carried away burning and shivering with fever. They were thankful to get him alive to the Jesuit house at Lyons, which had been stormed by the Huguenot mob three years before. The Legate, forced to hurry on, left Francis there, and there he was rejoined by his brother Thomas, who had arrived in Madrid too late to start for Rome with him.

The invalid reached St Jean de Maurienne more dead than alive, and the doctors sent to him by the Duke of Savoy treated him there for violent dysentery and fever, but entirely failed to diagnose the pleurisy which had attacked the weakened lungs. The Mont Cenis Pass was barely possible so early in the year, but somehow the dying man's litter was got over it and down the further slopes, where dead rushes showed dun and frozen pools steely against the snow—five or six miles a day was the utmost that could be endured—till Turin was sighted and the Jesuit house received its General.

Spring was here in Italy. A little further south the golden feathers of mimosa scented the warm air. Even in Turin it was soft and gentle. The Jesuits began to hope that, after all, their Father might recover. He was able to say Mass again, venerated the Holy Shroud which the bishop exposed for him, was begged to stay on over Easter and so get a longer rest. He had only one desire now, to reach Rome before Pius V died, and to die there himself, at home.

Alfonso, Duke of Ferrara (son of Ercole who had entertained him on the way to visit Ignatius) had the happy thought of sending one of his comfortable state barges to bring the sick man the two hundred miles from Turin to Ferrara smoothly and easily along the River Po. The barge was magnificently fitted up but, to Brother Marcos's superstitious horror, the *camarilla* (cabin) was all black! He was allowed by Francis to change the omen by sticking white paper over the black paint!

A few miles from Alessandria there was a violent return of fever and a fainting fit; little wonder, since the doctors' only idea of treatment was drastic bleeding. Thomas, thinking his brother dead, began to sob. Francis, recovering consciousness and seeing the tears, showed the same spirit as when he had scolded the weeping fathers round his bed at Evora. "If I had thought you such a coward, I should have left you at College at Salamanca."

Easter was spent at Bassignano till he was strong enough to go on, but bedridden as he was, Francis managed to drag himself up to say Mass every morning. The

Duke and his suite were on the river bank at Ferrara waiting to have Francis carried to the palace, but it was again the Jesuit house which received him (April 19, 1572). A little later he was moved to the Duke's villa outside the city, where the long summer days were cooler.

The Duke himself came out there to break to his cousin the news of the Pope's death on May 1. Other news was mercifully withheld. Thomas Borgia, sent on to Rome, had a conversation at Bologna in which the bishop, Cardinal Paleoto, told him it was urgent that the General should if at all possible, reach Rome before the Conclave, as many of the Sacred College considered him the most likely candidate for the Papacy. The shadow of the red hat had so often darkened Francis's horizon. He was kindly spared any knowledge of the likelihood of the triple tiara. The Conclave met and, within twelve hours, elected Gregory XIII. Nadal wrote to Ferrara an account of his first interview with the new Pope, who had spoken of little but the General's illness and had sent him his blessing. Francis, still too weak to be moved, sent Polanco to Rome at the end of May to present his homage to the Holy Father and to give Nadal some help and advice for which he had begged. His last letter (May 17, 1572), congratulations in Italian to the Pope on his election, was sent by Polanco. The faithful friend and right hand was back at Ferrara before the end of July, and to him Nadal wrote a month later, "The General must not set out till the doctors have consented and then *piano, piano!*"

The summer had drifted by in the ducal villa, with its views over the wide, fertile plain and the River Po winding east to the Adriatic. The terraced garden, its marble gods and goddesses white against the blackness of stone pines and cypresses, had that severe yet splendid architectural beauty of Italian gardens which rely for warmth and colour on blue sky and golden sunshine rather than on masses of flowers. Francis, lying out in cool shade during the noonday heat, was little conscious of outward things. His mind was clear, though when the fever from his poisoned lungs mounted, towards evening, past and future, absent and present, sometimes became merged. The past, with all its drama, its passion, its splendour and its renunciation was submerged. The pages were turned. There was no need to look back. Faults, imperfections, mistakes had been regretted, could not be undone. His noviciates, as always, were in his heart and his prayers. The little Polish saint, the greatest glory of Sant' Andrea, would be waiting to greet him in heaven, in the train of Her whom his dying lips had called his Mother. There were two other novices at Sant' Andrea now, Rodolfo Aquaviva and Matteo Ricci, whose future blazed in the East, Rodolfo, winning the martyr's crown in India, Matteo, Mandarin of the First Class at the Imperial Court of Pekin, to be venerated through the centuries by the Chinese as the western Confucius. And in Spain there were Saint Alfonso Rodriguez, author of *Christian Perfection*, and Francisco Suarez, with St Robert Bellarmine, now at Louvain, to be the greatest theologian of the Society, after Lainez and Salmeron. St Peter Canisius too, the Apostle of Germany, how blessed he, Francis, had been in his spiritual children. *Deo gratias.*

His shallow breathing was more painful, the throbbing of fever stronger at aching temples and burning hands. Westward the sky was the colour of a ripe orange. East, toward the sea, the long shadows were blue as those little wild flowers on the Basque hills. He was vaguely conscious of someone speaking, of gentle hands under his aching body. It was Brother Marcos come to take him in, to break his dreams and prayers. Instinctively he smiled and repeated those customary words, "A little more, Brother Marcos, a little more."

September came, with the promise of cooler days. There was a slight abatement of fever and dysentery. The iron will asserted itself again. One more visit to Loreto and then home to die, as Ignatius and Lainez had done, among the brethren. The doctors shrugged their shoulders. "Let him go. He will die soon anyhow." The Duke provided a litter that was practically a bed, so that the invalid need not be moved at the end of the day's journey. Special bearers were to carry it. Nadal in Rome ordered that all prayers in all Jesuit houses were to be offered for the General's journey, each priest to say three Masses, each brother three prayers for the same intention.

Ferrara was left on the third of September. Polanco wrote from Rimini that so far the three days' travel had been born well, but he himself went down with fever and had to be left behind in the Jesuit college at Macerata. Thomas says that his brother arrived at Loreto "more dead than alive," but the litter was carried into the Holy House and Francis lay there for a while in the quiet, golden gloom bidding his last goodbye on earth to his dearest Lady.

They wanted him to rest there a few days, but he felt the end near and cried with a flicker of his old impatience, "I must die in Rome, amid the holy places of the holy city. Hurry, hurry, for the love of God!" During most of those days being carried over the Apennines and down the Tiber valley he suffered such terrible internal agony, "as if a knife were piercing his entrails," that even his steely self-control could not prevent him from moaning. Unwilling that his companions should suffer with him he sent them out of earshot.

It was Sunday evening, the eve of Michaelmas Day, 1572, when Rome was reached. At the Porto del Popolo Francis bade the bearers set down the litter for a moment so that he might thank God Who had brought him home after he had accomplished the task set him by the late Pope. His thanksgiving took him out of time and space so that, after half an hour or more, Nadal stepped forward with a quiet order for him to be brought into the city.

A wild suggestion was made that he should be carried round to all the Jesuit communities in Rome. This was summarily vetoed by Father Hernandez, his confessor during the journey. Even now there was to be no escape from crowds and receptions. Outside the door of the professed house in la Strada were gathered all the Jesuit fathers, brothers and students, as well as other ecclesiastics. They pressed round Francis as he was lifted from his litter, unable to stand or speak, welcoming him, asking his blessing, trying to kiss his hands. Someone with a little mercy and sense (surely Brother Marcos) cried bluntly that if this were not stopped they would have a corpse on their hands.

At last Francis was laid in his own camp bed, in the little room so near the altar and the Blessed Sacrament. Still there was no peace. Day and night the cell was thronged with visitors, cardinals, ambassadors, princes and weeping Jesuits. The Pope sent his blessing and a plenary indulgence from Tivoli, where he was staying, "the loss to the Church of a faithful servant and a strong column of support," he said. Francis received the blessing with humble gratitude but begged the visitors to go. "Leave me, for now I have only time for God." He would allow no one to stay with him but Nadal, Hernandez, Brother Marcos and his own brother Thomas. Before they left him the fathers begged him to name a Vicar General. Neither Ignatius nor Lainez had done so and Francis shook his head with a smile. "I have enough to do settling my own account with God."

Polanco, who seemed the obvious choice, was not there. He struggled from his bed at Macerata and pushed on to Rome, but, for all his haste, arrived only in time to hear of Francis's death and his own appointment as Vicar General and to be "deeply afflicted by both these things."

Francis had always refused to have a portrait done, so, when they thought him unconscious, Thomas smuggled an artist into the room. The hurried sketch was hardly begun when Francis made a gesture of firm refusal, then, with a huge effort, turned on to his side and hid his face.

He received his Viaticum and Extreme Unction, rallied his forces to make a farewell speech to the fathers and superiors in Rome. Thomas, kneeling beside the bed, begged a blessing for sons, brothers and relatives. "Name them and I will pray for them." Carlos, Duke of Gandia, Francisco, Marquis of Lombay, the long list went on. "Don Juan." "Which one?" flashed the question. "My son or nephew?" Not one was omitted. Even a muleteer who had come with him from Gandia to Rome was remembered.

Brother Marcos bent over him to know if there was anything he wanted. "I want nothing but Jesus." It was September 30. He lay for two hours without speech or movement, lost in prayer. "He was conscious till the moment of death," Thomas wrote to Carlos a day later. "Nothing interrupted his deep and perfect prayer. He spoke only when questioned, then his eyes returned to his Crucifix. His beautiful serenity was witness of the peace he had always kept." Peace, serenity, union with God, these are the notes struck in all the descriptions of his deathbed. They had too been the inspiration and achievement of his life, the peace of God which is not stirred by outward action nor by the tongues of men.

"In Francis Borgia," says Father Martindale, "is all the human tragedy of the isolated spirit, moving untainted, like Christ, amid the jostling crowd, and all the splendour of the God-indwelt soul, supremely companioned all the while and imparting its virtue to those who, with the lightest touch of faith, enter into communion with its secret."

Night fell. Brother Marcos brought a little soup and held it to the dying man's lips. "I shall soon have finished," he murmured, but obedient to the last, swallowed a mouthful. Thomas knelt by the bed, holding his brother's hand. There was silence. The dying man's faint, shallow breathing was hardly perceptible. A little after midnight, early on the morning of Tuesday, October 1, 1572, it ceased and Francis Borgia reached what was for him, in Polanco's words, "the beginning of true life."

The official letter to the father superior in Sardinia says all in a few words. "He died as he had lived, with marvellous peace and serenity." Brother Marcos's letter to Carlos breaks off with a cry from the heart: "We are all overwhelmed with grief, I more than any . . . My eyes are so blinded with tears that I can write no more, only beg our Lord that He will grant your Grace and all of us such a holy end as that of our dear saint."

"I beg the Lord to forgive my mistakes, to make me a child of truth and an imitator of the virtues of Father Francis."

(End of *Vida del Padre Francisco de Borja, S. J.*, by Pedro de Ribadeneira, S. J. Madrid, 1592.)

NOTE

The death-mask at Rome is the only authentic contemporary likeness of the saint. The drawing of him on his deathbed has vanished, as have those mentioned as being at Gandia in the seventeenth century. Denis Vasquez criticises numerous portraits which he saw shortly after the saint's death as showing none of the living joy and devotion characteristic of the man. A strange El Greco-esque elongation is visible in the majority of portraits. The one above the altar of the English College, Valladolid, shows none of this, and the Seville statue has all the vitality of Spanish religious sculpture of the sixteenth and early seventeenth centuries.

The saint's body was brought to Madrid from Rome in 1617. It perished in the destruction of the Jesuit house and church during the Revolution of 1931. St Francis Borgia was beatified in 1624 and canonised by Pope Clement XI April 12, 1671.

BIBLIOGRAPHY

1. *Vida del Padre Francisco de Borja.* Pedro de Ribadeneira, S. J. 1592.
2. *Vida de San Francisco de Borja.* Juan Eusebio Nieremberg. (First edition 1624.) 1901.
3. *Ristretto della Vita del Beato Francesco de Borgia.* Virgilio Cepari. (First Edition 1625.) 1884.
4. *Vita di San Francesco Borgia.* P. Scipione Sgambati, S. J. 1688.
5. *Vie de S. François Borgia.* P. Verjus, S. J. 1672.
6. *La Heroica Vida del Grande San Francisco de Borja.* Cardinal Alvaro Cienfuegos, S. J. 1717.
7. *St Francis Borgia.* A. M. Clarke. 1894.
8. *St François Borgia.* Pierre Suau, S. J. 1905.
9. *St François Borgia.* Pierre Suau, S. J. 1910.
10. *Der Heilige Franz von Borja.* Otto Karrer. 1921.
11. *Vida de San Francisco de Borja.* Anon. 1923.
12. *Hechos politicos y religiosos del B. Francisco de Borja.* J. E. Nieremberg. 1882.
13. *The Practice of Christian Works.* St Francis Borgia (trs. by T. Everard, S. J.). 1620. (Spelling modernised)
14. *St Francis Borgia (Christ's Captains).* C. C. Martindale, S. J. 1917.
15. *Spiritual Works of St Francis Borgia* (trs. from the French). 1875.
16. *Vida de S. Ignacio de Loyola.* P. de Ribadeneira, S. J. 1863.
17. *Récit du Pélérin (Autobiographie de S. Ignace)* (trs. E. Thibault, S. J.). 1924.
18. *A Short Life of St Ignatius Loyola.* A. A. Astrain, S. J. (trs. R. Hull, S. J.). 1928.

19. *St Ignatius.* Christopher Hollis. 1931.
20. *St Ignace, Maître d'Oraison.* A. Brou, S. J. 1925.
21. *Spiritual Exercises of St Ignatius Loyola.* Joseph Rickaby, S. J. 1923.
22. *Directory to the Spiritual Exercises of St Ignatius Loyola.* (First edition 1591.) 1925.
23. *Ignatius Loyola and the Early Jesuits.* Stewart Rose. 1871.
24. *B. Robert Bellarmine.* James Brodrick, S. J. 1928.
25. *St Peter Canisius.* James Brodrick, S. J. 1935.
26. *La Santa Duquesa (Luisa de Borja y Aragon).* R. P. J. Nonell, S. J. 1892.
27. *Sainte Térèse.* Louis Bertrand. 1927.
28. *The Way of Perfection.* St Teresa of Avila. 1901.
29. *Life of St Teresa.* By herself (trs. David Lewis). 1904.
30. *Relations of her Spiritual Life.* St Teresa (trs. David Lewis). 1904.
31. *Monumenta Historica Societatis Jesu.* 1894 et seq.
32. *Historia de la Compañia de Jesus en la Asistencia de España.* A. A. Astrain, S. J. 1902-5.
33. *Storia della Compagnia di Gesu in Italia.* P. Tacchi Venturi, S. J. 1910.
34. *Histoire de la Compagnie de Jésus en France.* Henri Fouqueray, S.J. 1910-13.
35. *Histoire de la Compagnie de Jésus en France.* J. Crétineau-Joly. 1859.
36. *La Compagnie de Jésus.* Joseph Brucker, S. J. 1919.
37. *The Jesuits.* T. Campbell, S. J. 1921.
38. *Chronicles of the House of Borgia.* F. W. Rolfe. 1901.
39. *Historia General de España.* Don José Saban y Blanco. 1819.
40. *Historia General de España.* Don Modesto Lafuente. 1853.
41. *History of Spanish Civilisation.* Rafael Altamira (trs. P. Volkov). 1930.
42. *History of Spanish Literature.* J. Fitzmaurice Kelly. 1926.

43. *Cronica General de España, Valencia.* Don Vicente Boix. 1867.

44. *Historia de Valladolid.* Dr. A. S. Vitores. 1851.

45. *Viaje de España, Cataluña.* Don Antonio Ponz. 1788.

46. *Catalonia and the Balearic Islands.* A. F. Calvert. 1910.

47. *Handbook for Travellers in Spain.* Richard Ford. 1855.

48. *Obra de Averiguaciones Cantabricas y Ignacianas.* G. de Henao, S. J. 1895.

49. *Cambridge Modern History,* Vols. I and II. 1907.

50. *Europe in the Sixteenth Century.* A. H. Johnson. 1914.

51. *The Renaissance and the Reformation.* E. M. Tanner. 1915.

52. *The Renaissance in Italy.* Jacob Burckhardt. 1876.

53. *The Renaissance in Italy.* John Addington Symonds. 1898.

54. *Rome in the Middle Ages.* Ferdinand Gregorovius. 1902.

55. *La Cour Princière au Vatican pendant la Renaissance.* E. Rodocanachi. 1925.

56. *History of the Popes.* Ludwig von Pastor. 1930.

57. *Lives of the Popes.* Leopold Ranke. 1889.

58. *Lives of the Saints.* Alban Butler. 1838.

59. *Italy.* William Hunt. 1878.

60. *Histoire des Missions.* J. J. E. Roy. 1880.

61. *Missions and Missionaries.* Georges Goyau. 1932.

62. *L'Inquisition.* Vacandard. 1912.

63. *Histoire Critique de l'Inquisition d'Espagne.* J. A. Llorente. 1818.

64. *Conquest of Mexico.* W. H. Prescott. 1854.

65. *The Emperor Charles V.* E. Armstrong. 1902.

66. *Cloister Life of Charles V.* W. Stirling. 1853.

67. *Queens of Old Spain.* Martin Hume. 1911.

Catholic Encyclopedia, Encyclopedia Britannica, Enciclopedia Espasa Universal, Enciclopedia Italiana, &c.

NOTE: Vasquez's biography exists only in MS. at Gandia.

INDEX OF PRINCIPAL PERSONS